SOCIETY FOR NEW TESTAMENT STUDIES

MONOGRAPH SERIES

General Editor: Matthew Black, D.D., F.B.A.

Associate Editor: R. McL. Wilson

34

J. J. GRIESBACH:
SYNOPTIC AND TEXT-CRITICAL STUDIES 1776-1976

CONTENTS

JOHANN JACOB GRIESBACH
Professor der Theologie
1745 - 1812

THE JOHANN JAKOB GRIESBACH
BICENTENARY COLLOQUIUM
1776 - 1976

held at
Münster (Westphalia)
26–31 July 1976

under the joint patronage of
The Rector of the Westfälische Wilhelms-Universität zu Münster
Professor Dr Wolfgang Hoffmann

and of
The Rt Revd the Bishop of Münster
Heinrich Tenhumberg

and of
The Rt Revd the Präses of the Evangelical Church of Westphalia
D. Dr Hans Thimme

on the theme
JOHANN JAKOB GRIESBACH
and the
DEVELOPMENT
of the
INVESTIGATION OF THE SYNOPTIC PROBLEM
1776 - 1976

LIST OF PARTICIPANTS AND
SELECTED OBSERVERS

An asterisk indicates participants who were commissioned to write papers for distribution prior to the Colloquium and for possible publication in this volume or elsewhere.

The organizing committee

*Professor William R. Farmer, Perkins School of Theology, Southern Methodist University
*The Revd Bernard Orchard, O.S.B., Ealing Abbey, London (Hon. Secretary)
*Professor Dr K. H. Rengstorf, The University of Münster

The participants

Professor E. Bammel, Gonville and Caius College, Cambridge
Dozent Dr Klaus Berger, Heidelberg
Professor Matthew Black, St Mary's College, St Andrews
The Revd Père M.-E. Boismard, O.P., École biblique et archéologique française, Jerusalem
The Revd I. de la Potterie, S.J., Pontificio Instituto Biblico, Rome
Professor David L. Dungan, The University of Tennessee, Knoxville
Dr J. K. Elliott, The University of Leeds
*Professor William R. Farmer, Perkins School of Theology, Southern Methodist University
*Professor Gordon D. Fee, Gordon Conwell Theological Seminary
Professor Dr Albert Fuchs, Linz
Professor Reginald H. Fuller, The Protestant Episcopal Theological Seminary in Virginia
The Revd Francis T. Gignac, S.J., Catholic University of America
*Professor Dr Heinrich Greeven, Ruhr-Universität Bochum
Dozent Dr Tomas Hägg, Institutionen för klassiska spräk, Uppsala
Professor Dr Lars Hartman, The University of Uppsala
Drs W. M. A. Hendricks, O. Carm., Nijmegen

*Professor G. D. Kilpatrick, Queen's College, Oxford
Professor Dr H.-W. Kuhn, Heidelberg
Professor Dr H. Lausberg, The University of Münster
Professor Dr Fritzleo Lentzen-Deis, Philosophisch-Theologische
   Hochschule, Frankfurt
*The Revd Xavier Léon-Dufour, S.J., Centre Sèvres, Paris
Professor Thomas R. W. Longstaff, Colby College, Waterville, Maine
The Very Revd Carlo H. Martini, Pontificio Instituto Biblico, Rome
Professor Bruce W. Metzger, Princeton Theological Seminary
Professor Dr Frans Neirynck, The University of Leuven
*The Revd Bernard Orchard, O.S.B., Ealing Abbey, London
*Professor Dr Bo Reicke, The University of Basel
*Professor Dr K. H. Rengstorf, The University of Münster
Professor Harald Riesenfeld, The University of Uppsala
Professor E. P. Sanders, McMaster University, Hamilton, Ontario
Dr Werner Schäfke, Historische Museum der Stadt, Köln
The Revd George Soares Prabhu, De Nobile College, Pune, India
Professor Joseph B. Tyson, Southern Methodist University
Professor Dr W. C. van Unnik, Bilthoven

In addition to the official participants, whose numbers were limited by
the funds available to the organizing committee, other scholars were
invited to attend the colloquium as observers. Among those who (at the
invitation of the chairmen of the several sessions) made significant contributions to the discussion were Professor Dr Willi Marxsen, Dozent Dr
Martin Rese, and Dr Klaus Junack. A number of other scholars (including
Professor Dr G. Schneider, Professor Dr H. Lausberg and Akad. Oberrat
Dr Hubert Frankemölle) supported the colloquium by their presence
and participation.

PREFACE

The aim of this volume is to provide the reader with basic information about the life, work and influence of Johann Jakob Griesbach (1745–1812) and to indicate why an understanding of this scholar's contributions to New Testament criticism is important both for the history of New Testament scholarship and for contemporary research. Griesbach was perhaps the most noteworthy and influential Biblical scholar during the last quarter of the eighteenth century – the age of the French and American Revolutions. The editors of this volume are firmly convinced that, after being forgotten and ignored for more than a century, his ideas, suitably brought up to date, have a great deal to offer to twentieth-century New Testament studies.

Griesbach spent long hours in the attempt to find the best readings among the many variants in the New Testament. His work laid the foundations of modern text criticism and he is, in no small measure, responsible for the secure New Testament text which we enjoy today. Many of his methodological principles continue to be useful in the process of determining the best readings from among the many variants which remain.

But Griesbach was first and foremost a theologian concerned with the issues of faith and life in his own time. In this regard he firmly believed that theology requires a clear understanding of the sources from which it proceeds. Thus his greatest contributions to New Testament scholarship were his Greek *Synopsis* of 1774–6 and the theory about the interrelationships among the Gospels which resulted from it.

An examination of Griesbach's *Synopsis*, the bicentenary of which has been the occasion of the Münster Colloquium, reveals that he was under the influence of the Augustinian Hypothesis (that Matthew was written first, that Mark knew Matthew and that Luke was latest of the three and had knowledge of both Matthew and Mark) when he produced this work. A few years later, however, in his Easter Programme of 1783–4 (one of a series of Biblical essays which he issued annually at this season for the spiritual benefit of the citizens of Jena) he first outlined his belief that

Mark's Resurrection Narrative must have been dependent on those of Matthew and Luke.

In 1789-90 Griesbach issued his famous *Commentatio qua Marci Evangelium totum e Matthaei et Lucae commentariis decerptum esse monstratur* in which he listed in full his reasons for concluding that not only in the Resurrection Narrative but throughout his whole Gospel Mark was dependent on the Gospels of Matthew and Luke. This new theory, together with his *Synopsis*, was to enjoy considerable popularity and influence, not only through the work of his disciple, Wilhelm M. L. de Wette, but also as a result of its adoption by the Tübingen School under the leadership of F. C. Baur. (Until now this important essay has been available only in eighteenth-century Latin and thus has been relatively inaccessible. The English translation included in this volume was especially prepared for the Münster Colloquium.)

Griesbach's influence, however, although great, was also limited. His solution to the Synoptic Problem did not find universal acceptance, in part because at the time he was developing his own theory his contemporaries (and rivals) Heinrich E. G. Paulus, Gottlob C. Storr and Johann G. Eichhorn were developing another understanding of the relationships among the Synoptic Gospels which was eventually to become the theory of Marcan priority.

The reasons for the decline and eventual disappearance of Griesbach's solution to the Synoptic Problem have been considered in detail in William R. Farmer's *The Synoptic Problem* and need not be repeated here. We may note that Farmer has argued forcefully - and with some success - for the revival of Griesbach's theory, modified, of course, to take account of developments in New Testament criticism over the past 200 years. Thus the essays on the Synoptic Problem presented to the Münster Colloquium and the resulting discussion were timely contributions to New Testament studies.

The lasting influence of Griesbach's work on textual criticism can be seen clearly in the essay of G. D. Kilpatrick (included as chapter 7 below) and in the manner in which his principles and methods are still incorporated into contemporary New Testament text criticism.

This volume had its origin in the Griesbach Bicentenary Colloquium which was held in Münster in July 1976. The details of how the Colloquium was conceived and organized are related in W. R. Farmer's essay 'The genesis of the Colloquium' (chapter 1 below). The programme of the Colloquium was devised by an organizing committee and, with three exceptions, proceeded according to plan. (Prof. G. Delling was unable to come to Münster for the Colloquium. His paper was circulated in advance to all participants and, at the opening session, was accepted as read. Prof. C. M. Martini found it necessary, due to the unforeseen pressures of other duties, to decline the invitation to present a paper to the Colloquium. His contributions to the discussions, however, were of great value. Finally, Prof. G. D. Fee kindly and ably stepped into the void left by the late withdrawal of Prof. K. Aland. His paper (chapter 8 below) and his participation throughout contributed much to the Colloquium.)

After an opening session in which the Colloquium was formally convened, introductions made, etc, the discussions proceeded as follows. Two formal meetings were held each day.

The first day was given over to the consideration of the Gospel synopsis. Under the chairmanship of Prof. Matthew Black, papers prepared by Prof. Heinrich Greeven and Prof. Xavier Léon-Dufour were read and discussed.

The second day was given over to a discussion of New Testament text criticism. Under the chairmanship of Prof. Fritzleo Lentzen-Deis, papers prepared by Prof. G. D. Kilpatrick and Prof. Gordon D. Fee introduced the discussion.

The third day was reserved for a discussion of the Synoptic Problem. Under the chairmanship of Prof. Reginald H. Fuller, papers presented by Prof. Bo Reicke and Prof. William R. Farmer stimulated extensive discussion.

On the fourth day, the first session was devoted to a discussion of a paper by Prof. K. H. Rengstorf on Luke, and the second session given over to an evaluation of the Colloquium, including an attempt to define the progress which had been made and the questions raised but not resolved. Both of these sessions were under the chairmanship of Prof. Harald Riesenfeld. The final session is summarized in part in chapter 9 below.

The essays included in this book have been selected from those presented to the Colloquium. It is unfortunate that the limitation imposed by the need to produce a volume of manageable size has made it impossible to include all of the papers which were prepared for that meeting. (Not included are the following: W. R. Farmer's 'Modern developments of Griesbach's hypothesis'; G. D. Kilpatrick's (supplementary paper) 'Griesbach's place in the text criticism of the New Testament'; Xavier Léon-Dufour's 'The Gospel Synopsis of the future'; and K. H. Rengstorf's 'Griesbach and the problem of Luke'. G. D. Fee kindly agreed to an abridgement of his paper in accordance with the criteria used for selection. It was also impossible to include a number of written responses, prepared for and circulated at the Colloquium. Among these were: F. Neirynck's 'A new synopsis?', a response to Farmer's suggestion that it would be an advantage to have a synopsis illustrating the Griesbach Hypothesis; Neirynck's further response to Farmer in 'The Griesbach Hypothesis: a phenomenon of order'; and Bernard Orchard's response to Greeven's view that a modern synopsis, when properly edited, is entirely neutral.) Happily, some of these are published separately and thus available to interested scholars. (Thus, Farmer's essay appears in *New Testament Studies,* 23 (April 1977), 275–95. The editors hope that the remainder will also be published individually in the near future.) In making the selection the editors have attempted to produce a volume with a unified and coherent theme: Griesbach's contributions to, and subsequent influence upon, the critical study of the New Testament. Omitted were those papers (or parts of papers) where the author expressed his personal views with regard to the present state of the discussion of questions considered by Griesbach and still at issue. Accordingly, the intended value of this volume is that it provides an adequate background for understanding and evaluating modern developments of Griesbach's theories as they are proposed in contemporary scholarship.

On behalf of the organizing committee and themselves the editors wish to offer special words of appreciation to a number of people who contributed greatly to the success of the Colloquium.

A special word of thanks is offered to Prof. Gerhard Delling for his instructive biography of J. J. Griesbach and for his list of Griesbach's published writings, but no less also for the inspiration and assistance which he provided in the preparation of the exhibition of Griesbachiana which was featured in the library of the University of Münster throughout the Colloquium.

Warmest thanks are also expressed to the chief citizens of the historic and lovely city of Münster for the splendid welcome which they gave to all the participants: to His Excellency the Bishop of Münster, Heinrich Tenhumberg, for his patronage and support of the Colloquium from the beginning; to D. Dr Hans Thimme, Präses of the Evangelical Church of Westphalia; to the Rector and Pro-Rector of the University of Münster; to all of the personnel of the Universitätsbibliothek, to Dr G. Liebers, the Librarian, and Dr Hellmut Rüter his colleague and assistant, for their efforts in mounting the exhibition of Griesbachiana and to all of the staff for the courteous provision of the facilities necessary for a comfortable and efficient series of meetings; to the students and staff of the Institutum Judaicum Delitzschianum for their unobtrusive, generous and effective help at all times; to the Burgomaster of Münster for his welcome at the Rathaus on behalf of the citizens of the city; and to the Director of the Collegium Borromäum and his staff for the excellent arrangements which were made for the meals, accommodation and general comfort of the participants.

Our best thanks are also due to the scholars who came as participants and observers and who by their collegiality and contributions made the Colloquium a success; and above all our appreciation is expressed to Prof. K. H. Rengstorf whose personal prestige and influence at all times were an asset of immeasurable value.

Further, since no such gathering can take place without an ample supply of funds, appreciation is expressed to two German philanthropic foundations: to the Volkswagenwerk Stiftung of Hanover, and to an anonymous private charitable trust in Düsseldorf, for providing the essential financial support.

Finally, appreciation is expressed to the editorial board of the Studiorum Novi Testamenti Societas and to the editors and staff of the Cambridge University Press whose co-operation has made the tasks of the co-editors of this volume easier and much more pleasant.

Ealing Abbey, London   Bernard Orchard
January 1977   Thomas R. W. Longstaff

ABBREVIATIONS

AdBiog	*Allgemeines deutsche Biographie*
GCS	*Die griechischen christlichen Schriftsteller*
HTR	*Harvard Theological Review*
JBL	*Journal of Biblical Literature*
JTS	*Journal of Theological Studies*
NovT	*Novum Testamentum*
NTS	*New Testament Studies*
RB	*Révue Biblique*
RE	*Realencyklopädie für protestantische Theologie und Kirche*
RGG	*Die Religion in Geschichte und Gegenwart*
ThLZ	*Theologische Literaturzeitung*
VC	*Vigiliae Christianae*
ZNW	*Zeitschrift für die Neutestamentliche Wissenschaft*

1

THE GENESIS OF THE COLLOQUIUM

William R. Farmer

At the opening of the Colloquium on Tuesday 26 July 1976, the participants assembled in the main conference room of the reconstructed library of the University of Münster, where they received an official welcome from the Pro-rector, Herr Professor Dr Friedemann Merkel. In reply, Professor William R. Farmer, representing the organizing committee, spoke as follows:

We thank you for all that you have said and for all that has been done by this university and especially by Dr Liebers and his assistant Dr Rüter of this university library. We are grateful for this fine room and for all its appointments, which are ideal for the kind of discussions we intend to hold. We especially appreciate the painstaking efforts that have been taken to assemble the Griesbachiana which grace our deliberations and for the imaginative and tasteful manner in which these books and pictures have been arranged.

On this occasion it is fitting that something should be said about the genesis of this Colloquium and about the benefactors and patrons who have helped make what started as a dream four years ago become a reality at this time.

In 1965 in Göttingen a small-scale conference was held for the purpose of discussing the importance of Griesbach's solution to the Synoptic Problem. Out of this conference, which included Eugene Roesenstock-Hussey and Hans Conzelmann, came the idea for a large-scale international conference on Gospel studies. This led to the organizing of the 'Festival of the Gospels' which was held in Pittsburgh in 1970. In a brilliant and witty essay on Mark, prepared for that conference, Professor David Dungan brought the international community of New Testament scholars to a new awareness of the viability of the Griesbach Hypothesis. A year later in a second essay on Mark prepared for the Louvain Biblical Colloquium, Dungan further demonstrated the advantages of Griesbach's solution. Among those present to hear that paper discussed was Dom Bernard Orchard, to whom credit is due for the idea to organize a bicentennial

1

celebration of the work of Griesbach.

It was in the summer of 1972 that Orchard wrote a friend in the United States proposing that such a bicentennial should be held. To begin with, the idea was to increase appreciation for the contribution that Johann Jakob Griesbach had made to the solution of the Synoptic Problem. But, as is well known, this was only one of the areas of New Testament research to which this great German scholar had made a pioneering contribution. Therefore, from a very early stage in the planning for this Colloquium, provision has been made for acknowledging Griesbach's contribution to New Testament textual criticism and to his contribution to the development of the modern Gospel Synopsis, as well as to his contribution to the solution of the Synoptic Problem.

It was quickly recognized that plans for such a bicentennial could not succeed without two essential components. First, the Colloquium had to be international in its composition. Second, it had to have the sympathetic co-operation of highly respected members of the world of contemporary German New Testament scholarship. It was further decided that as far as possible, in keeping with the best of contemporary developments, the Colloquium would be ecumenical, and that, if possible, it would be held in East Germany at the University of Jena which was the principal sphere of Griesbach's scholarly career.

To this end an exploratory trip was made by Dom Bernard Orchard and Professor William R. Farmer to the University of Jena in July 1973. Preparatory to that trip several New Testament scholars were consulted about the feasibility of the idea for a Griesbach Bicentennial Colloquium. These scholars included Professor Lohse of Göttingen, Professor Bo Reicke of Basel, Professors Grässer and Greeven of Bochum and Professors Rengstorf and Aland of Münster.

The trip to Jena confirmed the desirability of such a bicentennial, but in the end it was deemed advisable to make plans to hold the Colloquium at some appropriate place in West Germany.

The financial uncertainties consequent upon the energy crisis of 1974 almost forced a postponement of plans to hold the bicentennial. Dom Bernard Orchard sent a letter to all who had been consulted, informing them that it was no longer feasible to proceed with plans unless some way could be found to assure the funding of the conference in face of the financial uncertainties that had unexpectedly developed. It was Professor Karl Heinrich Rengstorf of this university who responded that plans for the bicentennial should proceed at all costs, and who himself offered to help locate the conference, and find financial support. This made it possible to proceed without losing any of the momentum that is so essential to the success of a venture of this kind. At first it was thought feasible to hold the bicentennial in the famous and historic library in Wolfenbüttel. This would have been a very appropriate setting for our conference.

But we are very glad that as plans developed it has turned out that the host institution for the Griesbach Bicentennial Colloquium was to be this great university which through you, Sir, so graciously receives us on this occasion.

We are also very grateful that the ecumenical character of this celebration can be publicly apparent through the joint sponsorship of the Right Reverend Bishop of Münster, Heinrich Tenhumberg, and the Right Reverend the Präses of the Evangelical Church of Westphalia, Dr Hans Thimme.

It is appropriate that we acknowledge that the funding for our conference has come from two German foundations. Seed money for the planning of the conference was obtained from a private benefactor who wishes to remain anonymous. The funds necessary to turn the carefully laid plans into a living reality have been provided by the Volkswagenwerk Stiftung of Hannover. We are very grateful for the benefactions from both these sources.

From 1973 onward, Dom Bernard Orchard kept the officers of the international Society for New Testament Studies informed as plans for the bicentennial developed. From that beginning until now, those planning this conference have enjoyed the recognition and encouragement of this society. The international and ecumenical character of our conference was assured once Bernard Orchard, an English Roman Catholic, invited Karl Rengstorf, a German Lutheran, and William Farmer, an American Methodist, to join him to form the organizing committee for the bicentennial. Because of the location of the conference, it has been inevitable that the two Europeans on the committee have done the lion's share of the work.

Needless to say, there have been countless problems that have needed to be worked out in order to reach the happy result you see before you, an unprecedented gathering of scholarly talent to honor a great German New Testament scholar, whose work, after 200 years, continues to stimulate new research.

Those gathered here come from many different lands. They have come from as far south as Rome, Italy. They have come from as far north as Uppsala, Sweden. They have come from as far west as Hamilton, Ontario and Dallas, Texas. And they have come from as far East as Pune, India. They represent many different universities, such as Oxford, Princeton and

Heidelberg, and some very important centers of biblical studies such as the École Biblique in Jerusalem and the Pontifical Biblical Institute at Rome.

In an atomic age when the world is presently witnessing by live telecast both the Olympic Games in Montreal and a space-craft landing on Mars, we must seem to be a small and unimportant gathering. But in a world which has much to learn about how the human family can best live together, we think that there is some point in our coming together to do what we can to help ourselves and others better to understand the New Testament – and better to understand the central figure of the New Testament, who taught us to pray to a heavenly Father and to treat one another as brothers and sisters. You will be interested to know that it is our intention not only to work together, but also freely to pray together: in the morning before breakfast, at noon before lunch, and in the evening before supper. We sincerely hope that through our working and praying together in these days some good may come not only to ourselves but to others, not only to this land but to people in every land. To this end we pledge our common efforts and we begin by thanking you and all your colleagues who have helped make this day possible.

2

JOHANN JAKOB GRIESBACH:
HIS LIFE, WORK AND TIMES

Gerhard Delling[1]

Translated by Ronald Walls

Recalling his own youth,[2] Goethe says of the young Griesbach[3] and the brothers Schlosser,[4] that in Frankfurt 'everyone cherished the sure hope that they would accomplish outstanding things in State and Church'. 'Distinguished in those linguistic and other studies that open up the way to an academic career', by their own excellence they stimulated others 'to immediate emulation'. In this connection Goethe mentions that, 'subsequently he formed a closer tie with these men, a tie that endured unbroken for many years'. In fact Goethe moved to Weimar in 1775, the same year in which Griesbach moved to Jena; as a result, there grew up a frequent interchange between the two men.

Growing up as he did in an intellectually lively Frankfurt bourgeois family, Johann[5] Griesbach saw a wide horizon open out to him from his earliest days. Until 1806 Frankfurt was *de facto* a free imperial city;[6] it had a great market, was a centre of international trade, a city of banks;[7] it boasted also a busy book-fair, and was a city of both printing-presses and publishing houses. The *Römer* at Frankfurt was more than a well-known market-hall; it was distinguished by the part it played in the coronation of the emperor, which was solemnized in Frankfurt from 1562 to 1792. Goethe has given us a detailed description of his impressions of the events surrounding the coronation of Joseph II as 'King of the Romans' in April 1764.[8]

Our Johann Griesbach was the son of Konrad Kaspar Griesbach, a Pietist minister of Halle. His father had saved enough from his earnings as a chorister in Frankfurt to finance a three-year course of study at Jena. Then in 1730, in order first of all to finance his further studies, he went to the institute of Francke at Halle where he came in contact in particular with August Hermann Francke's like-minded successor at the theological faculty – Johann Jakob Rambach.[9] When in 1731 Rambach moved to Giessen he took Konrad Kaspar Griesbach with him as tutor for his children. After Rambach's untimely death in 1735 Griesbach continued in this office for some time longer. Soon – according to his *Vita*[10] – K. K.

5

Griesbach had become a much sought-after preacher. Until 1740 he remained in Giessen; in 1743 he went to Butzbach (Hessen-Darmstadt) taking with him as his wife Dorothea, eldest daughter of his patron Rambach. He had watched her grow up in her parents' home – she was twenty years younger than himself. Shortly after the birth of their only son on 4 January 1745 – not for nothing named after his grandfather, Johann Jakob – [11] K. K. Griesbach accepted a call to his birthplace, Sachsenhausen, a suburb of Frankfurt. In 1747 he became pastor of the Church of St Peter at Neustadt, Frankfurt. Goethe describes his wife, Dorothea, as 'pre-eminent' among the outstanding women of the Pietist circle in Frankfurt.[12] But, he comments, she was 'too severe, too arid, too learned'; 'she knew, thought, and comprehended more than the others'. In fact her knowledge of Latin[13] and Greek (*37* I: iv) allowed her a deeper penetration into theology. The Pietistic attitude of her husband is clearly evident in – among other things – his preface to J. J. Rambach's *Moral Theology*, published by his son-in-law in 1738 in Frankfurt/M (1434 pp.). In his view this is a work in which the author describes the corruption of nature and the way of grace; it presents a theology of conversion (para. 3 of the preface). In those days, within the markedly Lutheran Church of Frankfurt Pietism was fairly general. From 1743 to 1761 the leading clergyman (*Senior*) in Frankfurt was Johann Philipp Fresenius, who had met Rambach during his first ministry in Giessen (1734-6).

In his address to J. Griesbach when he was defending his first treatise (*1*), Semler, Griesbach's teacher, referred to the outstanding example of noble piety, especially that set by Rambach's daughter. 'I know', he said, 'and I rejoice, that here (in Halle) you have lost nothing' of that spiritual treasure which you inherited from your parents' home (*37* I: 165). Our Griesbach did not in reality think of himself as a Pietist; later on he explicitly dissociated himself from Pietism and from the 'enthusiastic and mystical parties' in general (*33*: 5). Nonetheless it has to be remarked, that his lecture on dogmatics in the concluding part 7 – under the title, 'How is the Christian led by his religion to his great destiny?' – treats specially of 'complete change of heart and mind', that is of conversion.[14] This is necessarily linked to 'a lively awareness' of 'the divine decrees concerning the redemption to blessedness, of sinful man' and to the ever-renewed devout contemplation of these decrees (para. 155), as well as to 'frequent renewal of feelings of love for God and for Jesus' (para. 160). At all events, during the five semesters when he studied at Tübingen, J. Griesbach was brought into contact with the Würtemberg style of Pietism, through Jeremias Friedrich Reuss.[15] By and large the theological faculty at Tübingen was moulded by Lutheran orthodoxy. Here Griesbach made a closer acquaintance with 'the older system of theology with its proofs'; this enabled him, 'as he progressed gradually, and without jumping hastily to conclusions, towards a freer style of theology' to reach – among other things – an objective and just judgement concerning orthodoxy (*35*: 537f.).

It was during the decade he spent at Halle (1764-75) that the development, which he himself has described, took a turn that decisively determined the course of his life. Here he soon came in contact with Johann Salomo Semler, with whom he lived as a student, and also after his great tour abroad (*40*: 18). Semler claimed him for an academic career, and marked him out for special research in the field of textual criticism of the New Testament. It is worth noting with what determination Griesbach took up the execution of the plan. In the course of a double semester at Leipzig he studied first the lecturing method of the professors there, and then devoted himself in particular to 'reading the ancient sources' of Church history (1766-7).[16] He continued this study in Halle 'joining with it the more exact critical investigation of the New Testament' (*35*: 538). After gaining his master's degree in the faculty of philosophy at the Regia Fridericiana (*2*), at twenty-three years of age, he set off on an extensive tour in order to widen his horizon, and, in particular, to get to know the teaching methods of a wider circle of professors, and to make use of the treasures of New Testament manuscripts contained in other libraries (*35*: 539). His sojourn in England and in Paris was devoted especially to this last objective. Griesbach travelled for a full half year in Germany, then went to the Netherlands. In England (September 1769 – June 1770) he spent long hours working in the library of the British Museum. An additional two months were spent at the Bodleian in Oxford, and a short spell at Cambridge. In Paris he buried himself chiefly (*34*: xiv) in the Royal Library, and in that of Saint Germain and others. The fruits of the months spent in these libraries determined Griesbach's work in textual criticism until the end of his life. Back home with his parents from October 1770 until Easter 1771, he continued to prepare himself for the work of university teaching. In Halle in October 1771 he won the *venia legendi* with his treatise on the importance of the Church Fathers (as exemplified in Origen) for New Testament criticism. This treatise concludes with six theses on New Testament textual criticism in general (*3*). Straightaway Griesbach took up his work of lecturing. In February 1773 he was nominated *extraordinarius* by Friedrich II. To this period belongs the oil painting of Griesbach by Johann Daniel Bager[17] of Frankfurt. The painting now hangs in the Schiller Memorial in Jena.

While in Halle Griesbach laid the foundation of his great editorial works, through which he made his mark in the history of research. 'He had scarcely returned from his tour to Halle when he provided New Testament criticism with a new style, so that... not long after he became *praeceptor Germaniae* (*37* I: v). In Halle he produced the manuscripts of his great editions of the New Testament – those of 1774 and 1775 (*4* and also *5* II) – and the *Synopsis* of 1776 [but see Greeven, chapter 3, n. 17]. The ground-plan of the *Symbolae criticae* (*22*) dates also from the Halle period.[18] Griesbach's publications of his last two decades were again devoted almost exclusively to the form of the text of the New Testament; the beginnings of these go back to the Halle decade of 1764–75 (including the grand tour; see the preface to *22* II, at the beginning).

Griesbach felt bound in many ways to Halle, not least through personal ties – through the 'quite unique goodwill of patrons and friends' – as he says (*34*: xv). However, as he had been assured that working in Jena[19] he would enjoy 'all such freedom in teaching', as 'an academic teacher can reasonably hope to enjoy at a Lutheran university', and as, on the other hand, the Curator at Halle 'seemed to avoid giving a positive answer on the subject of Griesbach's release from the King's service', which behaviour 'offended Griesbach's sense of freedom, he resolved to accept the call he had received' (*35*: 541). Here one sees the bourgeois pride of the son of a free imperial city. Chief among his Halle friends was Christian Gottfried Schütz[20] (in Halle 1769-79, then in Jena), whose sister Friederike became his wife on 16 April 1775, after an engagement of a year and a half (*40*: 21, 47).

On his installation as a regular professor at the 'Princely Saxon Comprehensive Academy at Jena'[21] (his installation took place in December 1775)[22] Griesbach embarked upon a concentrated spell of lecturing.[23] In the five semesters from the winter of 1777/8 until the summer of 1780 Griesbach actually offered four full lecture-courses.[24] He went systematically through Church history – the whole *historia ecclesiastica* indeed, divided out generally speaking over three semesters. From the time of its publication he based his lectures upon the outline of Church history by Johann Matthias Schroeckh.[25] Griesbach's earliest publications (1768) dealt with themes belonging to the field of historical research. His first, on the history of dogma, treated of the doctrine of Leo I on scripture, on Christ, on sin and grace, on the law, and on the sacraments, etc. (*1*); the second, Griesbach's dissertation for the master's degree, was basically an inquiry into norms for judgement of the reliability of historical records (*2*). Later, in the invitation to his inaugural lecture in Jena in 1776, Griesbach expounded the manifold uses of Church history in judging contemporary problems in theology and in the Church (*7*), and, finally, in a Whitsun programme for 1779 (*13*), discussed the position of the Church of Rome according to Irenaeus III.3. 1. Griesbach's far-reaching and intense interest in Church history is indicated by the catalogue of the library he left behind (*38*).[26] This contains some 2500 items on Church history (*libri exegetici*, Old and New Testament, amount to less than 1600, including straightforward texts, the 'apparatus for the interpretation of holy scripture', etc.); within the list is a special section for *patres et scriptores ecclesiastici* (almost 500 items) under which heading are no less than 200 quarto volumes concerning the early Church period, for example a 17-volume edition of the works of Gregory the Great (Venice, 1768-76) and – *nota bene* - the Delarue edition (1733-59) of Origen, following the volumes and pages of which Griesbach inserted New Testament variant readings in an interleaved working copy.[27] For the rest, by way of comment on the 12,526 items, it may be said, that there are a host of minor treatises that are not catalogued in detail, and – not least in importance – that by 1804 Griesbach – as he wrote to Gabler – [28] 'had twice already thrown out 1000 books'.

In addition to Church history, from the winter of 1779/80 certainly until the summer of 1790[29] Griesbach lectured on 'theologicam *dogmaticam* methodo populari, h. e. futurorum verbi divini ministrorum usibus accommodata',[30] from the time of its publication in his *Anleitung* (*23*). This was not intended as a 'theology for non-theologians', but, as the prospectus indicates, as a course for theological students (cf. *23*: 3).[31] This outlines certain hypothetical discussions of the traditional dogmatics of his time ('pure speculations'[32]) and treats the biblically based *theologumena*,[33] which are normative for the Church's preaching. The treatment most certainly goes beyond what is to be utilized in catechesis and preaching (preface of 1786). In this way Griesbach presents, among other things, the essence of 'authentic divine revelation' (para. 8), the doctrine of the two natures in Christ (paras. 54-8, 134f., 147), discusses man's fallen nature (para. 123) and, within a wide context of New Testament affirmations, expounds the Biblical interpretation of the cross (paras. 141-4, and cf. his footnote to para. 132). In his preface of 1786 Griesbach said that to some extent he would be referring to 'the precious "enlightenment" of many dogmas' provided by modern scholars, so that certainly some of his readers 'will shake their heads suspiciously at supposed heterodoxies – known now as neologies', whereas others 'will shrug their shoulders indulgently at the author's attachment to old-fashioned orthodoxy'.

Griesbach's *Anleitung* deals in great detail with New Testament texts – citing numerous authorities; in his view, 'popular' dogmatics must be 'firmly grounded upon' Biblical theology (*23*: 4f.).[34] Griesbach's New Testament courses were predominantly exegetical in content, and in fact he gives us an exegesis of what amounts to the whole of the New Testament, with the notable exception of the Apocalypse.[35] The whole cycle took from four to five semesters. The importance that was attached to exegetical courses can be estimated by a comparison with other disciplines. At Jena in 1800 one read Church Dogmatics in a single semester.[36] Between 1779 and 1803 Griesbach devoted one semester in each cycle to the Synoptics and another to John and Acts. As a rule Romans and the two Letters to the Corinthians were taken along with a number of the shorter Pauline letters, and more than once we find Hebrews and the Catholic Epistles; but we also find other combinations of the letters. Besides exegetical lectures Griesbach offered an introduction to the New Testament as a whole, at intervals of from three or four semesters – until a pause in 1800.[37] In addition, every fourth or fifth semester, he gave a course on the hermeneutics of the New Testament – with application to particular texts.[38] This was published in a transcript in his last years (*33*). On one occasion he gave an introduction to the rules of textual criticism (winter 1784/5).

In hermeneutics[39] Griesbach stressed the necessity not of dogmatic, but of 'historical-grammatical interpretation' (*33*: 48). The philological aids for this are the same as those used for all ancient texts (p. 53). Griesbach produces these sources of knowledge (pp. 56–63) in respect of other ancient authors. It is true that the purely Greek linguistic usage is not sufficient, for the New Testament is written in Hebraic Greek[40] (pp. 74–82, 85–7; for the LXX pp. 75–80). 'To begin with, the pure philologist and exegete alone is allowed to speak' (p. 47). Then he has to inquire further into the historical circumstances in which the book was produced (pp. 100–1, 92f.),[41] and into the purpose the author had in mind (pp. 91–4) in the context of the sentence, the passage, etc. (pp. 87–91, 93). But although the New Testament must be interpreted just like any other ancient book, 'constant regard' must be given to the 'whole peculiar character of the content and the form' of the New Testament (p. 53).

The way in which Griesbach applied the rules of hermeneutics can be seen from the numerous exegetical or Biblical-theological treatises which he published from 1776 to 1793. It is noteworthy that these works become more numerous especially in the decade and a half from 1778 to 1793. During the height of his work as a theological teacher it becomes evident that Griesbach saw his responsibility as that of a Biblical theologian. We ought at least to mention, as examples of the interpretation of longer passages, his expositions of Rom. 8 and 1 Cor. 12 (*8*; *14*); unfortunately the method used in these expositions cannot be explained here. The fact that the greater number of these treatises, of which we now speak, are almost entirely so-called programmes for the great Christian feasts,[42] does not in the least diminish their essential importance. And the fact that the key-word *pneuma* plays a part in eleven out of the twenty-nine Whitsun programmes (*8*; *14*; *17*; *19*; *21*) makes them no less interesting as an insight into Griesbach's work in the field of the theology of the New Testament.

In the most comprehensive of these works (*21*) he attacks the orthodox *theologumenon* that the text of the New Testament scriptures was directly (*amésōs*) inspired by God, attacks, that is, the doctrine of *theopneustia*, the inspiration of the individual words.[43] He discusses also the legitimation and the results of textual criticism.[44] In opposition to the above doctrine, Griesbach argues that the apostles at Pentecost received the gift of the Holy Spirit to be effective throughout their whole lives. The once-for-all event of Pentecost has to do with 'an extraordinary working of the Holy Spirit' through which the apostles 'were fitted for their teaching office, and endowed with gifts that surpassed the powers of nature' (*37* II: 299f.). 'They were briefed with exact and clear knowledge of the all-embracing totality of the Christian religion' in terms of its fundamentals (p. 307). Later, from time to time, the Holy Spirit revealed to them other things that they subsequently needed to know (p. 309, cf. p. 299). Knowledge of the *peristaseis*, on the other hand, referred to in the New Testament, is acquired by natural means (p. 349; cf. with this pp. 295–8). By the special Pentecostal gift 'the apostles were fitted through the Holy Spirit to both understand and transmit the doctrine without danger of error' (p. 342). The Christian people live in the light of the event of Pentecost, thus interpreted (pp. 342f.). It is worth noting that the core of the assertions sketched out above is to be found at the end of the set of Whitsun programmes (*37* II: 150, 185, 485f.; *12*; *14*; *27*). The Holy Spirit works in Christians through the word of the apostles (*37* I: 400); he comes alive in them through the Gospel (p. 418; *8*). God's *summa beneficia* come down to the whole of Christendom[45] from the first Pentecost, as from the Ascension (*37* II: 150; *12*), the Resurrection (*ibid,* p. 256; *18*) and from Christ's work in general.[46]

The word 'beneficia' plays, correspondingly, a part in the Whitsun programme for 1 Cor. 6: 11 (*19*; *37* II: 258f.); the three verbs in the verse – synonyms, according to Griesbach – express the thought, that Christians 'are given a share in all the benefits and privileges granted by God to the members of the community of Christ collectively' (p. 267). For the rest, *19* is a good example of the way in which Griesbach executes exegesis in terms of context (cf. *33*: 89f., 93, see above p. 10).

That Griesbach was constantly engaged theologically[47] becomes evident when, for example, he makes a historical-critical examination of the New Testament texts concerning the Resurrection and Ascension of Jesus. In the apostolic preaching of the Ascension the decisive factor is not a description of the process, but the proclamation of the exaltation and operation of him who has been exalted (*37* II: 484f.; *27*). Behind the several different accounts of Easter in the Gospels there lie varying reports by the women and apostolic eyewitness, those, that is, of Matthew and John. 'All that John writes, he created either from the report of Magdalene or from autopsy' (*37* II: 246). The picture which Griesbach, for his part, draws (pp. 249-51), comes from the comparison of John with Matthew (p. 249). Luke used partly Matthew's presentation and partly Joanna's account or that of one of Joanna's friends (pp. 248f.). Mark used Luke and Matthew (pp. 255f.). Here we already find the thesis that Mark depends upon Matthew[48] and Luke (see *24*). Clearly Griesbach regarded apostolic witness as important.

The same sort of thing applies to the apostolic authorship of most of the New Testament. At least twenty books[49] are 'certainly genuine, and unfalsified in respect of their essential content'[50] (*23* para. 10).[51] In his *Anleitung* (*23*) Griesbach presupposes that a considerable portion of the New Testament is genuine, on the grounds 'that the Christian religion... rests upon an authentic divine revelation' (notably para. 10). In this context the thesis of the priority of the Gospel of Matthew acquires special importance: according to Griesbach, the author of the oldest Gospel was an apostle.

From among Griesbach's Biblical-theological works let us at least name the treatise 'On the Jewish imagery used by the author of Hebrews to describe the office of the Messiah' (*25*). Our account must of necessity be fragmentary. Griesbach's fellow-citizen of Frankfurt, J. P. Gabler (born 1753), his pupil (from 1778) and his successor (at Jena from 1804[52]), states, in the preface to his edition of his master's *Opuscula*, that this highly gifted man, who 'could have mightily advanced the whole of theology, especially historical and exegetical theology', had instead turned himself to a totally different kind of task,[53] and for that reason 'in the course of more than thirty years.., apart from a little compendium of popular dogmatic theology, published nothing that was not ephemeral, except the *Symbolae criticae* and the new edition of the Greek New Testament with critical apparatus, and year by year specimen exegeses for feast-days' (*37* I: viif. - no mention of the *Synopsis*). Gabler has to admit, however: 'This clear-sighted man certainly did a great deal for the common good and for the economic affairs of the Academy, and of the city and region of Jena and of the state of Weimar in general' (pp. viif.). Moreover, Griesbach himself in 1790 admits that his additional duties along with 'his daily professional scholarly and academic work...fill up his time so completely...that scarcely any leisure is left for literary activity' (*35*: 542).

A certain restriction of his teaching activities from 1791 onwards may be partly connected with his having become burdened with special tasks. During the period from 1791–1804 Griesbach, in each of at least fourteen of the semesters, gave only two sets of lectures. From 1805 this became his regular practice. In his later years this undoubtedly was caused also by ill-health.[54]

At all events soon after his moving to Jena we see Griesbach becoming more and more involved in administration, not least in the finances[55] of the university and – after 1782 – of the provincial diet.[56] As deputy for the district of Jena he spent weeks in Weimar.[57] A physician called Loder (in Jena 1778–1803), and Griesbach, exerted great influence over university affairs,[58] for example in matters of appointments,[59] and especially in terms of their influence upon the man who had the last word in Weimar[60] – the Duke Carl August.[61] The expectations of the burgesses of Frankfurt concerning the young Griesbach, which we cited by way of introduction, from Goethe's self-portrait, were in many respects fulfilled in the man's activities.

The role which Johann Griesbach played in the social life of Jena and further afield obviously emerged from the totality of his personal qualities. According to contemporary descriptions, Griesbach made a striking impression: 'Of large, powerful physical build, Griesbach's outward appearance, even at first sight, announced his serious, discreet, upright and reliable character', as one *laudatio* puts it (*39*: 15). Koethe continues: 'Severity[62]...was softened by an almost hidden kindliness.' This is in line with an early saying of Schiller's:[63] 'At first sight Griesbach seems taciturn and precious, but soon he thaws out, and one discovers a most sociable and understanding man.' Gabler believed that Griesbach was by no means reluctant to assume functions of leadership, 'for his personality was inclined, and fitted, to command' (*37* I: viii); and Koethe agreed with this view: 'His resolute mind, his power of definite decision,[64] which became evident in all circumstances', appeared at times no doubt 'to those who did not know him so well, as arrogant self-will'; but these characteristics were 'but the expression of an individuality..., that was at one with itself' and was clear in its judgements (*39*: 19). We ought to heed also what H. E. G. Paulus has to say: Griesbach –

'this paragon of scholarly discernment, as of patriotic industry, was unsurpassed also in this quality: no matter how ardently he argued for his own view in a learned or a practical dispute, if the opposite view won the day he dropped all partisan spirit and worked wholeheartedly for the success of what had been agreed, as though he had never held a contrary view.'[65]

Jena and neighbouring Weimar could offer any man of marked character plenty of opportunity for contacts with intellectually important contemporaries. Griesbach's manifold contacts with Goethe were not only official[66] – from 1782 Griesbach belonged, as we observed, to the Weimar provincial diet; and in 1782 Goethe was chairman of the treasury-board,[67] etc.[68] Their families had already known each other. In later years Griesbach liked to speak of Goethe's father.[69] Goethe often stayed in Jena, at 'Griesbach's Garden'[70] often at the summerhouse (built at the latest in 1787).[71] Another visitor was the old Wieland (1733–1813),[72] who came over from Weimar in 1809 to spend a few weeks in Griesbach's three-storeyed summer residence;[73] and there was Voss,[74] who also stayed there as a visitor in 1811.[75]

During the last years of his activity in Jena (1795–9) Schiller took up residence in Griesbach's town house – 'one of the best houses in the city'.[76] It was built by the Weimar master-builder Johann Moritz Richter (1620–67).[77] Just four days before his celebrated inaugural lecture at Jena (1789) Schiller wrote:[78] 'I now have close links with the Griesbach house; I don't know how it is that I seem to have gained the good-will of the old Church councillor; but he seems to be very fond of me.' Schiller goes on to record his first impressions of Friederike Griesbach: 'His wife is a most intelligent, genuine and natural person – and very vivacious.'[79] In this Schiller is almost pointing to how she differed from her husband (see above). When after the birth of their third child Schiller's wife, Lotte, became seriously ill, their family friend Friederike Griesbach proved herself an understanding nurse. Schiller writes about this with deep appreciation.[80] Friederike's, and her husband's, quickness to give help was demonstrated in other ways too, not least in connection with the battle of Jena (1806), which brought great misery upon the city. Griesbach gives us a lively description of this in a letter dated 7 November 1806 (*40*: 56–60).

From the above-mentioned associations of Griesbach with the intellectual giants of his age[81] one forms the impression that they were of a decidedly personal and human sort. They were long-lasting. On his last longish journey (April/May 1810; *40*: 42f.) Griesbach visited Voss in Heidelberg, and Schnurrer (1742–1822),[82] the Chancellor at Tübingen, who had been his companion on the study tour to England and France, and H. E. G. Paulus in Nürnberg, his one-time colleague in the theological faculty at Jena from 1793 to 1803. Griesbach's friendship with Paulus was in no way damaged[83] by the fact that he had to raise serious objections to Paulus' theological position.[84] For his part Griesbach had supported Paulus'

nomination as *Professor Orientalium* at Jena, and, in Paulus' early days
there had shown himself to be – in Paulus' words – 'one of the enthusiastic promoters and protectors of my work'.[85]

Although in his day – even in the eyes of the Weimar government –
Griesbach was regarded as a representative of a more liberal theology,
and although he, for his part, saw himself to some extent in this light
(*35*: 537), nonetheless he expressly rejected extreme ideas – as represented,
for example, by H. E. G. Paulus. For Griesbach the basic affirmations of the
New Testament, as not only his *Anleitung*, but his whole programme for
feast-days, demonstrates, are *data* set before theology. Expressed in another
way that is: God's action in Jesus Christ is a *given*; the coming of the Son
(of the Logos, *Anleitung* paras. 55, 57f.), his preaching and that of the
apostles – both attested by supernatural miracles –[86] the redemptive act
of the cross, the Resurrection[87] and Ascension of Jesus, are facts presented
to theology. In these, God's great *beneficia* are given, and of these Griesbach
never tires of speaking. As the risen and exalted One, Christ works in many
and diverse ways in his people.[88] Griesbach no doubt was anxious to maintain, that *ratio* and revelation ought not to be thought of as in opposition
(*23* para. 8). In fact according to him a remarkable series of affirmations
about God are already accessible to man through reason (paras. 1, 4). In
paras. 8–9 Griesbach then sets out the features which distinguish a religion
of revelation from a rational point of view. In so doing he formulates the
expectations that one may direct towards such a religion, in such a way as
to show that in the religion of revelation in Jesus Christ they find their
fulfilment. And so one of the valid proofs of the authenticity of divine
revelation is, that 'God has caused to happen something extraordinary,
which is beyond human power to do, thus confirming his revelation' (para.
8*b*). Certainly, as an historical-critical expositor of the New Testament,
Griesbach is in a specific way an innovator – and he explicitly admits the
fact, as he is bound to do in his role as textual critic.[89] But it is also true
that he fully earned the comment of August Tholuck[90] of Halle, that he
followed the 'supernaturalistic line'. This reminds us of Griesbach's own
observation in his *Anleitung*, that he expected to be charged on the one
hand with being an innovator and on the other with being orthodox. Both
schools determined his theological thought and work. But as we look back
on his work we must keep clear in our minds this fact: the critic Johann
Griesbach was first and foremost a theologian, that is one who bore
witness to the gracious acts of God in Jesus Christ.

APPENDIX

I. The published works of J. J. Griesbach

1 Dissertatio historico-theologica locos theologicos collectos ex Leone
   Magno Pontifice Romano sistens. Halle, 1768. 4° 116 pp. [24] Feb.
   1768.   Gabler I, 1–162
2 De fide historica ex ipsa rerum quae narrantur natura iudicanda. Halle,
   1768. 4° 40 pp. Diss. mag. phil. 22 Oct. 1768 (pp. 41f. letter of
   Semler to Griesbach).   Gabler I, 167–223
   [In this treatise alone Griesbach made footnotes in the manuscript.
   Gabler incorporated these (I, x).]
3 Dissertatio critica de codicibus quatuor Evangeliorum Origenianis pars
   prima. Halle, 1771. 4° 62 pp.
   Gabler I p. xvii: pro impetranda venia legendi. 8 Oct. 1771.
   (Vol. II did not appear.)   Gabler I, 227–317
4 Libri historici Novi Testamenti Graece. Pars prior, sistens synopsin
   Evangeliorum Matthaei, Marci et Lucae. Textum ad fidem codicum,
   versionum et patrum emendavit et lectionis varietatem adiecit Io. Iac.
   Griesbach. Halle, 1774. xxxii+275(5) pp.
   Pars posterior, sistens Evangelium Ioannis et Acta Apostolorum.
   Textum... Halle, 1775. (iv+) 170 pp.
5 Novum Testamentum Graece. Textum ad fidem codicum, versionum
   et patrum emendavit et lectionis varietatem adiecit Io. Iac. Griesbach.
   Vol. II Halle, 1775. xxxii+303 pp. Vol. I Halle, 1777. xxxii+168 pp.
6 Synopsis Evangeliorum Matthaei, Marci et Lucae. Textum Graecum ad
   fidem codicum, versionum et patrum emendavit et lectionis varietatem
   adiecit Io. Iac. Griesbach, Theologiae prof. publ. Halle, 1776. xxxii+
   295(9) pp.
7 De historiae ecclesiasticae nostri seculi usibus sapienter accommodatae
   utilitate. Jena, 1776. 4° 58 pp.
   Invitation to the Inaugural lecture 6 July.   Gabler I, 318–77
8 De vera notione vocabuli πνευμα in cap. VIII. epistolae ad Romanos.
   Jena, 1776. 1777. 4° 16 pp. 12 pp. Whitsun Programmes.
                                                          Gabler I, 378–418
9 Curae in historiam textus Graeci epistolarum Paulinarum Specimen
   primum. Jena, 1777. 4° 3+98 pp.
   (pp. 1–72 down to 7 Feb., pp. 73–98 down to 13 Feb.) (Specimen
   secundum did not appear.)   Gabler II, 1–135
10 'Auszüge aus einer der ältesten Handschriften der LXX. Dollmetscher
   Uebersetzung': Repertorium für Biblische und Morgenländische
   Literatur 1. Leipzig, 1777. Pp. 83–141.

11 'Fortgesetzte Auszüge aus einer der ältesten Handschriften der LXX. Dollmetscher Uebersetzung': *Ibid.* 2, 1778. Pp. 194-240.

12 *Brevis commentatio in Ephes. cap. I comm. XIX seq.* Jena, 1778. 4° 12 pp. Whitsun Programme. Gabler II, 136-50

13 *De potentiore ecclesiae Romanae principalitate ad locum Irenaei libr. III. cap. III.* Jena, 1779. 12 pp. Whitsun Programme.
Gabler II, 151-68

14 *Commentatio ad locum Pauli 1 Cor. 12, 1-11.* Jena, 1780. 4° 12 pp. Whitsun Programme. Gabler II, 169-85

15 'Ueber die verschiedenen Arten deutscher Bibelübersetzungen': *Repertorium*... (see *10*) 6, 1780, Pp. 262-300.

16 *De mundo a Deo Patre condito per Filium.* Jena, 1781. 18 pp. On Heb. 1: 2. On the occasion of Ernst Adolph Weber's promotion to D. Theol. (Griesbach Dean.) Gabler II, 186-207

17 *De λογῳ προφητικῳ βεβαιοτερῳ 2 Petr. 1, 16-21.* Jena, 1781. 1782. 4° 12 pp. 12 pp. Whitsun Programmes.
Velthusen-Kuinoel VI, 1799, 419-53: *iam recognita et aucta*; see Gabler II, 208-40.

18 *Inquiritur in fontes, unde Evangelistae suas de resurrectione Domini narrationes hauserint.* Jena, 1783. 4° 12 pp. Easter Programme.
Gabler II, 241-56

19 *De Spiritu Dei, quo abluti, sanctificati et justificati dicuntur Corinthii 1 Cor. VI. 11.* Jena, 1783. 4° 8 pp. Whitsun Programme.
Gabler II, 257-68

20 *Nexum inter virtutem et religionem paucis illustrat*... Jena, 1784. 4° 16 pp. On the occasion of Johann Wilhelm Schmid's promotion to D. Theol. (Griesbach Dean.) Gabler II, 269-87

21 *Stricturae in locum de theopneustia librorum sacrorum i-V.* Jena, 1784-8. 4° 12 pp. 12 pp. 8 pp. 12 pp. 12 pp. Whitsun Programmes.
Gabler II, 288-357

22 *Symbolae criticae ad supplendas et corrigendas variarum N. T. lectionum collectiones. Accedit multorum N. T. codicum Graecarum descriptio et examen.* Halle, 1785. 1793. ccxxiv+388 pp. xvi+647 pp.

23 *Anleitung zum Studium der populären Dogmatik, besonders für künftige Religionslehrer* [Magistri verbi divini]. 2nd ed. Jena, 1786. 3rd ed. 1787. 12+252 pp. 4th ed. 1789.
1st ed.: *Anleitung zur gelehrten Kenntnis der populären Dogmatik.* Jena, 1779. (Not known in the booktrade.)
Anviisning til at studere den populare Dogmatik. Kiøbenhavn, 1790.

24 *Marci Evangelium totum e Matthaei et Lucae commentariis decerptum esse monstratur.* Jena, 1789. 1790. 16 pp. 16 pp. Whitsun Programmes.

Velthusen-Kuinoel I, 1794, 360–434: *iam recognita multisque augmentis locupletata*; see Gabler II, 358–425.

25 *De imaginibus judaicis, quibus auctor epistolae ad Ebraeos in describenda Messiae provincia usus est.* Jena, 1791. 1792. 4° 16 pp. 12 pp. Whitsun Programmes.
Velthusen-Kuinoel II, 1795, 327-59: *ab auctore recognita*; see Gabler II, 426-55.

26 *Quid Ebr. III. 7 - IV. 11 καταπαυσεως θεου imagine adumbretur, disquiritur.* Jena, 1792. 4° 12 pp. Christmas Programme.
Gabler II, 456-70

27 *Locorum Novi Testamenti ad ascensum Christi in coelum spectantium sylloge.* Jena, 1793. 4° 12 pp. Whitsun programme.
Gabler II, 471-86
[The programme (for Christmas) Jena, 1794: *Eutychis de unione naturarum in Christo sententia* is not by Griesbach (as Koethe, *39*: 3b, asserted - the first I think to do so) but by Johann Wilhelm Schmid. The programmes for the Christian Year throughout appear without stating the author.]

28 *Bemerkungen über des Herrn Geheimen Regierungsraths Hezel Vertheidigung der Aechtheit der Stelle I Joh. 5, 7 Drey sind die da zeugen im Himmel etc. mit Anmerkungen und einem Anhange, von Hezel.* Giessen, 1794. 104 pp. Griesbach's Text - in the form of a letter to Hezel - pp. 5-80, with 112 notes by Hezel; Appendix by Hezel pp. 81-98; Appendix II pp. 99-104. Author: pp. 105-12.

29 *Novum Testamentum Graece. Textum ad fidem codicum, versionum et patrum recensuit et lectionis varietatem adjecit D. Jo. Jac. Griesbach. Editio secunda emendatior multoque locupletior.* Halle-London, 1796. 1806. cxxxii+554 pp. xi+684, [40] pp. [These 40 pages counted in square brackets. Pp. 1-25 on 1 John 5: 7f; cf. *28*.]
Novum... adiecit D. Io. Iac. Griesbach. Vol. I, IV Evangelia complectens. Editionem tertiam emendatam et auctam curavit D. David Schulz. Berlin, 1827. cxxvi+668 pp. Schulz's preface pp. iii-lvi, then Griesbach's foreword and prolegomena *adiectis aliquot novi editoris adnotationibus.* Vol. II did not appear.

30a *Synopsis Evangeliorum Matthaei, Marci et Lucae una cum iis Joannis pericopis quae historiam passionis et resurrectionis Jesu Christi complectuntur. Textum recensuit et selectam lectionis varietatem adjecit D. Io. Iac. Griesbach. Ed. secunda emendatior et auctior.* Halle, 1797. xl+331 pp.

30b *... una cum iis Joannis pericopis quae omnino cum caeterorum evangelistarum narrationibus conferendae sunt. Textum... Editio* *tertia emendatior et auctior.* Halle, 1809. xxxii+340 pp.

31 *Commentarius criticus in textum Graecum Novi Testamenti.* Jena,
1798. 1811. 168 pp. lxix+206 pp.
Made up (partly revised, I, p. 7; II, p. iv) of:
I *Commentarii critici in Graecum Matthaei textum* [Matt. 1-20].
Specimina I-VI 1794-(8). I-IV Whitsun Programmes, 1794-7. 12 pp.
16 pp. 16 pp. 12 pp. V 1797 On the occasion of F. I. Niethammer's
Disputation.
II pp. vii-lxviii: *Meletemata de vetustis textis Novi Testamenti
recensionibus.* pp. 1-206: Programmes, 1799-1810 [pp. 1-44 comm.
on Matt. 21-8]. Pp. 20-30 = specimen VIII, programme, 1800, on the
occasion of Carl Christian Erhard Schmid's promotion to D. Theol.
(Griesbach Dean), pp. iii-ix. Pp. 45-64: Ἐπίμετρον *ad commentarium
criticum in Matthaei textum* (according to Koethe, *39*: 36, 1st ed.
1801). [Matthew 1f. belongs from the beginning to the Gospel
according to Matthew.] Pp. 65-206: *Commentarii in Graecum Marci
textum critici.* I, III-IX Whitsun Programmes, 1802, 1804-10. 8 pp.
16 pp. 8 pp. 8 pp. 8 pp. 10 pp. 12 pp. 8 pp. II Easter Programme,
1804, 8 pp.

32a Ἡ Καινὴ Διαθήκη. *Novum Testamentum Graece. Ex recensione Jo.
Jac. Griesbachii cum selecta lectionum varietate.* Leipzig, 1803. 1804.
1806. 1807. Large 4° xx+241 pp. iv+271 pp. 317 pp. 308 pp.

32b Ἡ Καινὴ Διαθήκη. *Novum Testamentum...* Vols. I, II Leipzig, 1805.
xxx (ii)+615 pp. (together.)

33 *Vorlesungen über die Hermeneutik des N. T. mit Anwendung auf die
Leidens- und Auferstehungsgeschichte Christi,* published by Johann
Carl Samuel Steiner. Nürnberg, 1815. 319 pp. Postscript of 1809.

34 Autobiography in Ernst Jakob Danovius: *Iudicii super integritate
Scripturae S. regendi iusti fines.* Jena, 1777, pp. xi-xv, on the occasion
of Griesbach's promotion to D. Theol.

35 'Johann Jakob Griesbach' (author not named, presumably Griesbach)
in *Allgemeines Magazin für Prediger nach den Bedürfnissen unsrer Zeit*
(published by J. R. G. Beyer) 3, (Leipzig, 1790), 537-44. [The literature here is speaking of Griesbach's 'not inconsiderable' (Koethe, *39*:
38) recensions in the *Allgemeine deutsche Bibliothek* and in the
Allgemeine Literatur-Zeitung or the *Jenaische Allgemeine Literatur-
Zeitung.* In my opinion, the older *ALZ* does not make any reference
to the recensions, the *AdBib* as a rule refers only by symbols that
clearly indicate the name, and the *JALZ* refers frequently by signs
chosen quite arbitrarily. Even with the second method (*AdBib*) nowhere is the probability suggested that the recension is by Griesbach.]

36 Iohannes Casparus Velthusen, Christianus Theophil. Kuinoel, Georgius Alexander Ruperti: *Commentationes theologicae.* Leipzig, 1794ff. Cf. *17; 24; 25.*

37 Io. Philipp. Gabler: *Io. Iacobi Griesbachii Opuscula academica.* Jena, 1824. 1825. xxvi+418 pp. xcviii+486 pp.

II. Early published works concerning J. J. Griesbach

38 *Catalogus bibliothecae Jo. Jacobi Griesbach Theologi nuper Jenensis celeberrimi, qua continentur libri ad theologiam universam, inprimis criticam et exegeticam S. S., historiam ecclesiasticam, politicam, literariam, philologiam et philosophiam spectantes, quorum auctio fit Jenae inde a die 19 septembr. anni 1814.* (12,526 numbered items.)

39 Friedrich August Koethe: *Gedächtnisrede auf D. Johann Jacob Griesbach, weyl. Herzogl. Sachs. Weim. Geheim. Kirchenrath, ersten Professor der Theologie zu Jena, der Königl. Bayersch. Academie der Wissenschaften zu München und mehrer gelehrten Gesellschaften Mitglied.* In addition a sketch of his *curriculum vitae.* Jena, 1812.

40 B. R. Abeken: Johann Jakob Griesbach, in Friedrich Christian August Hasse (ed.), *Zeitgenossen,* 3rd series, vol. 1 part 8, Leipzig, 1829, 3–64, with additions (mostly letters), pp. 45–64. [Abeken was a pupil of Griesbach (p. 3).]

Oberbibliotheksrat Hellmut Rüter (Münster) has kindly offered us the following additional titles, which are placed here for convenience of reference.

A. Three minor literary items of Griesbach:

1 Johann Jakob Griesbach [praeses] : *Commentatio historico-theologica exhibens historiae sententiarum Remonstrantium de rebus ad religionem et conscientiam pertinentibus, Specimen primum.*
[Resp.:] Christ. Julius Wilhelm Mosche. Jena, 1790.

2 Johann Jakob Griesbach: *Commentarius criticus in Matthaei textum. Specimen V.* Jena, 1797.
[Introduction to the promotion of Friedrich Immanuel to D. Theol. Niethammer, Jena, 28 Oct. 1797.]

3 Johann Jakob Griesbach: Foreword to: Wilhelm Martin Leberecht de Wette: *Beiträge zur Einleitung in das Alte Testament,* vol. I. Halle, 1806.

B. Note also the following editions of, and references to, the works of Griesbach:

4 Wilhelm Martin Leberecht de Wette and Friedrich Lücke: *Synopsis Evangeliorum Matthaei Marci et Lucae cum parallelis Joannis pericopis. Ex recensione Griesbachii cum selecta lectionum varietate.* Berlin and London, 1818.

5 Idem: *Synopsis...cum selecta Griesbachiana lectionum varietate atque enotata Lachmanniana lectione. Editio secunda emendata.* Berlin, 1842.

6 Rudolf Anger: *Synopsis Evangeliorum Matthaei Marci Lucae... Ad Griesbachii ordinem concinnavit, prolegomena, selectam scripturae varietatem, notas, indices adiecit Rudolphus Anger.* Leipzig, 1852.

7 Ἡ Καινὴ Διαθήκη. *Novum Testamentum Graece. Ex recensione Jo. Jac. Griesbachii cum selecta lectionum varietate. Editio nova non tamen mutata.* Leipzig, 1825.

8 *Verzeichnis von gebundenen Büchern, welche Mittwoch, den 24. August 1831... öffentlich versteigert werden sollen. In der ersten Abtheilung sind Nro. 1–2095 aus der berühmten Griesbach'-schen Bibliothek, meist ältere Werke aus dem Gesammt-Gebiete der Theologie und Geschichte. Auch die folgenden Nrn. bis Nro. 2133 und die zweite Abtheilung enthalten viele Werke aus derselben Bibliothek...* Jena, 1831.

3

THE GOSPEL SYNOPSIS
FROM 1776 TO THE PRESENT DAY

Heinrich Greeven

Translated by Robert Althann, S. J.

Introduction

This contribution to our Griesbach Colloquium does not give an exhaustive enumeration of all the Gospel synopses that have appeared within the period under review. This would have required years of time-consuming research and in the end one or another synopsis mentioned in scholarly discussion would still have had to be labelled as missing for the time being, until chance put a dusty copy from some cellar or attic that had been spared by war and fire into the hands of someone acquainted with the material. Furthermore, it is questionable whether a complete collection would impart more knowledge than is already provided by the material that could be obtained from European libraries[1] over a period of a few months. It is true that to some degree chance rather than careful, expert judgement made the selection. But this does not justify excessive scepticism. For in the first place even in what was fortuitously present, the chaff had to be, and could be, separated from the wheat. Secondly, the more important and progressive works, especially if they went through several editions, did not disappear so easily. Thirdly, it is the custom of learned authors in detailed prefaces to distinguish their work from everything comparable to it, so that it is possible basically to comprehend the landscape by means of a good survey from many mountain peaks, without having to wander through every individual contributory valley.

Griesbach's synopsis and its significance for Gospel research can be properly judged only when it is seen in the total context in which it belongs: namely that Christianity has never fully satisfied itself or been quite at ease with the fact that what it knows of its Master has been handed down to it in four books which – unanimous as their witness is – do differ from one another in numerous details. Whatever theological motives may underlie this, the Church has never, or at least never for long, wanted to accept the four Gospels simply as they are. The replacement, connected with the beginnings of the Syrian Church, of the four Gospels by Tatian's Diatessaron[2] is no doubt the most violent attempt up to now, and so one not repeated, to cut the Gordian Knot. But also the Eusebian Canons cautiously try to put some order into the Gospels' mixture of agreement, divergence and contradiction. The problem, here only sketched out, is discussed at length by Augustine. In his *De consensu evangelistarum* he shows that the Gospels present a clear and complete picture of the persons and things about which they narrate, and that the occasional contradictions are either no contradictions at all, are insignificant, or serve the purpose of clarification. His harmonizing is sometimes forced and can hardly prove acceptable to a critical reader, but he has no intention of turning the four Gospels into a single work, behind which the four Evangelists would have to retire. So the early Church already took in hand a theme of Biblical scholarship that was afterwards always with it, obviously not without being variously illuminated by the historical currents of the human spirit and of theology. The ways in which this theme is expressed are diverse. The trend of the scribes, more or less observable everywhere, to harmonize the text of the canonical Gospels (mostly with Matthew) belongs to it, as does a broad stream of harmonizing Gospel interpretation which is handed down in the exegetical tradition.

A. Early 'synopses' of the Gospels

1 Origen, Eusebius, Augustine

At first sight it does not seem to be too difficult clearly to define within this complex mass of material that which deserves the name 'synopsis': a presentation of what belongs together so that it is simultaneously in view. In the early period the Canons of Eusebius fit this definition of 'synopsis' best. For even though they give references to parallel texts only in the margin of the Gospels, without setting them out in full, they do put the corresponding chapter- and verse-numbers of the different Gospels together in their charts. It is all the more possible to see here the intention of a comparative juxtaposition, since Eusebius, the pupil of Origen's pupil Pamphilos, takes up and perfects in his Canons an idea stemming from the Alexandrine Ammonius and moves therefore entirely within the sphere of the great Biblical scholar, significant remains of whose famous *Hexapla*, with its six columns of parallel texts, have come down to us.

What Origen achieved in the *Hexapla* with the instruments of his time certainly deserves the name 'textual criticism'; and this in the real sense: a critical restoration of the original text. Something other again is Augustine's attempt – clearly with the aid of Eusebius'[3] Canons – to determine the agreement, not equally strong, of the individual Evangelists with each of the other three, and to draw conclusions as to their mutual dependence.[4] Here one may speak of a literary-critical interest, even if everything is subordinated to the aim of demonstrating the compatibility of the texts and so the unanimity of the Evangelists' witness.

2 Joannes Clericus (Le Clerc), 1699

In the next period, this last theme of exegesis is the only one that concerned scholars. Fabricius[5] counts nearly 150 harmonies and concordances which had appeared up to his time. It required the rise of modern Biblical criticism before the need for a synoptic presentation of the Gospel text made itself felt. But just as the critical study of the Bible did not appear all at once, but rather gradually had to free itself, with various trials and advances, from what had gone before, so too the first Gospel synopses of the modern period were principally concerned with obtaining from the juxtaposition of the texts the material for a uniform, complete, and consistent presentation of the course of the Gospel history.

An example of this is the only predecessor mentioned by Griesbach himself,[6] the Arminian Joannes Clericus (Le Clerc) with his *Harmonia evangelica, cui subjecta est historia Christi ex quatuor evangeliis concinnata* which appeared in Amsterdam in 1699. This work should have contained, according to the original intention of the author, the Greek text of the Gospels, arranged synoptically, and with it a continuous Gospel history, arranged as a paraphrase of the canonical texts. At the request of the publisher, the Latin Vulgate was placed opposite the Greek text,[7] incidentally without harmonizing divergent meanings in one direction or the other.[8] Every page is divided into four columns, one for each Gospel. Of two facing pages, the left one invariably has the Greek text, the right one the Latin text. If an Evangelist is silent, his column remains empty. For instance, pp. 235-323, on which Luke 9: 51 - 18: 14 and John 7: 1 - 10: 39 are printed alternately, remain three-quarters white - certainly already then no mean luxury. Where several Gospels appear together, great care is taken that the mutually corresponding parts of sentences and the words themselves stand on the same level. The lower third or quarter of every page is reserved for the continuous paraphrase. A much-used reference sign, a little hand, gives information on the upper part of the page as to the order in which the paraphrase on the lower part takes up the individual passages of the canonical Gospels. A text-critical apparatus is entirely lacking. Explicit quotations from the Old Testament are usually provided with an accurate reference in the paraphrase. Allusions to the Old Testament, even very literal ones, are disregarded.

The intention which Le Clerc pursues in his work arises from the experiences of the exegete in academic teaching. He wants to put into the hands of the student an instrument with the aid of which the narratives of the

Evangelists can be effortlessly compared and which, in addition, provides references so that the exegesis of scholars can be looked up. In the numerous harmonies of his age he finds three things to criticize: First, the question of the chronological course of the events is unacceptably neglected. The mechanical juxtaposition of similar texts often tears the parts of the several Gospels strangely apart, regardless of the fact that their authors must have had certain ideas about the chronological succession of events. In this way the Fourth Gospel, which alone would make it possible to distinguish the years of Jesus' public life, usually drops out entirely. Second, the explanations given were usually unsatisfactory, since they were too scanty or quite out of date, and in any case did not contribute sufficiently to a unified picture of the Gospel history. Finally, the parallel arrangement was usually very incomplete, so that everything had to be read several times before what was common or unique could be correctly discerned.[9]

It must be asked whether Le Clerc himself was able to avoid these difficulties. On the last point, that of making the corresponding texts exactly parallel, he certainly did his utmost with regard to even the smallest units. The second problem he doubtless tried to counter with the paraphrase which is also exegetical and allows the view of the author on the sequence of events to appear. However, those dangers mentioned in first place seem to have been least avoided by him. This is connected with his concern for a unified picture of events and with the method which he therefore employed. As expected, he makes John's Gospel basic and prints it in its column – including the pericope of the Woman Taken in Adultery – in its original order so that great empty spaces appear where the matter of the first three Gospels is inserted. This procedure is abandoned only in the Passion Narrative.[10] But since the Synoptic material is for the most part not included by John, the latter could give only the larger framework within which numerous decisions as to the correct placing of individual passages still had to be made. So e.g. the Genealogy of Luke 3: 23–8 is drawn forward and now stands between Luke 2: 20 and 21. Matt. 14: 3–5 and Mark 6: 17–20 are drawn far forward to stand parallel to Luke 3: 19a, 20, 19b, c and now stand after Matt. 3: 12 and Mark 1: 7 respectively. The Sermon on the Mount stands in one piece beside Luke 6: 20–6, 29, 30, 27, 28, 32–42, 31, 44, 43, 45–9; this means that the programmatic character of Matt. 5–11 has been dissolved. There is least transposition in Luke; Mark's sequence is also basically unchanged.

These examples show that Le Clerc himself had to disrupt considerably the connections between the narratives of the Evangelists. That he did this only reluctantly is to be expected after his preface, and it also shows itself

when some transpositions are omitted. Thus the Temple-Cleansing pericopes, John 2: 14-22 and its parallel, Matt. 21: 12-13, are for him two quite
distinct events.[11] That Luke 11: 2-4 comes so much later than the Lord's
Prayer of the Sermon on the Mount is explained by saying that the inquir-
ing disciple of Luke 11: 1 had not heard the directive on prayer of the
Sermon on the Mount, so that Jesus repeats it for him and uses the favour-
able opportunity to give further instruction on the necessity and efficacy
of prayer (p. 270). The Parables of the Talents and the Pounds are not
placed in parallel but are merely termed 'similar' in the paraphrase to Matt.
25: 14ff. Of the Anointing stories not only is Luke 7: 36-50 distinguished
from all the others, but also John 12: 3-8 is distinguished from Matt. 26:
6-13 // Mark 14: 3-9. It is therefore assumed that there are three different
anointings. Similarly, there is no hint that the narratives of the Royal
Official (John 4: 46-53) and of the Centurion of Capernaum (Matt. 8: 5-
13 // Luke 7: 1-10) might be related.

Against the obvious objection that his reconstruction of the correct
sequence of events is too arbitrary, Le Clerc has assembled a full arsenal of
weapons: in an appendix he puts together twenty-one canons according to
which he built up his harmony. Starting from the premise that the Gospels,
with quite minor exceptions, give an accurate account of the events and
taken together offer a complete picture of them, most of these canons are
obvious. Some sound rather banal,[12] and others are alternatives[13] and
therefore allow the harmonizer to make any decision he pleases. Even without the 'notulae' (pp. 547-51) given at the end of the volume it is easy to
recognize in each case on which canon the author relies.

If the whole work is judged not according to the criteria which the
author applies to his predecessors – and rivals – but according to what was
possible given his presuppositions, we should conclude that he produced a
serviceable instrument for the exegesis of the Gospels and for the study of
the Gospel history.[14] The compromises he had to make did not prevent
him but rather actually made it possible for him to maintain two principles
which he never explicitly set forth: (a) no word of the Gospels is omitted,
and (b) no word of the Gospels appears twice. (a) is obviously the duty of
the conscientious historian. (b), on the other hand, does not have the same
dignity and merely leads ultimately to numerous similarities and relationships in the texts not being made 'synoptic', that is they are not presented
to the eye simultaneously, but have still to be laboriously collected.

B. J. J. Griesbach's Critical Synopsis 1774-6

Only against this background does it become comprehensible how Griesbach – and others who agree with him – could understand his project as a

new beginning.[15] Let us allow him to speak for himself:

'The authors of harmonies have principally tried to determine the time and sequence in which the events written down by the Evangelists happened; but this lies far outside my purpose. For I freely admit – and I wish to draw the readers' attention to this – that a "harmonia" in the literal sense of the word is not the aim in this book. For although I am not unaware of how much trouble very learned men have taken to build up a well-ordered harmony according to self-imposed rules,[16] yet I still think not only that out of this minute care small advantage may be obtained, or even practically none at all that my synopsis would not also offer; but further I have serious doubts that a harmonious narrative can be put together from the books of the evangelists, one that adequately agrees with the truth in respect of the chronological arrangement of the pericopes and which stands on a solid basis. For what [is to be done], if none of the Evangelists followed chronological order exactly everywhere and if there are not enough indications from which could be deduced which one departed from the chronological order and in what places? Well, I confess to this heresy!'[17]

What Griesbach himself wants to present with his synopsis is a handy text for the hearers of his lectures, in which he interprets the first three Gospels, not one after the other but – as we would say today – 'synoptically', that is, always referring to the parallels. In this way not only could time-consuming repetitions be avoided, but also the individuality of each Evangelist, his style and vocabulary, his basic idea and structure, his method and sources, could all be made more visible. But for this it was necessary that despite the synoptic arrangement of the comparable texts of the Evangelists, each Gospel could be read continuously on its own.

Griesbach takes account of this by making transposed texts recognizable (usually Matthew, because he mainly follows Mark and Luke in his arrangement) by means of a line drawn on the left-hand side and with a reference to the section to which the passage belongs according to its original position. There, however, the full text is usually no longer to be found. Instead, the beginning and end are printed with a reference to the section where it appears in full. Only very short pericopes (e.g. Matt. 8: 19–22) are printed more than once, or such logia as yield a different sense in a different context (e.g. the Sermon on the Plain, the text of which for the most part had already been printed opposite the corresponding parts of the Sermon on the Mount). Such passages usually have – in their 'synoptic' position – instead of the line on the left-hand side a complete frame ('box'). Also in boxes are the (rarer) references to a comparable text which provide only the Gospel chapter and verse and the number of the section but no text.

(This is how, for example, the two Parables of the Banquet, Matt. 22: 1ff. and Luke 14: 15ff., are connected. Clearly, to the author they did not look similar enough for a full 'synopsis'.)

From this description of the appearance of Griesbach's synopsis it might seem difficult to obtain an impression of the continuous text of an individual Gospel without being disturbed by the necessity of continually turning backward and forward. This difficulty did in fact exist and the author first tried to lessen it by indicating at the head of each page where a Gospel, not represented there or represented only through a transposed text takes up again the thread of the continuous text (chapter, verse and section). Next, he places a *conspectus sectionum* in front of the text, which permits the rapid finding of any pericope and in addition gives an overall view of the structure of the several Gospels both in their relationships and in their differences. To the honour of Griesbach it must here be stressed that neither in this conspectus nor anywhere else in his synopsis does he lay before the user a particular theory about the mutual relationship of the Gospels (unless the exclusion of John's Gospel – except for the Passion Narrative – is to be judged the consequence of a 'theory'). And this, although Griesbach's hypothesis of the dependence of Mark on Matthew and Luke[18] must have been in his mind at least in outline at the time of the appearance of his synopsis. But even in 1797, in Griesbach's preface to the second edition of the synopsis, his *Commentatio,* which had already appeared in a second, significantly enlarged edition,[19] is mentioned only in a footnote. Therefore, just as the 'historia', i.e. the sequence of events in the Gospels, is left entirely to the judgement of the reader, so too is their mutual relationship. The reader receives, at least for the latter task, the most complete material possible to assist him in forming a judgement, a process which is reserved for later consideration by the user. It seems that we obtain here a glimpse of the scientific ethos and academic teaching method of a great scholar. In this way Griesbach set standards for the future of the Gospel synopsis, which, although they were often not attained, could not thereafter be forgotten.[20] His synopsis appeared in a third edition in 1809 and a fourth (posthumously) in 1822. The second edition is distinguished from the first, apart from text and apparatus, mainly by the inclusion of the Passion Narrative of the Fourth Gospel (12: 1-8; 18: 1 – 21: 25), which was printed in full.

C. Gospel synopses from 1776 to the present

1 H. L. Planck, 1809

In the same year as Griesbach's third edition there appeared a small book by H. L. Planck.[21] It is in fact no real synopsis, but offers only tables displaying the arrangement of a synopsis that he intended to publish later. However, it is interesting because it considers Griesbach critically and takes up a position opposed to him. Planck gives[22] three possible principles for the arrangement of a Gospel synopsis, and these have been widely accepted even if they have not always been accurately connected with his definitions. He distinguishes an historical, an exegetical and a critical synopsis. *Historical* synopses are the traditional harmonies. Unlike Griesbach, Planck did not wish to deny the possibility of an 'historical-pragmatic treatment of the life of Jesus', which had obtained a significant impetus through the writings of H. S. Reimarus.[23] But he questioned the value of such a synopsis for the interpretation of the Gospels. Griesbach had achieved an *exegetical* synopsis determined by the Gospels' content alone. But such a synopsis does not consider the questions of which parallels between the Gospels are important for a judgement about their mutual relationship or to what conclusions they lead. Accordingly, Planck asks for – and outlines – a *critical* synopsis, which

> 'takes account not only of similarity in content, but also of the similarity in form of the several passages, a form deriving from the use of similar sources. Passages which are parallel only according to content but not with respect to external form and presentation cannot be placed together in this synopsis, but remain independent of each other, each one in its special place.'[24]

Therefore those texts only are 'critically parallel' in which there can be demonstrated *either* the direct dependence of one Evangelist on another *or* the dependence of two or more Evangelists on a common source. The critical synopsis follows 'naturally... the results of the presupposition according to which anyone who wishes to use it thinks he can best explain the relationship of the Gospels'. Planck came to the final conclusion that the unmistakable relationship of our first three Gospels 'could be most naturally attributed only to common use of the same sources'.[25]

Given the aforementioned presuppositions he counts forty-two passages[26] in which all three Gospels agree. Taken together they contain the earliest Gospel which all three Evangelists translated independently from the original Aramaic into Greek. A second group contains forty-two passages which appear in two Evangelists only (nineteen in Matthew–Mark, sixteen in Matthew–Luke, seven in Mark–Luke). Here we have either expansions of the original text, which the two witnesses found in their copies of it, or we have further common sources. The remainder of the text, attributed in each case to only one Evangelist, in its turn also consists of augmentations of the original text which stood only in one of the copies used, or as special additions from the Evangelist's other sources. The limitation to a 'demonstrable' relationship has for a consequence that not only the two genealogies, Matt. 1: 1–17 and Luke 3: 23–38, but also the Parables of the Lost Sheep, Matt. 18: 12–14 and Luke 15: 4–7, are not placed in relation to each other.

The groups of texts distinguished by Planck are, however, in no way treated each by itself alone. Rather he arranges them – showing this by distinct indentation – in a normal synopsis, the structure of which for exegetical reasons – 'for criticism the choice was immaterial' – is guided by Matthew. For Matthew had rearranged the order of the original text, an order still visible in Mark and Luke, evidently because he wanted to produce a more accurate chronological arrangement. But such a concern deserves trust. In this way too the greatest and fullest[27] Gospel is not torn apart and gives exegesis a sure guiding-line. It is not immediately clear from Planck's tables how he imagined the arrangement in detail of the print for the completed synopsis. But it can safely be assumed that his planned grouping of the matter, made according to whether three, two, or only one Evangelist included it, would have been obvious. In this manner, and also because of the limitation of what was considered parallel to the demonstrable relationships, the user of the synopsis – and this was also the declared intention of the author – would have received from the beginning with the texts also a definite hypothesis, namely that of the 'Proto-Gospel' (Ur-Evangelium). In order to check other suggested solutions of the Synoptic Problem he would laboriously have to collect the texts to be compared and make tables for himself. Exegesis too could not abandon comparing material divergent in form but related as to content; but exegesis would be let down by Planck's synopsis e.g., in the case of the Parable of the Lost Sheep. Planck's criticism of Griesbach's synopsis and his improvement of it is therefore rather a step backward than a gain: the user is pushed to a particular solution from the beginning, and the formation of one's own judgement is made more difficult. On the other hand Griesbach's arrangement allows the hypothesis put forward by Planck and any other too, to be tested.

2 W. M. L. de Wette and F. Lücke, 1818

Six years after Griesbach's death de Wette and Lücke[28] issued their synopsis. The text for it they took entirely from Griesbach's third edition, including the text-critical signs in the text which were to direct the students to Griesbach's full apparatus. De Wette–Lücke for their part note only a few variants and those without naming the witnesses. If it be asked what moved the authors to bring out a new synopsis when they follow Griesbach so closely then the preface reveals – after ample praise for 'Griesbachius noster' – that his work was no longer adequate for the progress of learning, because it no longer allowed the course of the narrative of the individual Gospels to be sufficiently clearly discernible and in general – a surprising statement – impaired freedom of judgement in questions of source criticism. Therefore what Planck felt to be a deficiency in clarity of attitude had the effect on de Wette–Lücke of tutelage! In order to assist freedom of judgement they therefore undertook a presentation of the texts with numerous repetitions. As a result the textbook expanded to such an extent that, as they themselves admitted, they had for this reason to omit almost entirely the text-critical information for which they directed the reader to Griesbach.

The material is divided into six parts: (I) The pre-history (1) of Matthew, (2) of Luke; (II) John the Baptist; Baptism and Temptation of Jesus; (III) Deeds and teaching of Jesus in Galilee (1) according to Matthew, (2) according to Luke, (3) according to Mark; (IV) Deeds and speeches of Jesus on the last journey to Jerusalem and in Jerusalem: (1) journey-narrative of Luke, (2) common journey-narrative of the three Gospels, (3) entry into Jerusalem, words and deeds there; (V) Passion and Death; (VI) Resurrection and Ascension. The inclusion of the Fourth Gospel is somewhat expanded over Griesbach (e.g., with the Witness of the Baptist, the Feeding of the Multitude with the Walking on the Sea, the Cleansing of the Temple – but not the Call of the Disciples, the Royal Official and the Healing of the Blind). The parts and their subdivisions (sections) are arranged in passages of narrative, and at the head of each a Latin title is placed as an indication of its content. The authors were not satisfied with Griesbach's procedure of printing out the texts in their original position but with only the first and last words. They would then have had the complete individual Gospel in its own sequence, interrupted only by those parts[29] printed again elsewhere for the purpose of the synopsis. But that this did not satisfy them is clear especially in part III, where in three successive sections they print everything from the first three Gospels subsequent to the story of the Temptations and prior to the start of the (last) journey to Jerusalem, each time with all of the parallels from the other Gospels. Consequently, everything that Matthew, Mark and Luke have in common is printed out juxtaposed three times with the full text, including the meagre text-critical apparatus. But the striving for completeness goes further still. Not only are 'overshooting' parts of the relevant pericopes of the parallel texts printed out – undoubtedly a necessary procedure (e.g. Mark 2: 4 and Luke 5: 19 beside Matt. 9: 2) – but so also are 'appended accounts' (e.g. Mark 1: 45 and Luke 5: 15f. after Matt. 8: 4, or Mark 9: 49f. after Matt. 18: 9), so that in section 1, which is reserved for the continuous Matthean text, there is sometimes

only a Marcan and/or Lucan text, but no Matthean text. The same is true
of the other sections, although the combination of putting related texts
parallel and the presentation of the continuous text is not always carried
out as extravagantly as in part III. Thus, for example, the closely related
passages Matt. 7: 7–11 and Luke 11: 9–13 are found together only in part
III at Matt. 7, whereas in part IV a bracket reference '(cf. Mt 7, 7-11)'
suffices. From the Lucan journey-narrative onward the Synoptic Gospels
could basically be printed parallel to each other without the addition of
earlier or later parts of the text – except for three places: (i) Luke, in the
introduction to the Last Supper and the Announcement of the Betrayal,
diverges from Matthew and Mark. The authors respond to this by envisaging
two Lucan columns: in the first the Lucan material is printed in the
Matthean–Marcan order, in the second in the sequence peculiar to Luke.
(ii) The rest of the Lucan 'Farewell Speeches' (22: 24–38) would have
required some parallels. But the authors here too contented themselves
with references. And so we nowhere find – although here a real deficiency
of the Griesbach synopsis could easily have been eliminated – Luke 22: 25f.
next to Matt. 20: 25–7 // Mark 10: 42–4 though they are certainly related.[30]
Similarly, Luke 22: 28–30 is not put in parallel with Matt. 19: 28. It seems
especially strange that a section with the title 'Lapsus Petri praenunciatur',
containing Luke 22: 31–8 and next to it John 13: 33, 36–8, is followed by
a second with the title 'Petro lapsus praedicitur', with Matt. 26: 30–5 //
Mark 14: 26–31 and Luke 22: 39. (iii) The pericope containing the Questioning of Jesus and the Denial of Peter required a decision because of certain
Lucan peculiarities. De Wette–Lücke first give the Matthean and Marcan
text of the (Night) Questioning and Mocking together, the latter with a
reference to Luke 22: 63–5 in brackets. Then come the Matthean, Marcan
and Lucan texts of the Denial (without putting in parallel the Johannine
account, which was instead printed in the text-block John 18: 12–27 before
its parallel, Matt. 26: 57), followed by the Lucan presentation of the Mocking (with a bracket reference to Matt. 26: 67) and Questioning (in the
Morning). In this way any putting in parallel of Luke 22: 67–71 with the
corresponding Matthean and Marcan texts is abandoned; not even the cross-
references are given. This is a not-insignificant loss for the overall view as
compared with Griesbach. Incidentally, almost all the texts put in boxes
were taken over from Griesbach, and, if only the reference was given, were
printed out in full. A few further portions of text in boxes were added by
the authors of their own accord, e.g. Luke 10: 6 to Matt. 10: 13. On the
other hand Griesbach's reference at Matt. 10: 21 to Luke 21: 16 is can-
celled and so all connection between these parts of the text is severed.

On the whole improved clarity must be conceded to the synopsis of de

Wette–Lücke as compared with that of Griesbach. However, real progress beyond Griesbach can hardly be observed, and in some details there is even regression,[31] even if the almost total abandonment of text-critical information is disregarded. It is true that a second edition of this work was produced after twenty-four years (1842), but Griesbach's publisher could still risk a posthumous fourth edition in 1822, a sign that the older work had in no way been pushed aside by the more recent one.

3 M. Roediger, 1829

This statement is fully confirmed by another successor of Griesbach, the candidate for the office of preacher, Moritz Roediger.[32] His point of departure was not that of the academic teacher, but of the student whom he wished to equip with an aid arranged for an easier over-view and reasonably served by text-critical material, which would be also – in comparison with the works of Griesbach and de Wette–Lücke – cheaper (!). Indeed, a glance at this handy little book shows that it surpasses its predecessors with regard to clarity. It takes some things (e.g. the division of the material into six principal parts)[33] from de Wette–Lücke, but for the most part follows Griesbach, but not without improving him as much as possible. As far as I can see, Roediger is the first – no doubt owing to the progress of printing technique – to use a smaller type than the one used in the main text for those parts of the text which appear outside their original sequence.[34] He makes fuller use of references; a table of the continuous text of the individual Gospels makes it easier to find a place rapidly. However, each part of the text is printed only once. In the appendix the distribution of the text by de Wette–Lücke is printed as well as the 'Muthmassliche Angabe der Ordnung in den Abschnitten' in the outline of Professor Kaiser[35] of Erlangen which had just appeared. There follow excursuses on the genuineness of the doxology to the Lord's Prayer and on the Marcan ending (16: 9–20).

Roediger's synopsis is admittedly a serviceable book for students; but he himself regretted not having had enough time and strength to produce a synopsis that satisfied all scholarly demands. What it should look like is for him best described in a letter from his teacher and patron, David Schulz, which he quotes:

'I wish there existed or that you should produce a synopsis of all related Gospel passages, not only of the first three Gospels but of all, including the apocryphal Gospels and of those that appear in the Fathers. Only when everything that still remains of the Gospel tradition has been brought together for one over-view, will a sure result in respect of the

original relationship of these Gospel books appear, and – at least nega-
tively – some things will be more clearly defined.'[36]
It can be seen that goals are being envisaged here which modern Gospel
criticism cannot formulate more comprehensively.

4 H. N. Clausen, 1829

Simultaneously with Roediger's synopsis appeared Clausen's *Tabulae
synopticae.*[37] Although they offer no synopsis of the text they do deserve
brief mention because the prolegomena contain a full pre-history, beginning
with Tatian, and a balanced discussion of the 'Synoptic Problem'. Here the
author reveals his hesitation about separating the historical aspect from the
exegetical and so establishing over against the traditional harmonies a new
kind of over-all view which the new synopses would serve.[38] The texts
themselves – according to Clausen – do not permit abandonment of the
attempt to reconstruct the course of what was narrated. Not only do the
Evangelists have definite ideas about this,[39] but also the individual pericopes betray clearly enough their position in the course of the history and
could not be adequately interpreted without regard to this. The fact that
with regard to the 'historia' clear conclusions, assured in every detail, had
not been obtained, by no means meant that this question should, even
could, be put aside. And so he arranges the matter 'juxta rationem temporis', as well as he can. His book gives the synopsis only in table form, but it
does offer a brief commentary which does not aim to replace the commentaries on the individual Gospels but to discuss the correct chronological
arrangement of the pericopes, to draw out the material and stylistic differences among the Gospels and to offer assistance at places which are more
difficult to interpret. Just as he has a definite idea about the sequence of
events, so too he holds a literary-critical position from the beginning, namely
the dependence of Mark on Matthew and Luke. Clausen's basic excursuses
are also interesting *inter alia* because they show that on the threshold of an
historical-critical investigation of the life of Jesus[40] no thoroughgoing
division existed between those scholars using the Gospels as sources for
history and those who wanted to use them 'merely' exegetically or who were
even exclusively interested in the literary-critical problem of their mutual
relationship. Rather, one affected the other and whoever wanted to write a
'life of Jesus' not only could but had to take all these aspects into account.

The spectrum of aims, of arrangements and of literary-critical hypotheses to which the different synopses corresponded which had shown
itself up to the time of Clausen, also remained fully intact subsequently.
Here a synopsis might principally serve interpretation of the Gospels,[41]
there the solution of the Synoptic Problem,[42] or elsewhere – as before –

the reconstruction of the true 'Historie'.[43] The authors see their task either
as a neutral presentation of the material[44] or, to the contrary, as work in
support of a definite hypothesis about the relationship of the Gospels one
to another.[45] Apart from the synopses of texts that are fully set out, there
are outlines in the form of tables.[46] According to the aim in view, the
Gospel of John is either fully included,[47] or included only in some parts
(especially the Passion Narrative),[48] or not included at all.[49] In the arrangement of the texts there also continue to be differences. Griesbach's principle,
to print each text only once, however, has hardly any following.[50] The
parallel parts of the Gospels are usually printed in columns next to each
other.[51] Those parts that are brought for comparison from earlier or later
sections of an Evangelist are usually clearly distinguished, even if in different
ways.[52] The comparison of individual sentences and words in parallel passages is partly left entirely to the user,[53] partly made easier by the arrangement of the type,[54] and, with the passing of time, worked out increasingly
subtly by means of exact juxtaposition.

5 R. Anger, 1852

In a certain way, the synopsis of the Leipzig professor Rudolf Anger[55]
marks a significant step forward; he includes in the synopsis all comparable
text material not only from the rest of the New Testament,[56] but also from
the apocryphal ('Judaeo-Christian') Gospels, the Apostolic Fathers, Justin
and other pre-Irenaean sources. In this way he largely fulfils the demands
of David Schulz, (given above on p. 33) which he expressly mentions.[57] In
the arrangement of the text he follows with few changes Griesbach's division
into 150 sections, which was also taken over by Roediger. However, he
gives up the principle of printing each text in full only once. Instead he
gives (a) a full comparison of related texts at the place where one of these
first occurs in the sequence of sections, (b) the full text of most of the
compared passages in their original position in the Gospel with a reference
(chapter and verse) to the parallel texts.[58] The texts or references inserted
for the sake of comparison always stand in 'boxes', which consist of unbroken lines when they are to distinguish a text from another Gospel, and
dotted lines when the comparison is with the text of the same Gospel. The
texts for comparison from John and the rest of the New Testament are
printed in smaller type on the right next to the column of the synoptics,
and are distinguished from these by a somewhat thicker line. All these texts
are printed continuously, i.e. without the gaps which would be bound to
appear if the words were placed exactly parallel. To each column belongs a
corresponding one in the first apparatus which offers the text-critical material, including that for texts from John, Acts, etc. Furthermore, there is a

column next to Luke's which notes the situation in Marcion and the divergences. The second apparatus contains in four columns the material from outside the New Testament mentioned above. In the third apparatus are found notes to the second, and in the fourth there are also notes, mainly to Marcion's text. At the end of the work follow appendixes with the ancient testimony of the Fathers about the Gospels and further notes with Patristic content on the individual places in the synopsis. There also follows in Index 1 a synopsis in the form of tables, which shows the total arrangement of the texts in the synopsis, and in Index 2 an index of passages (a) from the Synoptic Gospels, (b) from other New Testament texts, (c) from the Apocrypha and the Fathers (the latter expanded by addenda). Anger's synopsis will have been for its time not the handiest or easiest to use, yet the most thorough and comprehensive instrument for study of the Synoptic Problem.[59]

6 W. G. Rushbrooke, 1880

The appearance of Rushbrooke's *Synopticon*[60] must be termed a spectacular event in the history of the synopsis. The *Synopticon* was not only suggested by E. A. Abbott, but represents the carrying out of a suggestion which he made in his article 'Gospels' in the *Encyclopaedia Britannica* and developed in the example of the Parable of the Wicked Husbandmen. The aim is to refute the opinion that Mark compiled his Gospel out of Matthew and Luke, and instead to show that he is their source. In pursuit of this aim – and this occurs for the first time – the material common to the three synoptics[61] is presented in the order of Mark, now understood in the main as the actual core of the synoptic tradition ('the triple tradition'). Meanwhile the Matthean–Lucan material as well as the matter unique to Matthew and Luke is relegated to three appendixes (A' - Γ'). Where there exists doubt as to the attribution, all possibilities are presented next to each other. Luke 10: 1-12 appears, for example, not only as a parallel reference to Mark 6: 8-11; Matt. 10: 9-15; Luke 9: 3-5 in the main part, but also next to Matt. 10: 5-16 in Appendix A' (Matthew–Luke) and for the most part also in Appendix Γ' (matter unique to Luke); Luke 7: 36-50 stands next to the stories of the Anointing in Bethany (see n. 61), but also in Appendix Γ' as matter unique to Luke. Agreements between Matthew and Luke are brought out by special typeface in Appendix A', but are not mentioned at all in the Introduction – which had already appeared a year earlier with the main part as the first instalment. The principal interest is in the material shared with Mark and, in the opinion of the author, derived from Mark. This material, 'the triple tradition', is made to stand out with red print.[62] Next, special types of print ('capitals' and 'spaced type') are used for those parts of the text which two of the three Evangelists have in common. Only what is unique to the individual Evangelist appears in normal black type. In this way the author wants (i) to demonstrate the dependence of Matthew and Luke on Mark (by showing that the material common to Matthew and Luke but not in Mark is quite slight – a *reductio ad absurdum* of the theory that Mark was the compiler), (ii) to discuss the question of whether the material handed down thrice is to be considered as the common source document of the three synoptics, or whether the quantity of material common only to Matthew and Luke (even if slight) points to an already changed basic document which lay before both, and (iii) to bring out better the characteristics of each Evangelist (better than they appear in the matter unique to them) for in the treatment of a text that has to be taken over, the intention of the author (according to Rushbrooke) is more visible than where he narrates freely without a written source.

This work is impressive in a number of ways and has often been praised down to the present day,[63] but it seems, nevertheless, to have had no very strong influence. It underwent – so far as I can see – no further editions, nor did it find real imitators.[64] What is the reason for this? Apart from the costly presentation which put the work beyond the means of most students and must surely have made a new edition more difficult, the one-sided emphasis on the 'triple tradition' seems to have found no support. Literary judgement was too prejudiced by it, and the principle, frequently repeated by critics, that it was always necessary to begin with the given material, the Gospels, was taken too lightly. In addition, the aim of providing a clear view was hindered rather than forwarded through the use of different colours and typefaces. Rushbrooke uses his four typefaces (normal red, normal black, black capitals, and black spaced) in such a way that the normal type always shows the triple tradition (red) or what is unique to the respective Evangelist (black). Capitals on the other hand denote in the Marcan column what is common to Mark–Luke, in the Matthean column what is common to Matthew–Mark, and in the Lucan column what is common to Luke–Matthew. In the same way, spaced type in the Marcan column stands for Mark–Matthew, in the Matthean column for Matthew–Luke and in the Lucan column for Mark–Luke. It is true that this is adhered to without change from beginning to end, but this consistency need not have led to the unfortunate situation that fully identical parts of the text appear in different kinds of type; for example, what is common to Mark and Matthew appears in the Marcan column in spaced type, and in the Matthean column in capitals. How easy it would have been to draw attention to the same parts of the text with the same type! It is true that then five kinds of print would have been used rather than four (((1) Mark-

Matthew–Luke, (2) Mark–Matthew, (3) Mark–Luke, (4) Matthew–Luke, (5) Mark or Matthew or Luke alone), but in the Anointing story (see n. 61) the author even uses seven different typefaces (with two colours) of which spaced-out capitals (for example) could easily have yielded the fifth typeface. The different typefaces lead to different extensions of the text so that the accurate placing in parallel of differently printed texts runs into difficulties.[65] But this is not even attempted. Instead, the text is printed continuously, verse by verse. Periodic gaps do not draw attention to a divergent parallel text, but arise from the requirements of composition in narrow columns.[66] The limited effectiveness of Rushbrooke's *Synopticon* may well have been due also to the very scanty contact, in comparison with today, between the teaching of Biblical exegesis in the universities of the different language areas, nations, and denominations. In any case Huck's Synopsis, which will now be discussed, appeared on German soil next to the great *Synopticon* from England, which did not seriously rival it since its circulation was too small.

7 A. Huck, 1892–1950

It is true that H. J. Holtzmann says in the preface to his commentary on the synoptics:[67] 'Among the synopses in print, the most serviceable is the *Synopticon* of Rushbrooke which is, at least for scholarly research, indispensable.' But he continues: 'For normal needs Mr Albert Huck's synopsis, which follows the principles of the present commentary and is shortly to appear in the same publishing house, should suffice.' In fact the work[68] hereby announced had the primary purpose of serving as a text book for the readers of Holtzmann's commentary as well as the hearers of his lectures on the synoptics. This commentary's arrangement of the material is therefore also followed (apart from a few unimportant exceptions). Further, Huck provides no texts from John, but prints the text of Matthew, Mark and Luke in three columns in such a way that he gives Mark in strict sequence, whereas Matthew and Luke are transposed according to the requirements of comparison. Each text is printed only once. The longstanding demand that the text of each Gospel should be capable of being read in its original order remains unfulfilled. This deficiency can be explained only from the limited aim of its being a textbook to Holtzmann's commentary on the synoptics;[69] here each text's own context plays the subordinate role. But already the second edition of 1898 tried by means of four appendixes to improve the first. There were added lists of Old Testament quotations (which are printed in different type in the text), of the Johannine parallels, and a collection of 'parallels and doublets' as well as supplements and corrections to the initially very modest text-critical apparatus. The text used for the first edition was the one which also underlies Holtzmann's commentary, namely the *Novum Testamentum recensionis Tischendorfianae ultimae*, repeatedly brought out by O. von Gebhardt with Tauchnitz in Leipzig from 1873 onwards. When Holtzmann, or B. and J. Weiss[70] in their commentaries, or Tischendorf in his *editio octava maior* (1869), diverge from Tischendorf–Gebhardt then this is noted in the footnotes. Huck furnished his synopsis from the first edition on with a table of parallels in which the text of the Synoptic Gospels is adduced in three columns in the order in which they are printed (with reference to the pages of Holtzmann's commentary!) as well as an index of Gospel passages which shows for each verse where it is to be found in the synopsis.

With the third edition in 1906 'Huck', so to speak, quits its matrix. The former textbook to Holtzmann's commentary[71] has become an independent instrument for the study of the Synoptic Gospels – they now stand in the sequence Matthew, Mark, Luke – and of their problems, which tries to avoid any pre-judgement. Each Gospel can now be read in the original sequence of its text.[72] Despite this, all comparable parts of the text are printed next to each other in one place, some even in several places. Texts outside their original context are recognizable by way of smaller print. Where an Evangelist is silent his column is no longer simply continued empty, but is reduced to a narrow empty column. The text of Tischendorf–Gebhardt is retained, but the text-critical apparatus has been thoroughly revised. The variants referred to are increased, as are the manuscripts, etc (not the editions). Old Testament quotations, synoptic doublets and references to Johannine parallels are transferred from the appendix (second edition) to the apparatus of the passage concerned. Comparable texts from the Apocryphal Gospels and similar writings are added, so that at the foot of some pages there is a fivefold apparatus. In the index of parallels appears 'parallels and doublets' in three special columns in their place. New prolegomena give information about the oldest witnesses to the Synoptic Gospels, explain the text-critical apparatus (a short introduction to textual criticism) and, finally, give the minimum necessary information about the Apocryphal Gospels and the Agrapha. From the third edition on, Huck's synopsis has therefore the same basic form it has today (tenth edition 1950). A number of little aids to its use have been added in subsequent editions and the text-critical apparatus has been regularly improved. From the fifth edition on, the text of the Johannine parallels has been given as a loose supplementary fascicle and the arrangement of the print has served to make the juxtaposition of the same or corresponding words in the parallel columns ever more exact, something that can, however, hardly be achieved with the use of smaller typefaces and varying spaces between the lines.

With the ninth edition (1936) the care of this widely used textbook was handed over to H. Lietzmann, assisted by H. G. Opitz. The tenth edition (1950), a photo-mechanical reproduction of the ninth is generally known; its innovations need only to be outlined. The supplementary fascicle with the Johannine texts has been abandoned. Instead the references to the corresponding places in John are inserted beside the titles of pericopes or are put in a frame within the text of the pericope. The distinction in type-face between main and parallel texts has been abandoned, which allows for a more exact equalization of the corresponding words in the different columns. The Greek manuscripts have been rechecked against photographic reproductions, and the translations against the most modern editions. The number of variants referred to has been decreased throughout - except for thirteen pericopes which have been equipped with the full apparatus for practice; unfortunately, however, not all the witnesses have always been included. About seven-eighths of the text of Gebhardt-Nestle has been changed over to that of Nestle's fifteenth edition of 1932; but this is not said anywhere and only emerges after careful examination. Huck's full description of textual criticism in the prolegomena is reduced to a few explanations of the apparatus. This can be understood and welcomed in view of the books on textual criticism that now exist.

8 A. Wright, 1896

Having followed the changes in 'Huck' up to the present, we shall now turn back to the synopses which appeared contemporaneously and subsequently. The first to be mentioned here is Wright[73] who like Rushbrooke divides up the material, though not into three but into five groups ('sources'), giving preference, however, to the theory of an oral tradition ('oral hypothesis'). At the same time he declares that his principal aim is to give, with regard to the study of the Synoptic Problem, the facts from which any solution must begin. His five 'sources' are: (1) the Marcan material with its parallels in Matthew and Luke, (2) the five great speeches in Matthew together with the Parables of the Unjust Servant, the Workers in the Vineyard and the Two Sons, (3) ('Pauline') the (approximately) 19 parables from the material unique to Luke, (4) 140 anonymous fragments, mainly in Matthew or Luke, 9 of which are contained in both, 6 of which are 'agrapha', (5) the Nativity story in Luke 1 and 2, together with 3: 23-38 (Genealogy); 4: 16-30 (Rejection in Nazareth) - all of this deriving from the family of Jesus, to-gether with 7: 11-17 (Raising of the Young Man in Nain). When they were worked into the Canonical Gospels these sources were given all kinds of 'editorial notes', which are the responsibility of the respective Evangelist alone. In this way 'proto-Mark', 'trito-Mark', 'deutero-Matthew' etc are distinguished. The author emphasizes repeatedly that the attribution to particular sources is not always certain; but he firmly holds to the five sources and in his synopsis he offers them separately, although with all the conceivable material for comparison, not only from the Gospels (including John) but also (in an apparatus) from the other New Testament writings and from the LXX (the latter being usually printed in full). In addition to this, the text is accompanied by numerous notes concerning the origin and arrangement of the passages. The text is not printed continuously but is divided into smaller material or grammatical units, whereby a more accurate juxtaposition of the parallels becomes possible. Page by page Wright's synopsis gives a view - often fascinating - into an effort concerned above all with the recognition of the different sources, their historical connection with the disciples or other first-generation Christians and so with their reliability. The Synoptic Question is viewed together with the historical one with great force. However, if the author thought he was giving only the 'facts' and offering every other hypothesis the same chance as his own, he deceived himself mightily - even if charmingly - and no one reveals this more clearly than he himself.

9 K. Veit, 1897

Soon after Wright's synopsis there appeared in rapid succession two works which distinguished themselves by using a special comparative technique. The first to be named here is Veit,[74] who is principally concerned in his book with 'puzzling out' the synoptic parallels. For us it is most important that in the first part he prints the text of the synoptics in three lines running below one another. The sequence is determined by Mark, and, where he is missing, by Matthew, without thereby implying anything about the relationship among the Gospels or the course of the Gospel history. Material unique to any one Gospel is not included, nor is the text of John. As far as I can see this is the first attempt to undertake a comparison of the text of the synoptics vertically instead of horizontally, in lines placed one below the other instead of in juxtaposed columns. This method can certainly have advantages in some circumstances, especially when a higher number of lines forms a broader band.[75] But this is not the case with Veit's three lines. On the contrary, his system makes a general view more difficult since the absence of an Evangelist is not shown by one continuous empty column but by a multiplicity of empty lines, between which lines with text are continually appearing. It is not only the *fact* that an Evangelist is silent that comes less quickly to the eye but also *which* of them it is; and above all, it is not clear at first glance[76] whether it is the *same* one throughout.

10 R. Heineke, 1898

The same technique as Veit's is employed by Heineke[77] for his synopsis which is otherwise differently arranged. Following Rushbrooke (see above p. 36) he divides the material into three parts: (I) Mark with Matthean and Lucan parallels, (II) Luke with Matthean parallels, (III) matter unique to Matthew. A judgement about the relationship among the Gospels is not to be given but only to be made possible. An apparatus contains not only the comparative material from John's Gospel, but also doublets and further parallels (e.g. Mark 6: 32–44 is compared in the main text with Luke 9 and Matt. 14, and in the apparatus also with Mark 8: 1–10). Heineke and Veit are also alike in omitting any text-critical apparatus and in printing only the Tischendorf–Gebhardt text. Heineke says in the preface with regard to his method of presenting the parallels (hardly different from that of Veit): 'The reader may judge for himself whether there has been a step forward'. The reader has judged: neither Veit nor Heineke have found successors.

11 W. Larfeld, 1911

In contrast to the Huck synopsis, expressly termed 'excellent', Larfeld[78] wishes to offer a synopsis constructed 'according to literary–historical points of view'. However, what this means remains rather obscure. The author does not wish to enter into source analysis. Instead his synopsis is to present 'our total canonical source material[79] about Jesus so that the content may be compared and carefully considered' and therefore the Fourth Gospel also has to be included. From these meagre statements in the preface, and while testing the synopsis, one's impression grows that the author is really concerned with the time-honoured 'harmony' of the story of Jesus, only it is no longer assumed that everything must fit together without contradiction. The fitting together of the Marcan and Johannine structure succeeds through two transpositions (Mark 14: 3–9 after 10: 52 and 14: 26 after 14: 31), but at the cost of presenting the Cleansing of the Temple [in the synoptics and John] as identical and (with an appeal to Tischendorf) as occurring both at the beginning and at the end of Jesus' public life.[80] 'Where Mark failed, Matthew had to take the lead.'[81] No passage in the main text is printed more than once; therefore Matthew and Luke cannot be read continuously. Doublets and more distant parallels appear in one apparatus. Allusions to, and quotations from, the Old Testament are not indicated, in fact not even references are given. Otherwise the end result is much the same as in the Huck synopsis, except that Mark stands in the furthest left of the three columns and that homonymous words and parts of words are made to stand out through heavy type. The text is that of Nestle, not (as till Huck's eighth edition) that of Tischendorf-Gebhardt. The text-critical apparatus however follows that of Tischendorf's eighth edition, with far-reaching abandonment of all merely formal variants. At the beginning there is an introduction to New Testament textual criticism. There is also an index to the synopsis and to the Gospels. It would be hard to understand why Larfeld's synopsis appeared next to Huck's in the same publishing house at the same time if one were not permitted to assume that its harmonizing character and above all the exactly corresponding German part[82] could ensure extensive interest among the public.

12 E. D. Burton and E. J. Goodspeed, 1920

The synopsis of Burton–Goodspeed[83] aims to meet the need, up to then – in the opinion of the authors – never quite satisfied, that the texts should through their parallel print make possible a most accurate comparison 'sentence by sentence, phrase by phrase, word by word'. In fact the text is divided into small parts in such a way that with parallel printing the same or corresponding words always stand at the same height.[84] The authors leave the text of each Gospel, with quite minor exceptions, in its original order. Parallel passages 'brought' from other places stand in smaller print in their columns, sometimes also in a special apparatus. But the distance between the lines is the same as in the main part, despite the smaller print, so that no doubts can arise about the line to be compared. The authors stress that they are not aiming at a 'harmony' nor a reconstruction of the 'life of Jesus' or at defending a particular theory about the relationships among the Gospels, but wish only to present the facts for a study of the Synoptic Question. They are themselves convinced of the priority of Mark. In their judgement of the non-Marcan material in Matthew and Luke they come fairly close to the 'classic' two-source theory. They print the text of Westcott–Hort, and give their marginal variants in the apparatus as well as adding some which represent instances of 'harmonistic corruption' important for the Synoptic Problem. Here the first beginnings of an attempt to take the special character of synoptic textual criticism into account are becoming visible.[85]

13 M. -J. Lagrange, 1926

The synopsis of Lagrange[86] arose from his exegetical work. Only after the publication of his great Gospel commentaries[87] did the founder of the École Biblique de Jérusalem, of *Études Bibliques* and of *Revue Biblique*, again take up his plan, long cherished but repeatedly abandoned, for a Gospel synopsis. He had long doubted the possibility of determining the course of the Gospel history more or less correctly. But in the course of his exegesis he became increasingly certain that the order now presented in his synopsis came closest to the truth with regard both to content and to chronology. In fact he wanted to provide not only an instrument for comparing the texts, but also a harmony of the four Gospels. This task is made easier by the fact that he does not consider all Gospels to be equally reliable: with regard to chronological order he follows John[88] on the whole, inserts Luke - unchanged apart from some slight exceptions - into this frame and adds the corresponding passages from Matthew and Mark in parallel. Since he prints the transposed texts of Luke (marked with a †) a second time in their original place (with an *), it is possible to read Luke - and of course John - in its original sequence, but not Mark and Matthew. Texts printed only for the purpose of comparison stand in square brackets; references with the numbers of the pericopes serve to complete this. Although Lagrange's work does not breathe the spirit of wooden harmonizing, yet the Anointing stories in Luke 7: 36-50 and in Bethany remain unconnected, as do the Healings at a Distance of the Servant (Luke 7: 1f.) and the Son (John 4: 46f.). The columns are arranged in the order Luke, Mark, Matthew, John. It is rather irritating that what is unique to each is also printed in two columns, although without a dividing line in the middle. No value is put on exact juxtaposition of corresponding parts of the text - a regrettable step backward. The text is taken from the editions of Tischendorf, Westcott-Hort, von Soden, and Vogels, and the apparatus notes the editors who offer in their editions the variant preferred or rejected by Lagrange. The reader is referred to the author's commentaries for the justification for these decisions. Witnesses are not given. No word or reference indicates that the pericope of the Woman Taken in Adultery, as also Mark 16: 9-20, are text-critically insecure, although this is done for Mark 9: 44-6. In the prolegomena there follows, after a synoptic table ('Index fragmentorum juxta ordinem fere chronologicum'), a 'Textus evangelici index', an indispensable means for finding individual passages. The work of Lagrange already bears the thoroughly conservative stamp which was also noticeable in the French Gospel Synopsis with popular commentary that followed in 1928.[89]

14 P. Benoit and M.-E. Boismard, 1969

Lagrange's synopsis underwent - so far as I have been able to determine - no further editions and only in its French form did it find a certain popularity. But now it has been replaced (to say this at once here) by the far more serviceable synopsis of Benoit-Boismard.[90] Although our account is really only concerned with the Greek synopsis, this work, presented by professors of the École Biblique de Jérusalem, deserves brief mention by reason of its special characteristics and advantages. Throughout, the authors are guided by the principle that each of the four Gospels must be capable of being read in its original form, and they accept the resulting frequent repetitions. Not seldom the full material to be compared in a pericope appears in three different places (e.g. Matt. 5: 32 in § §56, 235, 246; the story of the Anointing in § §123, 272, 313).[91] The relationships that La-grange ignored are of course made apparent to the eye, and doublets are printed in generous numbers. Striking is the strong emphasis on internal Johannine parallels, though this might be less a literary-critical problem than one of the Johannine way of thinking and speaking. The most import-ant text-critical information, and above all exceptionally rich comparative material from the Apocrypha and the Fathers, is found in the apparatuses. The technical arrangement of the book (arrangement and identification of the text, references, indexes and so on) allow the rich pedagogical experi-ence of the authors to appear at every step for the benefit of the French-speaking reader of the Bible.

15 J. Weiss, 1913

The use of red (and gold) print, introduced by Rushbrooke to denote the different sources is logically developed by J. Weiss in his Synoptic Tables[92] which he brought out as a supplement to his commentaries[93] following Huck's synopsis (fourth edition). The Mark material is printed black, red denotes Matthew–Luke (Q); brown, matter unique to Matthew; green, matter unique to Luke. John is not considered. The sequence in the Gospels remains unchanged. Also printed are the pericope numbers of the full synopsis (Huck) which refer to divergences in sequence from the other synoptics. Later editions underline in black those places where Mark is unique. The third edition adds all the comparable material from John's Gospel in appendixes.

16 W. R. Farmer, 1969

The use of coloured type also characterizes Farmer's *Synopticon*.[94] This work is not really a synopsis and does not claim to be one, but is for use together with one of the current synopses (introduction, p. 2). It merely consists of an expanded reproduction of the first three Gospels from Nestle–Aland (20th ed., 1950), in which, however, the text is overprinted with coloured bands or underlined in colour. The colours distinguish both full agreement among Matthew–Mark–Luke, Matthew–Mark, Matthew–Luke, and Mark–Luke, and marked but incomplete agreement between Matthew–Mark, Matthew–Luke, and Mark–Luke. Everything else, that is the matter unique to each Gospel in the widest sense, remains uncoloured.

Combinations of different colours are frequent; they always occur when there is a partial agreement next to a full agreement, or when two partial agreements are observed in the same part of the text. Agreement and divergence in the word sequence are marked. Farmer who has elsewhere expressed himself to be a critic of the two-source hypothesis[95] and who has again defended Griesbach's hypothesis (Mark dependent on Matthew and Luke) keeps his promise not to influence the reader in the direction of any possibility with regard to the solution of the Synoptic Problem 'one hundred per cent' as does no other author of a synopsis. The price is that the user never finds the texts put together in his book; for this he is referred to other synopses which have to decide, for better or for worse on this or that arrangement of the parallels.

In connection with Farmer's book one may be permitted a comment about the use of colours. They are – there can be no doubt about this – an excellent and essential means for letting agreement and difference in the 'synopsis' spring at once to the eye. It is another question whether the synopsis as a tool should be given colours from the beginning. It can hardly be denied that the user of the different colours gains much in knowledge and understanding if he adds the colours himself.[96] A work-book for students should therefore contain no coloured print; instead there should be sufficient space between the lines to allow multiple underlinings. Coloured synopses can however be useful for rapid orientation.[97]

17 B. de Solages, 1959

Colours were, however, used in the Greek Gospel synopsis of B. de Solages.[98] For the history of the synopsis this work is very important, but for another reason: it represents the first significant attempt to apply systematically the quantitative methods of the new literary science to the Synoptic Problem. Shortly before there had appeared Morgenthaler's Statistical Dictionary[99] which showed how much this step was 'in the air'. But in no way did it lead into totally new methodological country. The 'hapax legomena' had already long played a role in the argument about the provenance of New Testament texts; this is already a quantifying concept.[100] This is not the place to describe de Solages' work more closely, still less to do it justice.[101] His contribution aims at a statistically based solution to the Synoptic Problem. The synopsis is only a tool for this, although one obviously especially prepared for this use. Anticipating his conclusions, de Solages therefore groups the synoptic material into five principal groups (with various sub-groups): (1) threefold tradition (Mark-Matthew-Luke), (2) Q double tradition (Matthew-Luke), (3) Marcan double tradition (Mark-Matthew and Mark-Luke), (4) unique material

(Mark, Luke, Matthew), and (5) doublets. These five groups or sub-groups
are presented one after the other – as earlier in Rushbrooke – and the
word-position of each passage is analysed by determining how many words
are identical when the parallel passages are compared, how many identical
with divergent declension etc, synonymous, analogous or additional. It
should be said about the actual synopsis that it prints Lagrange's text[102]
but omits any text-critical apparatus. It is in no way a book for students,
unless the student has already decided to study the evidence for the two-
source theory *more mathematico*.

18 R. Morgenthaler, 1957

The work of de Solages is continued, even if in another way,[103] and in
many respects more completely and convincingly by Morgenthaler's
statistical synopsis.[104] The text no longer appears at all in the actual
synopsis, but is represented by the number of the words of the text. Only
in chapter 3a, in which the sequences of words are discussed, does the
Greek text (Nestle–Aland; 24th ed., 1960) appear in the thirty-four
examples, all of them very short. Although he too suggests a solution to
the Synoptic Problem, an 'expanded two-source theory', nevertheless
Morgenthaler's synopsis is arranged in such a way that with its help other
solutions can also be presented, or rather one should say, 'calculated'.
Since the principal significance of this book lies so much in the application
of statistical methods to the Synoptic Question, and since this in turn
belongs to a much more comprehensive context of the new linguistics, we
shall have to leave the matter with the remark that also in this situation,
new with respect to scientific method, the synopsis shows its significance
as a new presentation of the problem.

19 K. Aland, 1963

Aland's synopsis[105] has been put at the end of this paper. It has won its
place in the German-speaking world next to Huck – unchanged since
1936 –[106] and also outside it. A full description is hardly necessary here; all
of us will have long been familiar with this book. Its place in the history of
the synopsis during the last 200 years may nevertheless be sketched briefly.
The full inclusion of John's Gospel means that this synopsis is intended to
serve as a tool not only for the study of the Synoptic Problem but also for
that of the extra-synoptic Jesus tradition. A rich presentation of apocryphal
and Patristic material – the Gospel of Thomas is printed in full as appendix
1, and in Latin, German and English – fulfils everything that David Schulz[107]
could have dreamed. The sequence of the events also receives an emphasis
again – simply because the Johannine material must somehow be ordered

together with the synoptic material. For this reason several Journeys to Jerusalem are distinguished. The principle that each Gospel must be capable of being read in its own sequence means that the Temple Cleansing is narrated twice and the story of the Anointing three times, but reference is always made to the parallels. Elsewhere too, care is taken to avoid the appearance that a connected sequence of events could be reconstructed, by adding to the titles of individual passages, for example, The Sermon on the Mount, The Sermon on the Plain, or The Farewell Speeches, 'according to Matthew', 'according to John'. The synopsis distinguishes between principal and secondary parallels. All parallels are as a general principle presented with the full text, the principal parallels in normal type, the secondary ones in smaller type; the doublets of the latter within the same Gospel are, however, never printed next to each other in two columns but under each other in the same column. The printing of all the comparative material for each pericope, even distant comparative material, makes this synopsis rich in content and also rather bulky. The text-critical apparatus partly contributes to this since it is given for each principal text and for the juxtaposed principal parallels. The text and apparatus are those of the *Novum Testamentum Graece* of Aland–Nestle, in the improvement of which the synopsis shares.[108]

D. Conclusions

Does looking back over 200 years of Gospel synopsis allow any profitable result to emerge? I think so. The most important seems to me to be the fact that this undertaking – without prejudice to secondary results – has from its beginning been basically directed toward the 'Synoptic Question' for the study of which it presents the facts that require explanation. Griesbach's conception has therefore been shown to be basically correct. Secondly, it has been shown, in my opinion, that it is not worthwhile to prepare a synopsis designed from the beginning to prove a particular theory, but that, on the contrary, continuous, untiring attention is needed to avoid this if the usefulness of the instrument is not to suffer. The most convincing example for this point is Griesbach himself. His Synoptic Theory is today overwhelmingly rejected, but his synopsis has dominated the field with respect to intention and conception. Thirdly, our look into the past has also shown that no synopsis can provide a really clear view of the relationship among the Gospels, unless, in addition to the comparison of the texts, there is also a comparison of the structure, which can only be given by a general tabular view. Further, one can learn from the history of the synopsis that care and improved printing techniques have been able to bring about continued improvements in the possibilities of comparison. Finally, it can be recognized (at least in these early stages) that the rise of quantitative linguistic methods will not make obsolete synopses of the Gospels - and, *vice versa*, that the above methods will be indispensable for research about the Synoptic Problem, even if the synopsis would then have to assume the form of the contents of a computer bank.

4

GRIESBACH'S ANSWER TO THE SYNOPTIC QUESTION

Bo Reicke

Translated by Ronald Walls

Johann Jakob Griesbach (1745–1812) was active in Halle when he published his epoch-making *Synopsis* of 1774 which appeared separately in 1776. This instrument enabled him to apply himself to an exhaustive study of the literary relationships among the Gospels of Matthew, Mark and Luke. He later moved to Jena, and in 1783 gave scholars of Germany a hint of his Synoptic Theory.[1] In 1789–90 this was fully elaborated and published under the title of *Commentatio*;[2] in 1794 the study was republished with supplements.[3] Similar theories had been put forward in Great Britain by Henry Owen in 1764 and in Germany by Anton Friedrich Büsching in 1766; but Griesbach mentioned neither of these.[4]

I. The background of Griesbach's Synoptic Theory

The Synoptic Hypothesis of Griesbach was a *modification* of a theory which had prevailed down to his time, viz., the hypothesis of Augustine according to whom Mark had to be seen as the epitomizer of Matthew, but not of Luke (Augustine, *De consensu evangelistarum*, i. 2. 4: 'Marcus eum, scil. Matth., subsecutus tamquam pedisequus et breviator ejus videtur'; i. 3. 6: 'non habuit tamquam breviatorem conjunctum Lucas sicut Marcum Matthaeus'). Griesbach contradicted the second, negative proposition of Augustine, and affirmed that Luke had also been used by Mark.[5] It was his synopsis that led Griesbach to this conclusion. For by refraining from the usual attempts at harmonization, and by retaining in his parallel columns the sequence of pericopes characteristic of each Gospel, he permitted the similarities or differences in general order and immediate sequence between Matthew and Mark, as well as those between Mark and Luke, to stand out clearly. With regard to Mark's sequence of pericopes, the Second Gospel often displayed agreement with Matthew or Luke or with both. Griesbach found that the simplest explanation of this intermediate position of Mark was to regard the Second Gospel in the Canon as a compilation of the First and Third Gospels.

This relatively new solution of the Synoptic Problem was presented in a country where, for almost half a century, the literary problems of the Gospels had been discussed with unparalleled enthusiasm and energy. An adequate understanding of the hypothesis put forward by Griesbach requires that account should be taken in the first instance of solutions attempted by his predecessors and contemporaries, against whom Griesbach directed his arguments.

Augustine's hypothesis, which held the field in Griesbach's day, and the latter's own modification of it, represented different alternatives to an hypothesis that has always played a leading part in exegesis. It may be treated as no 1, and is called the Utilization Hypothesis since it presupposes a literary dependence of one Gospel upon the other. However, this includes various possibilities of combination, chiefly three:

(1*a*) Matthew influenced Mark, and both influenced Luke;
(1*b*) Matthew influenced Luke, and both influenced Mark;
(1*c*) Mark influenced Matthew and Luke.

Hypothesis 1*a* had been put forward in Griesbach's time for example by Hugo Grotius at Amsterdam in 1641 and by other advocates of the priority of Matthew who did at the same time allow for an influence of Mark upon Luke.[6] Hypothesis 1*b* was the solution that Griesbach supported. Hypothesis 1*c*, suggesting the priority of Mark, assumed dominance in the nineteenth century but was already introduced in 1786 by Gottlob Christian Storr of Tübingen,[7] that is, between the first hint of Griesbach's Hypothesis in 1783 and its elaboration in 1789–90. After *c* 1835, and independently of Storr, the latter's idea developed into one of the main supports of the presently dominant two-source theory. Against the priority of Mark, Griesbach adduced several arguments to be described below. Decisive was his conviction that Matthew had been an eyewitness, whereas Mark had not personally experienced the events recorded.[8]

Besides these principal configurations of the Utilization Hypothesis found in the history of synoptic research, there are also some important *alternatives* to it rejecting any literary use of the one Gospel by the other. That is to say, if dependence of the Evangelists upon each other is altogether denied, the scholar is obliged to trace their partial agreement with one another back to a common foundation or source. In the history of the problem, three such source theories have played important parts. By the contemporaries of Griesbach two of them were represented, whereas the last one was made public only after the final version of his *Commentatio* had appeared. The three source-theories referred to are these:

(2) the Proto-Gospel Hypothesis;
(3) the Fragment Hypothesis;
(4) the Tradition Hypothesis.

No 2, the Proto-Gospel Hypothesis, stems from a remark of Papias implying that Matthew had compiled the λόγια in Hebrew (Eusebius, History III. 39. 16). Following this, Epiphanius and Jerome held that there was an older Gospel of Matthew in Hebrew, and claimed that it had re-appeared in the Hebrew or Nazarene Gospel of the Syrian Judaeo-Christians. This theory was taken up in 1689 by Richard Simon in Normandy, the pioneer of New Testament text criticism. He asserted that an old Gospel of Matthew, presumed to have been written in Hebrew or rather in Aramaic and taken to lie behind the Nazarene Gospel, was the Proto-Gospel.[9] In 1778 Gotthold Ephraim Lessing in Wolfenbüttel identified the Nazarene Gospel as the common source of all the Synoptic Gospels, and his study on the subject was edited posthumously in 1784 by his brother.[10] Lessing's notion of an Aramaic Proto-Gospel was taken up in 1794 by Johann Gottfried Eichhorn in Göttingen.[11] But this scholar linked his theory in an eclectic manner with J. B. Koppe's below-mentioned assumption of several documents (no 3), and in this complex form the Proto-Gospel Hypothesis was rebuked by Griesbach – about which more later.

No 3, the Fragment Hypothesis, had been conceived in 1783 by Johann Benjamin Koppe in Göttingen. He assumed the existence of a number of shorter and longer accounts in Hebrew and Greek no longer accessible, but which had been used by the Synoptists.[12] A similar hypothesis was pro-pounded in 1817 by F. Schleiermacher in Berlin and became more widely known, but this was after Griesbach's death. Griesbach argued only against the original form as put forward by Koppe.

No 4, the Tradition Hypothesis, was made public in 1796–7 by Johann Gottfried Herder in Weimar.[13] Rejecting both the Utilization Hypothesis and the Proto-Gospel Hypothesis, he preferred to see the whole tradition (called the Gospel-legend) as a *vox viva*. Its protoplasm was supposed to be an Aramaic Proto-Mark, which had developed *c* 34–40 A.D. orally in Jeru-salem, and later been written down. This emphasis on the formation of oral traditions – appreciated by the Romantics, and important a hundred years later for the pioneers of form criticism – was still unknown to Gries-bach in 1794 when he expanded his *Commentatio* of 1789–90.

Griesbach's hypothesis thus emerged in competition with a series of critical attempts at a solution to the Synoptic Problem. In his argumenta-tion the distinguished professor of Jena discussed in detail some of the divergent views represented by his industrious and prolific contempor-aries.[14] Whereas the others wrote mostly in German, he preferred the scholarly Latin which he used fluently and elegantly, in polemics always remaining extraordinarily proper and courteous.

II. Griesbach's theory explained and illustrated

(a) Griesbach presented the hypothesis preliminarily in his study called *Fontes*, published at Easter in 1783, in which he discussed the sources of the Gospel accounts of the Resurrection (n. 1). He started from the conviction that John and Matthew were apostles, and therefore were able to report on events which they had in part experienced themselves after the death of Jesus and in part come to know through other eyewitnesses.[15] According to Griesbach, the Gospel accounts of the Risen Christ vary for the simple reason that the Evangelists were confronted with the testimony of different eyewitnesses. In particular the women involved, who discovered the empty tomb, were excited and began to run hither and thither. The Evangelists were therefore compelled to use different traditions. John proceeded from the testimony of Mary Magdalene (John 20: 1), Matthew from the report given by Mary the mother of James (Matt. 28: 1).[16] Luke utilized Matthew's narrative, omitting a few things but on the other hand providing expansions on the basis of information supplied by Joanna, an eyewitness especially mentioned by Luke, or by some of her acquaintances (Luke 8: 3; 23: 49, 55; 24: 10).[17] The line supposed to run from Matthew to Luke was then extended to form a triangle by the inclusion of the Second Gospel, other lines being drawn from Matthew and Luke to Mark.

In his essay on the Resurrection stories Griesbach only indicated his view of Mark's dependence on Matthew and Luke by two statements:[18] (1) In general Matthew served as a model for Mark; (2) but in the reports on the Risen Christ it was rather Luke who played the primary part for Mark. In the latter context Griesbach had also the ending of Mark in mind, although its textual foundation is uncertain; only later did he declare these verses to be secondary (Mark 16: 9–20).

(b) Griesbach developed his Synoptic Hypothesis definitively in his *Commentatio* of 1789–90, published with additions in 1794 (above, n. 3). He wanted to elaborate his theory about Mark, only hinted at in the earlier study, by taking the whole Gospel into account. The dispute carried on by contemporary scholars over the relationship among the sources could, he believed, be settled by reference to circumstances to which little attention had been paid earlier.[19] He was thinking particularly of Storr, Koppe and Eichhorn, who had recently put forward theories about the priority of Mark, about a plurality of sources, and about a Proto-Gospel (above, pp. 51–2). Griesbach proceeded to discuss the problem of Mark in four parts: (i) to present his opinion; (ii) to substantiate it by conclusive arguments; (iii) to answer various objections; and (iv) to draw some conclusions.

(i) Griesbach's fundamental thesis was this:[20] 'In composing his book,

Mark had before him not merely the Gospel of Matthew, but also that of Luke, and from them he extracted what he recorded about the acts, words, and experiences of the Saviour.'

Then he worked out his thesis in fifteen points:[21] (1) Chiefly and most frequently Mark followed Matthew as his authority. (2) From time to time he parted company with Matthew and took Luke as his guide. (3) Yet even where he followed in Matthew's footsteps, he never lost sight of Luke, but reconciled him with Matthew, and *vice versa*. (4) Above all Mark aimed at brevity, and wanted to write a book of limited scope. (5) Therefore, he left out elements not belonging to what our Lord had taught in public (Matt. 1-2; Luke 1-2). (6) In addition Mark omitted several longer speeches of Christ (e.g. Matt. 5-7; 10: 16-42; 11: 20-30; 12: 33-45 etc; Luke 6: 17-49; 19: 11-28). By leaving out the travel narrative in Luke 10: 1 - 18: 14, Mark even sacrificed about one-third of the Gospel of Luke, since this section of the Gospel consists almost entirely of speeches of Christ. (7) In making his excerpts from Matthew and Luke, Mark considered his readers, people living outside Palestine who had little precise knowledge of the dogmas and customs of the Jews and especially of the Pharisees, or who simply did not need to know or to learn about them. (8) Hence he cut away many details - but certainly not everything - from units present in Matthew and Luke which referred only to the Jews, and especially to the Pharisees, or were adapted to their manner of thinking (e.g. Matt. 16: 2-3; 19: 28; Luke 4: 16-30; 23: 28-32). (9) Similarly he did not quote as many Old Testament passages as the First Evangelist (cf. Matt. 4: 14-16; 12: 17-21; 13: 14-15). (10) Occasionally he added by way of illustration what he considered to be necessary or useful for a correct understanding of the narrative by his readers (e.g. Mark 7: 3, 4, 8, 11-13; 12: 42). (11) Frequently, however, he retained the same phrases, expressions, and constructions used by Matthew or Luke, including many that were somewhat unusual (e.g. Mark 2: 10 λέγει τῷ παραλυτικῷ; 10: 22 ἦν γὰρ ἔχων κτήματα πολλά; 12: 14 οὐ μέλει σοι περὶ οὐδενός, οὐ γὰρ βλέπεις εἰς πρόσωπον ἀνθρώπων; 13: 14 τὸ βδέλυγμα τῆς ἐρημώσεως together with the parenthetic expression ὁ ἀναγινώσκων νοείτω; and similar cases). (12) Mark by no means copied the books of the others literally, but only related in his own manner what he read in them, using other phrases and expressions. (13) Not seldom he unfolded and exposed more elaborately and distinctly what the others had handed down in shorter form, although by selecting the deeds and sayings of Christ for inclusion in his presentation he aimed at brevity, and, as has been said, left unmentioned many valuable pieces of both Gospels (such unfolding can for instance be recognized in Mark 6: 17-29, 30, 31; 9: 14-29, 38-50; 11: 11-26). (14) He expanded the accounts of Matthew and Luke with several individual features which, in his opinion, would be of interest to the reader (e.g. Mark 2: 14 ὁ τοῦ Ἀλφαίου; 5: 42 ἦν γὰρ ἐτῶν δώδεκα; 6: 3 ὁ τέκτων; 6: 13 ἤλειφον ἐλαίῳ πολλοὺς ἀρρώστους; 10: 46 ὁ υἱὸς Τιμαίου, Βαρτίμαιος; 13: 3 Πέτρος καὶ Ἰάκωβος καὶ Ἰωάννης καὶ Ἀνδρέας; 14: 51-2 καὶ εἷς τις νεανίσκος συνηκολούθει αὐτῷ, etc; 15: 21 τὸν πατέρα Ἀλεξάνδρου καὶ Ῥούφου; 15: 40 and 16: 1 καὶ Σαλώμη; and numerous other examples). (15) Mark added some episodes also (although not many and quite brief) which had been omitted by Matthew and Luke (to be mentioned below). His reasons for adding these would easily be discerned by an attentive reader, if he were only willing to compare the Gospels carefully.

(ii) For a more exact foundation of this view, Griesbach adduced three arguments (below *a, b, c*).

(*a*) What stands in Mark is also found in Matthew and Luke, with the exception of twenty-four verses only. Synoptic tables make it evident that Mark followed the other Evangelists alternately. An oscillation of parallels emerges which begins in the following way:

Matt.	Mark	Luke
3: 1 - 4: 22 =	1: 1-20	
	1: 21-39 =	4: 31-44

Griesbach continued this list over seven pages, and illustrated it by a detailed commentary.[22] Without any artificial hypothesis, so he maintained, his view should be able to explain why Mark had placed what we read in his book just at the relevant point. Mark has sometimes preserved in the appropriate context a section which Matthew had presented in an arbitrary connection, for example the story of the execution of John the Baptist which is recounted only after the reference to Herod Antipas' speculation on the reincarnation of the Baptist in Jesus.[23]

(*b*) Mark was a son of the hostess of a house-congregation in Jerusalem, and had been in contact with Peter and Paul. He would therefore have had considerable opportunity to collect information beyond the material available to Matthew and Luke. The fact that he made so little use of this opportunity is explained by his intention to provide a selection that would especially suit the needs of his readers. Mark's special material is contained in only twenty-four verses, distributed among three short accounts of miracles and two small parables (Mark 3: 7 - 12 Multitude and Unclean Spirits; 7: 32-7 Ephphatha; 8: 22-6 the Blind Man of Bethsaida; 4: 26-9 the Seed Growing Secretly; 13: 33-6 the Door-Keeper). But two of the short miracle stories in Mark were clearly suggested by phrases in Matthew, and the two small parables in Mark were simply meant to replace verbose parables in Matthew. It is only the Healing of the Blind Man of Bethsaida (8:

22–6) that has no model in Matthew, but the episode is analogous to the two other miracles and corresponds to the fundamental principle of the 'messianic secret' which is also present in them.[24]

(*c*) Time and again Mark passes in sudden jumps from agreement with Matthew to agreement with Luke and then back again, or *vice versa*. For example, there are these zigzag patterns:[25]

Mark 3: 1–5	= Luke	Mark 10: 22, 26–7	= Matthew
3: 6	= Matthew	10: 28–9	= Luke
Mark 5: 25–7	= Luke	Mark 13: 24–5	= Matthew
5: 28	= Matthew	13: 26	= Luke
5: 29	= Luke	13: 27–32	= Matthew
Mark 8: 37	= Matthew		
8: 38	= Luke		
9: 1–2	= Matthew		

(iii) Various objections had been made to Griesbach's hypothesis, and these were refuted in detailed arguments.

It had already become clear, Griesbach maintained, that Mark cannot be conceived in Augustine's sense as being only an epitomizer of Matthew. By taking into account Mark's additional dependence upon Luke, the reasons for the variations between Mark and Matthew or Luke are explained. This was emphasized to reject the counter-argument of Eichhorn, based on the Proto-Gospel Hypothesis (above, p. 52).[26]

Storr, the inaugurator of the preference for the priority of Mark (above, p. 51), said he could not see how Griesbach's hypothesis would agree with the information of Papias concerning Mark. For had Mark been in the sense of Papias the interpreter of Peter, then he would not have subordinated himself with such lack of originality to the authority of Matthew and Luke. Against this Griesbach appealed to the difficulty of believing that Papias and his followers had reliable traditions at their disposal. In reality Mark had not been the translator, but only the assistant (ὑπηρέτης), of Peter.[27] Storr further asked why Mark produced any presentation of his own, if this were only meant to be an extract from earlier sources. Griesbach answered by repeating his appeal to Mark's readers and their interest in having a convenient summary.[28] Above all the priority of Mark is excluded by the fact that Matthew was an eye witness.[29] It must only be admitted that Mark has often expressed more clearly what was not so clear in the Gospel of Matthew. And here again there are those frequent transitions of Mark from agreement with Matthew to agreement with Luke and *vice versa* (e.g. from Matt. 4: 22 to Luke 4: 31; from Luke 6: 11 to Matt. 12: 15; from Matt. 13: 35 to Luke 8: 22). The assumption of the priority of Mark can in no way explain why Matthew has either omitted or recounted differently several circumstances that appear in Mark (most notably in the sections of Matthew which should have corresponded to Mark 1: 21 - 3: 6.[30]

Nor would it be correct, Griesbach argued, to assert with Koppe (above, p. 52) that a shorter tradition must at any given time be older than a longer one. The eventual dimension of a writing depends upon the stance of the author: one writer may be inclined to expand his material, another likes to condense it.[31]

Griesbach then dealt with another objection made by Storr, implying that if Mark had read the writings of Matthew and Luke, it would have been irresponsible of him to omit so many elements which ought to have been worthy of note.[32] Griesbach wanted to show that Mark had always had good reasons for his abbreviations, and he did this in nine points:[33]

In describing (1) the Baptism and (2) the Temptation of Jesus, Mark refrained from mentioning details in Matthew which presupposed special contact with Judaism and familiarity with the scriptures. Concerning (3) the Sermon on the Mount, one has to note that Luke had already much shortened the tradition represented by Matthew, and in this respect Mark only went a step further because he wished in general to avoid longer speeches. The same applies to the continuation of the defence against the Beelzebul Accusation. The fact that (4) the Centurion at Capernaum and (5) the Question of the Disciples of John were not mentioned by Mark is accounted for by his transition in the use of the sources (a jump from Matt. 4: 22 to 12: 15; then from Luke 6: 16 to 8: 16). (6) Mark was able to leave unmentioned the walking of Peter on the lake, because he was not so much dependent upon Peter as is claimed by scholars who accept the doubtful remarks of Papias. (7) Contextual counterparts to several Matthean narratives about Jesus in Perea and Jerusalem (Matt. 19: 27; 20: 1-16; 22: 1-14; 23: 2-39; 25: 1-46) are lacking in the Gospel of Mark, but this is accounted for by his dependence on Luke who does not provide any contextual parallels either. (8) Matthew described a confrontation with the Risen Christ in Galilee, but Mark left this out in the concluding section of his chapter 16, although twice in what precedes Jesus had aroused the expectation of such an epiphany (Mark 14: 28; 16: 7). In explanation Griesbach took into account the possibility of a different original ending to Mark, because the last twelve verses are unreliable from the point of view of text criticism. (9) It was also for quite intelligible reasons that Mark omitted the sections of Luke which are missing from his Gospel. The chronological data concerning the first activity of John (Luke 3: 1-3) would not have interested Mark's readers. Shortly before the Sermon on the Plain, Mark was following Luke, then refrained from mentioning this discourse because he wanted, as a general rule, to avoid longer speeches.

Instead he linked up again with the First Gospel (Matt. 12: 15, 22), and therefore a large section of the Third Gospel was excluded (Luke 6: 17 - 8: 3). Similarly, in the Perean section Mark followed Matthew, and therefore omitted Lucan material (Luke 19: 1-27).

Storr had also quoted apparent contradictions between Matthew, or Luke, and Mark in order to criticize Griesbach's hypothesis. In seven points Griesbach attempted to prove that there were no contradictions, but that Mark had deliberately harmonized, clarified or expanded the data supplied by the other Evangelists:[34]

(1) Mark knew that Levi was the son of Alphaeus (Mark 2: 14), a fact not mentioned by the other two. (2) By quoting the saying of Jesus on the Sabbath as having been created in favour of men (2: 27), he merely clarified the statements found in the context and supported by the parallels about the Son of Man. (3) Unlike Matthew, Mark connected the Election of the Twelve with the Beelzebul Accusation (3: 7-30); this was caused by his dependence first upon Luke and then upon Matthew. (4) The chronological discrepancy between Matthew and Mark with respect to the Lord's sojourn in Capernaum and his journeys across the lake can be explained generally with the aid of the divergent arrangement in Luke. (5) According to Matthew and Luke, Jairus reported that his daughter had died, but according to Mark he only said that she was going to die (Mark 5: 23). In this alteration by Mark, Griesbach discovered a correction occasioned by reading the Third Gospel, for according to Luke the news of the girl's death came to hand later (Luke 8: 49). (6) On the Healing of Bartimaeus, Mark was in possession of a more precise narrative than the others so that he was able to improve on Matthew and Luke. (7) Similarly concerning the Cleansing of the Temple and the Cursing of the Fig Tree, Mark was able to correct the chronological order of Matthew because concrete data were available to him (Mark 11: 11, 12, 15, 19, 20, 27).

(iv) In thirteen definitive points Griesbach summed up the consequences of assuming the order of precedence to be Matthew-Luke-Mark:

(1) Mark composed his Gospel only after the versions of Matthew and Luke were completed. Storr's assertion of Marcan priority is to be rejected. (2) Papias' tradition about Mark and Peter is sheer fabrication. (3) On the whole the early Fathers of the Church did not provide us with historical reports, but with personal conjectures about Mark and Peter. At most Peter could be the source of certain data in Mark which go beyond those supplied by Matthew and Luke; but other sources are conceivable, too. (4) Augustine incorrectly described Mark as being only a follower of Matthew. (5) In general the Fathers seem to have received no secure tradition concerning the genesis of the New Testament. (6) Griesbach's explanation does not

exclude the postulation of an older Hebrew Gospel of Matthew; yet the existence of such a Gospel remains highly improbable. Mark at all events used a copy of Matthew in Greek. (7) The view of several people, that the Evangelists were not personally the authors of the Gospels attributed to them, is wrong. (8) But the least probable conjecture, especially with respect to Mark, is that the Evangelists compiled their books out of un-known, long-lost reports in Hebrew or Greek. (9) The original Gospel of Mark has been preserved whole and entire except for the last verses, which point toward a lost concluding section. (10) Already in the time of Mark, the Gospels of Matthew and Luke contained the same material in the same order as in the form before us now. Elements which Mark did not take over were not previously absent from these Gospels. (11) One must not look to Mark for a harmony of the Gospels. He was not con-cerned with chronological sequence, but moved from Matthew to Luke or *vice versa* without regard to the timing of the episode in question. From this it becomes evident that in the days of the apostles there was no kind of necessity to respect chronological sequence when recounting the acts of the Lord. It may further be supposed that none of the other Evangelists took on the task of writing annals or diaries. (12) At any rate Mark had a different conception of the purpose and use of Gospels than most theo-logians of later centuries. Had it occurred to him to explain Matthew by a regular history, this would certainly have turned out to be quite different from secular histories. No doubt it would have appealed to men like Lessing and all who have sharpened their minds through the study of classical literature, and have learned by long practice how to deal correctly with ancient records. This is not the case with authors of harmonies and too-industrious expositors. (13) Those who emphasize that Mark wrote under divine inspiration must portray him as a rather unimportant man.

With these somewhat ironic observations Griesbach concluded his argu-mentation, in other respects analytical throughout. He was convinced that his modification of the Utilization Hypothesis had solved the literary problem of the Synoptic Gospels once and for all.

III. The influence of Griesbach's theory on subsequent New Testament study

The immediate *effect* of Griesbach's hypothesis was not extensive. It is true that in 1795, just after the publication of the enlarged version of the *Com-mentatio* (in 1794, see n. 3), one of Griesbach's colleagues at that time in Jena declared that he found Griesbach's hypothesis to be superior. This was Heinrich Eberhard Gottlob Paulus, and he developed similar ideas in later publications.[35] But the notorious rationalist Paulus was not highly

regarded by his contemporaries. Somewhat later Griesbach was supported
by younger German theologians. He also found influential advocates in
Wilhelm Martin Leberecht de Wette of Basel and Ferdinand Christian Baur
of Tübingen.

In 1825 Griesbach's hypothesis was taken up and received its first
defence in the academic treatises of two young German theologians.

One of them was a student of Friedrich Schleiermacher in Berlin,
Heinrich Saunier. He regarded the assumption of a secondary abbreviation
of tradition by Mark as the best explanation for the fact that Mark provided no account of the birth of Jesus.[36] From the very beginning, Jewish
Christians in Palestine as well as Gentile Christians living in remote countries had to be instructed about the circumstances of the Lord's birth as
the foundation of his messianic ministry. The earliest Christian preaching
certainly did not suppress this important Christological information, but
the hypothesis of Marcan priority must have such a consequence. Only if
we grant that Mark, in the interest of his particular readers, omitted what
other Evangelists had already described in detail, is the absence of the
Nativity Narratives in his Gospel explained. The literary procedure of Mark
in relation to the other Evangelists provides confirmation of this assumption. In the rest of his work Saunier thoroughly compared each section of
Mark with the parallels in Matthew and Luke. The result of his exposition
showed that in the report on the discourses of John the Baptist, for example, the shorter form of Mark proves to be secondary, and in the Temptation pericope (1: 12–13) the Marcan account is even unintelligible without knowledge of the parallels.[37] On the other hand, in Mark's account of
the Lord's activity at Capernaum (1: 21 – 3: 6) where he is following Luke,
Mark enriched the narrative with several details, but this is evidence of his
practice of retelling ('Nacherzählung').[38] The omission of the Sermon on
the Mount and the Sermon on the Plain was sufficiently explained by
Griesbach as due to a change of sources.[39] In the parable chapter, too,
Mark was evidently the one who practised 'retelling'.[40] For these reasons
and because of similar analyses of the following units, Saunier reached the
conclusion that Mark was largely dependent upon Matthew and Luke. Out
of a total of seventy-nine pericopes Mark has fifty-one in common with
Matthew and Luke, fifteen with Matthew alone and eight with Luke alone,
whereas four pericopes are peculiar to Mark.[41] A partial dependence of
Mark upon Peter is conceivable, Saunier thought, but the remark of Papias
that Mark was Peter's translator rests upon the desire to link Mark with an
apostle, just as Luke was linked with Paul.[42] Each of the Synoptic Gospels
emerged in its own special way, although neither upon the basis of a purely
oral tradition nor after the model of a single Proto-Gospel; Mark was based

on the other two Synoptic Gospels which it unified and reconciled.[43]

The author of the second academic treatise supporting Griesbach's hypothesis in the same year, 1825, was the rationalistic Leipzig theologian Karl Gottfried Wilhelm Theile. He had planned two parts of his dissertation, but only the first appeared. In this he declared himself to be a supporter of Owen and Griesbach,[44] and then analysed the problem logically. He still owes the scholarly world some proofs from the texts, since the second part was never published.

In 1826, however, Griesbach was to gain the support of a more influential authority in his former pupil, Wilhelm Martin Leberecht de Wette (1780–1849). After studying in Jena and teaching in Heidelberg and Berlin, de Wette had to spend three years in political exile, but in 1822 received a call to Basel where he blossomed into unexampled productivity in every theological discipline. Here it is a question of his *Introduction to the New Testament* of 1826, which appeared in Berlin. He expanded this work in the fourth edition of 1842 and the fifth of 1848; in 1860 it reappeared in a sixth edition prepared by others. In the second main part of this textbook de Wette presented, with extraordinary clarity and objectivity, a detailed plea for Griesbach's theory.[45] Quotations given below are from the sixth edition, the editors of which have expanded the authentic text of de Wette by adding in square brackets several Biblical passages not quoted, but clearly intended, by the author, and references to recent literature.

First, de Wette established the undeniable kinship between the Synoptic Gospels. Not only the events described, but also the expressions used often show a striking agreement which cannot depend primarily upon the history of Jesus, because this is portrayed in a different way in the Fourth Gospel.[46]

Especially noteworthy is Mark's reconciling position between Matthew and Luke. With regard to particular material, Mark only goes beyond the other Gospels in four pericopes and in a few additions. Mark follows the others alternately and frequently provides 'a text that seems to be woven together out of the other two'. De Wette supplied his observations with several tables and numerous quotations. In his view Griesbach's hypothesis offers the best explanation of the phenomenon. According to his remark in the fifth edition of 1848, this hypothesis had also found the support of many scholars and was still acknowledged to a great extent.[47]

Storr's conjecture about the priority of Mark (above, p. 51) 'condemns itself by the additional postulate that in its present form the Gospel of Mark is not without interpolations'.[48] Furthermore, the Proto-Gospel advocated by Lessing (above, p. 52) can by no means explain all the phenomena that have to be explained, and it is made repugnant by Eichhorn's artificial elaboration of it (above, p. 53). Koppe's theory that there are a plurality of sources (above, p. 52) leaves unexplained the affinity found in the whole arrangement of the material.[49] On the other hand, Herder's assumption of an oral tradition (above, p. 52) should in part be worthy of recognition, for concerning the relationship between Matthew and Luke it might be combined with Griesbach's Utilization Hypothesis. De Wette tried to establish this by a very detailed and differentiated analysis.[50] Here an interesting circumstance is found in the fact that de Wette had been Herder's disciple at the Gymnasium of Weimar and Griesbach's student at the university of Jena. In his opinion the effect of primitive oral traditions upon Matthew and Luke is still visible to some extent, both in the narratives they have in common (e.g. the story of the Centurion at Capernaum and the various followers) and in the discourses (e.g. the Sermon on the Mount and the declaration against those who expected miracles). De Wette was nevertheless inclined to lay greater stress on the effect of literary redaction, and in considering possible oral factors he left Mark out of account. He was firmly convinced of the priority of Matthew to Luke, and found confirmation of this in the composition of the First Gospel, said to have been written from a Jewish-Christian standpoint and particularly evident in the speech-complexes with reference to the apostles; the beginning and completion of the Messiah's life according to a pre-established economy; the fulfilment of the Law; the inauguration of the heavenly kingdom; the attack on the hypocrites; and the consummation through Resurrection and proclamation. Luke took over this plan but altered it at several points, partly under the influence of his universalism and Paulinism and partly by adding oral traditions.

For de Wette, however, the decisive point was the literary dependence of Mark upon Matthew and Luke. He assembled a considerable amount of material, far more than Griesbach had collected, and he was convinced that it supported this view. In many regards de Wette's observations are still worth noting.

'According to ecclesiastical traditions, Mark wrote his book later than the other two [see the quotations from Irenaeus and Clement]. His later standpoint is also disclosed by a harmonizing tendency and a selection of material that displays a lesser interest in the discourses of Jesus. For the same reason the understanding of the "Gospel" appears to be less apostolic (the word "Gospel" placed at the head in Mark i. 1, and repeated in i. 15; viii. 35; x. 29 as the summary of historical facts about the revelation of the "Son of God", i. 1). The absence of reports of the supernatural birth of Christ is by no means evidence for the originality of the Second Evangelist, for Mark shares the notion of Christ's fatherless generation (vi. 3; cf. Matt. xiii. 55) and of the divinity of Christ (i. 1;

iii. 11; v. 7; xv. 39).

By comparing the parallel accounts, especially those of Matthew, one will discover in the Gospel of Mark unmistakable notes of non-originality: both in the presentation of Jesus' discourses which are partly recounted [1] in a context not quite correct, partly [2] in a form somehow garbled; and in the historical reports which are partly [3] altered in an arbitrary way, partly [4] embellished with more or less questionable additions.'[51]

After the second of the observations quoted above, de Wette presented a series of textual examples intended to prove that Mark had taken a logical text of Matthew and reproduced it in a somewhat confused form. Only a few of his examples can be quoted here. [1] Whereas in Matt. 12: 31f. a blasphemy against the Son and a blasphemy against the Spirit stood in a dialectical relationship to one another, Mark 3: 28f. has illogically made the first term of the comparison disappear. [2] According to Matt. 19: 3 Jesus was explicitly asked whether divorce were permissible for any reason, but Mark 10: 2 omitted the last-mentioned condition and thus related the question to the possibility of divorce in general, which was never disputed among the Jews. [3] According to Matt. 15: 24 it was Jesus' primary mission to the children of Israel that caused his hesitation with regard to the Syro-Phoenician woman; the explanation Mark 7: 24 gives is secondary because it is based on the principle of the messianic secret. [4] As examples of arbitrary embellishment, de Wette quoted remarks such as Mark 1: 13 (he was with the wild animals) and 15: 44 (Pilate was amazed that Jesus was already dead).

The simultaneous dependence of Mark upon Matthew and Luke is especially shown in his abbreviation of the story of the Temptation (Mark 1: 12–13.[52]

In addition to de Wette's comments on this passage, the following points may be emphasized to support his argument: Mark has in fact provided such a brief account of the Temptation that his description is not understandable without some knowledge of a more detailed tradition like that available in the Gospels of Matthew and Luke. The concluding remark, 'and angels served him', is only comprehensible to a person who has read in Matthew about the Saviour's triumph over the devil and his being served by angels. Mark cannot possibly have been a source for Matthew and Luke in this context. On the other hand, the contrary is not the only conceivable alternative, for one can also posit a common tradition followed to some extent by Matthew and Luke, but abbreviated by Mark. At all events de Wette rightly cited, as Saunier had done (above, p. 60), that remarkably short form of the Temptation Narrative in Mark as an objection against the general theory of the priority of Mark.

Then de Wette pointed out several obscurities in the Marcan story caused by the parallel accounts.[53] In what follows, the most forceful of his arguments will be discussed with the addition of details not specified by de Wette, but simply indicated by references to the Bible.

In the list of the apostles Mark gave their names in the accusative case without any corresponding verbal form (Mark 3: 16–19), and he did so according to de Wette because the Lucan parallel had the accusative, but correctly by reason of the participle ἐκλεξάμενος. The briefly formulated purpose of speaking in parables: that people although seeing must not see, etc. (Mark 4: 12 // Luke 8: 10), can only make sense in the light of the quotation from Isaiah found in the Matthean parallel. Here de Wette would have been able to stress that ἐπιστρέψωσιν in Mark must also derive from that Isaiah text only quoted by Matthew. Mark said about the Gadarene demoniac that he, after being cured, appeared dressed in a cloak and in possession of his senses (Mark 5: 15). Luke also emphasized this, using the same word as Mark (ἱματισμένος). But in contrast to Mark, Luke had at the beginning of his narrative mentioned the previous absence of a cloak (Luke 8: 27), and this alone makes sense of the concluding observation. On the rejection of Jesus in Nazareth, Mark remarked: 'And he could work no miracle there ... καὶ ἐθαύμασεν διὰ τὴν ἀπιστίαν αὐτῶν' (Mark 6: 5f.). This use of διά in place of ἐπί is unique in the New Testament but depended upon the parallel in Matthew: 'And he did not work many miracles there διὰ τὴν ἀπιστίαν αὐτῶν.' Mark mentioned three facts about the reaction of Herod Antipas to the reports on the success of Jesus (Mark 6: 14–16): (1) Herod believed that John had risen from the dead; (2) others said that Elijah or one of the prophets had appeared; (3) Herod meant that John had risen. Matthew offers an analogy to (1), Luke analogies to (2) and (3). According to de Wette, the careless repetition of (1) at (3) is explained by Mark's alternating dependence on Matthew and Luke. The strange Marcan expression 'the people and the disciples' (Mark 8: 34) is a conflation of the Matthean parallel 'the disciples' and the Lucan 'all people'. Immediately after the exclamation 'it is good to be here', Peter was in Mark's version overcome with quite groundless fear (Mark 9: 6). Luke ascribed this fear more naturally to the appearance of the cloud, but Matthew most reasonably to the divine voice, which is corroborated by the subsequent word of Jesus: 'Fear not.' Mark and Luke form parallels in their account of the question raised by John the son of Zebedee concerning the alien exorcist (Mark 9: 38–41 // Luke 9: 49–50), and then Mark has incorporated a parallel to Matthew (Mark 9: 42–50), but only Luke continued the narrative in an orderly manner with the reaction of the sons of Zebedee in Samaria (Luke 9: 51–6). Mark permitted the information about the scribes: 'no one dared any more to question him', to form a conclusion to the question of a scribe about the greatest commandment although this man had showed friendly intentions (Mark 12: 34); the corresponding passage of Luke occurs in a more appropriate way after the discussion with the Sadducees (Luke 20: 40). In his report on the preparations for the Last Supper, Mark first followed Matthew and let the disciples ask Jesus about the place. But then he followed Luke and indicated that one of the disciples was sent into the city (Mark 14: 12f.), and in this way the outcome of the original search did not emerge. Jesus was blindfolded and struck by the servants of the High Priest, and then according to Mark the guards cried: 'Now prophesy!' (Mark 14: 65). In this abrupt command de Wette discovered a too-concise abbreviation of the Lucan parallel: 'Prophesy now: Who was it that struck you?'

Following these observations, de Wette presented – in an extension of Griesbach – a survey of the sections in Mark 1–9 which prove to be parallel to Matthew and Luke alternately, so that a zigzag pattern emerges.[54] In conclusion he quoted several additional examples to corroborate his contention that Mark's indications of the situation, his concretions, and other peculiarities, were partly based upon his taste, plan and literary style, partly upon his paying attention to the parallel narratives he wanted to abbreviate. According to de Wette, such details found in Mark do not represent primary material.[55]

The consistent and logical application of Griesbach's hypothesis in de Wette's textbook is still impressive. Against every wholesale assumption of the priority of Mark, de Wette produced arguments that ought not to be ignored. Certainly the presumed influence of the Evangelists on each other was conceived by de Wette in a purely literary and mechanical sense, and that was anachronistic for it took little account of oral tradition and psychological factors. Nonetheless, his presentation was a masterpiece, and if the exegetes of the nineteenth century had paid more heed to the strict empiricism of de Wette, later research into the Synoptic Problem would have been spared many derailments and cul-de-sacs.

During the nineteenth century, Griesbach's hypothesis survived for a rather long time among Roman Catholic authors like Johann Kuhn in Tübingen or Adalbert Maier in Freiburg. These scholars defended the priority of Matthew, but also emphasized the dependence of Mark upon Peter.[56]

In the Protestant School of Tübingen, however, a dogmatic abuse of Griesbach's hypothesis began in about 1840. Here literary criticism was combined with the so-called trend criticism, by which each Evangelist was to be placed in a scheme of historical development according to a trend ascribed to him. First of all Eduard Zeller stressed the Paulinism of Luke,[57] and then Albrecht Ritschl endeavoured to show that the Gospel of Marcion with its Paulinism was the source of the Gospel of Luke with its alleged combination of Paulinism and Judaism.[58]

The chief manipulator of such trends or '-isms' was the leader of the school, Ferdinand Christian Baur, in Tübingen. In accordance with Griesbach he regarded Matthew as the oldest among the Synoptic Gospels, yet by no means on account of Matthew's apostolic status or because of the literary relationship of the Gospels to one another, but merely because of the Jewish tendency supposed to be represented by the First Gospel.[59] Since the Gospel of Luke had to imply a Greek antithesis to Jewish Christianity,[60] the original bulk of it was said to be dependent upon Matthew.[61] Then the Gospel of Mark was said to depend upon both, because here one would detect a reconciling trend.[62] On account of its apocalypse (Matt. 24: 1–51), the First Gospel was finally said to belong to the years of Bar Kochba, A. D. 130–4.[63] The other Gospels were supposed to have been written even later.

For a long time the Tübingen School remained a powerful factor. Many students admired the way in which the literary history of the Gospels was laid out in accordance with general philosophical concepts. The theoretical starting-point was Hegel's dialectic, implying a process of thesis, antithesis, and synthesis. But in practice Matthew, Luke, and Mark were also portrayed as representatives of a theological struggle comparable to the discussion between conservative, liberal and intermediary theologians so characteristic of Germany in the days of Baur. This anachronistic view of the Evangelists as conscious representatives of dialectical standpoints – Judaism, Universalism, etc – represented a *metabasis eis allo genos* for the Synoptic Problem and brought Griesbach's hypothesis into disrepute among scholars with empirical interests.

Meanwhile the so-called Two-Document Hypothesis won the field. Bourgeois realism wanted to see historical documents without elaborate theology as the starting-point for the Gospel literature. Karl August Credner of Giessen proposed in 1836 to start on the one hand from the *Logia* of Matthew, of which Papias had written, now understood as sayings of Jesus, and on the other hand from the Gospel of Mark.[64] Christian Hermann Weisse sought a documentary support against the Tradition Hypothesis which he regarded as dangerous, since David Friedrich Strauss had based his radical concept of myth on it. For this reason Weisse, in 1838, presented in a similar manner the *Logia* of Matthew and the Gospel of Mark as the two sources.[65] Christian Gottlob Wilke explicitly attacked Griesbach's hypothesis, and in the same year zealously defended the priority of Mark.[66]

These two assertions, the priority of Mark and the existence of a *Logia* source, soon became popular in Protestant Germany, and even took on the character of an article of faith that later spread to other countries and churches. Many scholars accept them as if they were axioms. But such *idola theatri* should always be called into question. Among younger scholars the Two-Document Hypothesis has rightly turned into a problem. In this context the renewed interest in Griesbach makes good sense, and the detailed argumentation of de Wette may also prove instructive (above pp. 61-5).

5

Commentatio qua Marci Evangelium totum
e Matthaei et Lucae commentariis
decerptum esse monstratur

J. J. Griesbach
Introduction by Bo Reicke

Introduction

Johann Jakob Griesbach lived from 1745 to 1812, went to school in
Frankfurt and worked as a professor of theology in Halle, moving in 1775
to Jena. His life coincided with a classical period in the history of German
literature. Goethe in Weimar was his friend since the years in Frankfurt;
Schiller in Jena was even his neighbour in the same dwelling for some years.

Griesbach also lived in a period when modern historical studies of the
New Testament began to flourish in Germany, and he was among the
pioneers of the critical empiricism which has dominated New Testament
scholarship since the nineteenth century. He took over this approach from
his main teacher in Halle, Johann Salomo Semler (1725–91). In his
scholarly production and university lectures, Griesbach was mainly occupied with New Testament Introduction and Church History. His practical
talents and reliable character were the reasons why he was compelled to
spend much of his time in Jena on the finances of the university. But his
scholarly publications also gave him a great reputation, far beyond the
limits of his country.

I

It was especially the problems of the New Testament text which interested
Griesbach, and in this context he gave fruitful impulses to all later New
Testament scholarship in three ways: (1) by his critical editions of the
Greek text; (2) by his *Synopsis*; (3) by his Synoptic Theory.

(1) On the basis of extensive travels and exhaustive studies of manuscripts and translations, Griesbach collected a wealth of material for a new
edition of the New Testament in Greek. Its two first editions were differently entitled:

Libri historici Novi Testamenti graece. 1. Synopsis evangeliorum
Matthaei, Marci et Lucae. 2. Evangelium Joannis et Acta apostolorum.
Textum ad fidem codicum, versionum et patrum emendavit et lectionis

varietatem adiecit J. J. Griesbach (Halle, 1774-5).

Novum Testamentum graece. II [counting *Libri historici* 1-2 as I. 1-2].
Epistolae apostolorum cum Apocalypsi. Textum ad fidem... [as above]
(Halle, 1775).

Novum Testamentum graece. Textum ad fidem... [as above]. 2nd ed.,
enlarged. *I. Evangelia. II. Acta et Epistolae apostolorum cum Apocalypsi*
(Halle, 1786-1806).

This publication appeared later in several new editions prepared by
Griesbach and others. For textual studies of the New Testament it meant
an innovation, and this is characterized in the title by the verb 'emendavit'.
Significantly, Griesbach was the first editor of the New Testament in Greek
who, not only in footnotes, but also in the main text, paid attention to
readings found in older manuscripts than those on which Erasmus had
based his printed text of 1516, a text often reproduced.[1]

(2) In the first part of Griesbach's text edition, the *Libri historici* of
1774, the editor presented the Gospels of Matthew, Mark and Luke in
parallel columns, keeping the sequence of the units within each Gospel
intact. This implied another innovation. Earlier attempts to harmonize the
Gospels were given up, and instead their individuality and interrelation
were made obvious.[2] Griesbach called his presentation a 'synopsis', and
the Gospels of Matthew, Mark and Luke have since then been called
'synoptic' because they can be studied in such parallel columns as in
Griesbach's first edition of Matthew, Mark and Luke in Greek.

A reprint of this first part of the edition appeared separately in 1776
under the following title:

Synopsis evangeliorum Matthaei, Marci et Lucae. Textum graecum ad
fidem... [as above] (Halle, 1776).

Of this *Synopsis*, too, several new editions were published by Griesbach
and others. Numerous similar presentations of the parallels between the
Synoptic Evangelists were published later. On the other hand, when
Griesbach enlarged the first volume of his general publication of the New
Testament text in that second edition of 1786 called *Novum Testamentum*
graece. I. Evangelia (see above (1)), he abandoned the synoptic arrangement and preferred an individual presentation of each Gospel in order to
facilitate the study of textual variants. He regarded his separate *Synopsis*
of 1776 as sufficient for the study of synoptic problems. And in fact all
scholarly discussion of the relations between Matthew, Mark and Luke
which has taken place during the last 200 years goes back to Griesbach's
publication of his *Synopsis* in 1776.

(3) In the first instance, the *Synopsis* of Griesbach inspired the editor
himself to further studies of the interrelationship among Matthew, Mark

and Luke. His parallel columns, in which the usual harmonizing transpositions had been avoided, gave a concrete impression of Mark's alternate
similarities with Matthew, with Luke, or with both. In his judgement, the
simplest explanation of this oscillation was to conclude that Mark had
sometimes followed Matthew, sometimes Luke, sometimes both, and
combined the material of his sources in a shorter form.

This Synoptic Hypothesis of Griesbach was developed in two Latin
essays:

> *Fontes unde evangelistae suas de resurrectione Domini narrationes*
> *hauserint: Paschatos solemnia...* (Jena, 1783). Reprinted in J. J.
> Griesbach, *Opuscula academica*, ed. J. Ph. Gabler, Vol. II (Jena, 1825),
> pp. 241–56.
> *Commentatio qua Marci evangelium totum e Matthaei et Lucae*
> *commentariis decerptum esse monstratur*, I-II (Jena, 1789–90).
> Enlarged edition in J. C. Velthusen *et al.* (eds.), *Commentationes*
> *theologicae*, vol. I (Leipzig, 1794), pp. 360–434. Reprinted in
> Griesbach, *Opuscula* (see above), pp. 358–425.

In his preliminary essay of 1783 called *Fontes*, Griesbach desired to
explain the differences between the Evangelists in their description of the
events connected with Christ's resurrection. He sought the explanation in
the confusion of the women after their discovery of the empty tomb.
Since these eyewitnesses ran hither and thither, the Evangelists had to use
the reports of different women. John relied upon Mary Magdalene, Matthew upon Mary the mother of James. These Evangelists were apostles.
Matthew's narrative was used by Luke with some abbreviation, but also
with some additions based on the experiences of Joanna. Mark combined
the narratives of Matthew and Luke.

In his definitive study of 1789–90 called *Commentatio* and republished
with additions in 1794, Griesbach endeavoured to demonstrate the dependence of Mark's whole Gospel upon Matthew and Luke. He was convinced
that Mark had taken over nearly everything from Matthew and Luke,
following them alternately. Only three short healing stories and two short
parables are found in Mark without parallels in the other Gospels, but four
of these units were influenced by Matthew, and the remaining story about
the blind man at Bethsaida was formed by analogy with the other miracles.

Griesbach's detailed, elegant and sensible argumentation can be followed
in the English translation of his Latin text presented below. Dom Bernard
Orchard has done a great service in making this important synoptic study
available to modern readers. Griesbach's Synoptic Hypothesis is of historical interest because it represents one of the classical synoptic theories
developed in Germany by the pioneers of modern research on the Synoptic

Gospels. It is also interesting because it was taken over by distinguished scholars in the first half of the nineteenth century (see above, pp. 60ff.), and is supported again by independent scholars in our own time. Even those who prefer other theories should be able to admit that Griesbach's hypothesis was consistent and uncomplicated in so far as the inclusion of unknown external factors was avoided.

II

Critical historical studies of the Bible were a relatively new field when Griesbach was a student. But they were presented in Germany with an unparalleled enthusiasm by a number of distinguished writers and scholars including such men as Lessing and Herder. Many of Griesbach's countrymen were also concerned with the Synoptic Question, and some of them suggested other solutions. For this reason Griesbach had to include a discussion with his opponents in the second edition of his *Commentatio* on the Synoptic Problem. The arguments can be studied below in section III of his treatise.

Some preliminary information about the principal scholars, men virtually unknown today, may be added here. The chief opponents were (*a*) J. G. Eichhorn, (*b*) J. B. Koppe, both of Göttingen, and (*c*) G. C. Storr, of Tübingen.

(*a*) Johann Gottfried Eichhorn (1752–1827) had been a student and later a colleague of Griesbach in Jena, but taught at the University of Göttingen from 1788. He was a veritable polyhistor who published numerous books on oriental languages, Biblical history, political history, the history of literature and other fields of learning.[3]

It was Eichhorn's study of the Synoptic Gospels published in 1794 that brought about Griesbach's criticism.[4] Eichhorn had taken over a theory suggested by Richard Simon in 1689[5] and later represented by other scholars, especially in a paper written by Gotthold Ephraim Lessing in 1778 and published in 1784 after his death.[6] This was the hypothesis of an Aramaic Proto-Gospel no longer extant, but supposed to be the common source of the Synoptic Gospels. Eichhorn, however, combined the Proto-Gospel Hypothesis with another theory suggested by a colleague of his in Göttingen to be mentioned below, that is, J. B. Koppe, who had argued that there were a plurality of shorter and longer sources now lost. The result of Eichhorn's eclecticism was a very complicated picture implying development on different levels. Griesbach found Eichhorn's construction unnecessarily complex, and was convinced that Mark's occasional deviations from Matthew should be explained by his intermittent dependence on Luke.

(b) Johann Benjamin Koppe (1750–91) had studied in Leipzig and was a professor of theology at the University of Göttingen from 1775 to 1784. During these years he was occupied with Biblical exegesis and wrote a Latin commentary on the New Testament which appeared in four volumes from 1778 to 1783. It was republished by others in several new editions. He also edited a German translation of Bishop Robert Lowth's commentary on Isaiah which appeared in four volumes from 1779 to 1784, and contributed to it by additional explanations. In 1784 Koppe left Göttingen to serve as a church superintendent in Gotha and then as a chaplain of the court in Hannover until his death at the age of forty-one in 1791.[7]

Koppe was dead when Griesbach entered into a discussion of his Synoptic Theory which had been presented in a university programme of 1782, a year before the publication of Griesbach's preliminary study of the Synoptic Question in his *Fontes* of 1783. In this programme Koppe opposed the Utilization Hypothesis as it had been represented by Augustine and many later writers, implying that Mark had epitomized Matthew. He preferred to regard the Synoptic Evangelists as dependent on a plurality of earlier sources, like those alluded to in Luke 1: 1. More exactly he supposed that Matthew, Mark and Luke had collected longer and shorter reports, spread among the Christians in oral and written form and moulded into narratives, speeches, parables, sayings of Jesus and other categories.[8] By his assumption of several fragmentary sources Koppe anticipated the so-called Fragment Hypothesis propagated by F. Schleiermacher in 1817; and by his reference to categories first developed in oral form he anticipated the inauguration of form criticism by M. Dibelius in 1919. Griesbach did not accept Koppe's inclination to regard shorter reports as older than longer ones.

(c) Gottlob Christian Storr (1746–1805) was the son of a Lutheran prelate in Stuttgart and studied in Tübingen where he became a professor of divinity in 1786. In the history of theology Storr is well-known as the founder of the so-called Older School of Tübingen. He developed a supranaturalistic Biblicism in discussion with Kant, and wrote a textbook in dogmatics published in 1793 and then used for a long time in Württemberg. In 1797 he was made a chaplain of the court in Stuttgart. As a preacher he combined his inherited Pietism with an intellectual moralism.[9]

Storr's Synoptic Theory was developed in a book on the Four Gospels and the Epistles of John published in 1786, just between Griesbach's two studies (*Fontes* and *Commentatio*) of 1783 and 1789. He turned Griesbach's hypothesis upside down by regarding Mark as the source of Matthew and Luke.[10] Storr is accordingly to be regarded as the pioneer of the theory of Marcan priority so popular later. Independently of Storr, this hypothesis was suggested again in 1836 by K. A. Credner and in 1838 by C. H. Weisse and C. G. Wilke. It gradually spread throughout the world. Griesbach realized that Storr was his most powerful opponent, and in the second edition of his treatise published in 1794 he devoted several pages to a refutation of Storr's arguments. In particular he pointed out: (1) that Papias had not given a reliable picture of Mark; (2) that the sections of Matthew and Luke missing in Mark were left out because the Second Evangelist wanted to give his readers a condensed report; and (3) that Mark is not to be seen as contradictory to Matthew and Luke, but rather as combining and sometimes illustrating or completing their reports.

NOTE. In the Latin text that follows the numbers in the lefthand margin are the page-numbers of the Gabler 1825 edition. The page-references in the text itself are either Griesbach's own or are those of Gabler. The page-numbers in the Notes refer to the present edition. The numbering of the Notes is the Editors'.

358 *Io. Iac. Griesbachii Theol. D. et Prof Primar in academia Jenensi com-*
mentatio qua Marci Evangelium totum e Matthaei et Lucae com-
mentariis decerptum esse monstratur, scripta nomine Academiae
Jenensis, (1789. 1790.) *jam recognita multisque augmentis locupletata.*[1]

Ad historicorum libros accurate interpretandos, fidem auctorum iusta lance
trutinandam, et veram eventuum, quos literis illi consignarunt, indolem
perspiciendam subtiliterque iudicandam, magni prae aliis momenti est,
fontes nosse, e quibus ea, quae in commentarios suos retulere, hauserint.
Hinc alio iam tempore[2] de fontibus, unde Evangelistarum de resurrectione
Christi narrationes promanaverint, disseruimus. Verum tunc unice ad

359 Evangeliorum partem eam, qua historia de Iesu in vitam reditu continetur,
respiciebamus et tantum de Matthaeo, Luca ac Ioanne paullo copiosius
agebamus, de Marco autem vix paucis verbis velut in transcursu exponeba-
mus nostram sententiam. Quare, cum de Marco potissimum, unde sua
desumserit, disceptetur, nec tantum de historiae resurrectionis sed de totius
Evangelii fontibus dubitetur, virique docti, qui hanc quaestionem, nuperrime etiam, tractarunt, ea argumenta, quae liti dirimendae maxime idonea
nos quidem arbitramur, neglexisse fere videantur; huic rei declarandae
operam nunc dabimus.

Antiquissimi scriptores, inde a PAPIA, uno fere ore Marcum ea, quae a
Petro, cuius interpretem ipsum nominant, audivisset, litteris mandasse
tradiderunt. Primus, quod sciamus, *Augustinus*, Marcum tanquam pedissequum et breviatorem subsecutum esse Matthaeum,[3] iudicavit. Ex eo tempore plerique viri docti utramque sententiam coniungere, et Marcum
partim e Matthaei libro partim e Petri ore ea quae scriberet derivasse,
statuere solebant. Recentiores vero nonnulli scite observarunt, tantam
esse Marci cum Luca etiam convenientiam, ut huius quoque Evangelium
ille ad manus habuisse videatur. Contra vero *Lardnerus*[4] Matthaeum a
Marco lectum plane non fuisse multis argumentis vincere studuit, quibus

360 *Koppius*[5] plura addidit, ut efficeret saltim, Marcum non esse Matthaei
epitomatorem. Hisce argumentis, speciosis sane, etiam *Michaelis*, qui antea
vulgarem sententiam defenderat, inductus fuit, ut in novissima introduc-
tionis suae in libros N. T. editione eam retractaret, et Matthaei librum
Marco, dum scriberet, praesto fuisse negaret. Cum vero tantus sit inter
Matthaeum et Marcum in rebus non solum sed in verbis etiam et phrasibus
consensus, ut nemo infitiari eum possit, variis modis ii, qui Marcum
Matthaei libro usum esse negant, talis et tantae consonantiae originem
et rationem explicare sategerunt.

S. V. [sic] *Storrius*[6] hypothesin vulgari e diametro oppositam exornare
studuit: nimirum, Marcum Evangelium suum eo iam tempore, quod Act.

11. 17–30. indicatur, scripsisse; post hunc Lucam commentarios suos
exarasse et Marci librum diligenter consuluisse; denique Matthaeum etiam
animum ad scribenda memorabilia Iesu Christi appulisse, et e Marci
Evangelio in suum multa transtulisse. *Koppius* commentarios de rebus ad
Iesum pertinentibus complures, breviores amplioresve, hebraice graeceque
conscriptos, olim extitisse putabat iam deperditos, e quibus Matthaeus,
Marcus et Lucas suos libros compilaverint; atque hinc existimabat intelligi
facile, non solum, cur Marcus plerumque concinat cum Matthaeo, verum
etiam, cur alter ab altero interdum et verbis et sententiis et ordine dis-
sentiat, atque cur Marcus multa notatu dignissima, quae apud Matthaeum
leguntur, omittat, contra vero nonnulla etiam, a Matthaeo praetermissa,
habeat. Nempe ubi eadem eodem modo narrant, ex eodem fonte hausisse
putantur; ubi autem vel addendo vel omittendo vel aliter rem narrando
inter se discrepant, diversis usi esse libris antiquioribus statuuntur. Hancce
coniecturam egregie nuper exornavit, perpolivit et novarum observationum
ex Evangeliorum inter se comparatione deductarum ingenti copia con-
firmare ac commendare studuit Cel. *Eichhornius.*[7] Sumit vero Vir doctissimus, extitisse primis iam temporibus Evangelium quoddam primitivum,
ebraico seu syrochaldaico sermone conscriptum, quod ea fere complexum
sit, quae nostris Evangelistis communia sunt. Hinc de eius argumento et
indole probabilem coniecturam e concordantibus nostrorum Evangeliorum
pericopis fieri posse. Ebraicum illud scriptum varie a pluribus in graecum
sermonem magis minusve accurate fuisse translatum. Hasce libelli primaevi
versiones saepius iam fuisse transscriptas,[8] et ab interpretibus vel librariis
vel lectoribus passim variis additamentis auctas, qualia etiam in ebraicum
archetypum, antequam in graecam linguam transferretur, irrepserint. Quin
plurium exemplarium augmenta in unum esse conflata ab iis, qui exemplar
habere cuperent quantum fieri posset πληρεστατον.[9] Huiusmodi igitur
exemplaria trium primaevi scripti versionum, sed non purarum, verum
diversimode iam commixtarum et adiectis multis auctariis interpolatarum,
ad manus fuisse tum tribus nostris Evangelistis,[10] qui e sua penu additamenta nova adiecerint, tum etiam aliis similium de vita Christi libellorum
auctoribus. – Superstructa est haec Clar. *Eichhornii* hypothesis argumentis
potissimum his; nec Matthaeus Marco aut Luca nec Marcus Matthaeo aut
Luca, nec Lucas Matthaeo aut Marco usi fuerunt; consensus igitur inter
ipsos repetendus est a communi quodam fonte, e quo omnes hausere;
ebraicum hunc fuisse, plura produnt indicia, (alio deinceps loco a nobis
commemoranda;) attamen nostra Evangelia, quippe quae per plures
στιχους in graeca phrasi saepenumero consonant, ex ebraico isto textu
immediate non videntur profluxisse;[11] ante igitur, quam nostra Evangelia
conscriberentur, ebraicus archetypus in graecam linguam iam erat con-

versus; plures autem versiones extitisse necesse est, quia Evangelistae, licet eandem rem eodem modo ac ordine narrent, phrasibus tamen plerumque utuntur diversis; tandem exemplaria tam ebraica quam graeca posterioribus curis aucta novis additamentis fuisse, ex eo cogitur, quod auctaria, quae primitus abfuerant ab ebraico archetypo, iam uniformiter comparent mox 364 in Matthaeo et Marco, mox in Matthaeo et Luca, mox in Luca et Marco.[12] - Denique, ut aliorum cogitata praetereamus, anonymus auctor[13] persuadere nobis conatus est, primum omnium scriptum esse Evangelium Ebraeorum; huius diversas recensiones, sed minus perpolitas, esse Nazaraeorum et Ebionitarum Evangelia; postea prodiisse Evangelium illud, quo Marcion usus fuit, nec non libellum Marci; tum secuta esse ἀπομνημονευματα των ἀποστολων, a Iustino M. laudata, et Matthaei commentaria; deinceps Lucae Evangelium evulgatum esse; de Ioannis autem Evangelio, utrum istis omnibus posterius, an nonnullis eorum prius sit, haud liquere.

Tantum doctissimorum virorum dissensum non mirari non possumus, cum, nostro quidem iudicio, vel ex sola triuum Evangeliorum inter se comparatione attenta abunde patescat, quonam cognationis gradu se invicem 365 contingant. Quod ut planum faciamus Lectoribus, I. sententiam nostram distincte exponemus, II. paucis, sed selectis, argumentis eandem confirmabimus, III. ad obiectiones, quibus impugnari ea posset, respondebimus, et IV. consectaria ex nostra hypothesi derivanda indicabimus.

Sectio I

Sententiae quam defendimus summa haec est: *Marcum in conscribendo libro suo ante oculos positum habuisse non solum Matthaeum sed et Lucam, atque ex his decerpsisse quicquid de rebus gestis, sermonibus et fatis Servatoris memoriae mandaret*, ita tamen, ut

(1) Matthaeum quidem potissimum et plerumque sequeretur ducem, at

(2) interdum tamen, relicto Matthaeo, Lucae sese adiungeret comitem;

(3) ubi Matthaei insisteret vestigiis, Lucam tamen ex oculis non dimitteret, sed hunc cum Matthaeo compararet, et vicissim;

(4) brevitati studeret, quippe qui libellum mole exiguum conscribere vellet; hinc non solum

(5) omitteret, quae ad munus doctoris, quo Dominus publice functus est, non pertinerent, Matth. 1 et 2. Luc. 1 et 2. sed etiam

(6) praeteriret sermones complures Christi verbosiores,[14] e. gr. Matth. 366 5, 6 et 7. 10, 16 - 42. 11, 20-30. 12, 33-45. 13, 37-54. 18, 10-35. 20, 1-16. 22, 1-14. 23, 2-39. 24, 37-51. 25, 1-46. Luc. 6, 17-49. 19, 11-28. imo inde a Luc. 10, 1 ad cap. 18, 14. tertiam fere Evangelii Lucae partem intactam praetermitteret, quoniam tota fere sermonibus Christi constat. Porro in excerpendis Matthaei et Lucae Evangeliis ita versatus est, ut

(7) rationem haberet suorum lectorum, hoc est, hominum a Palaestina remotorum, quibus Palaestinensium Iudaeorum, nominatim Pharisaeorum, placita et instituta minus cognita nec scitu admodum necessaria essent; eamque ob causam partim

(8) resecaret nonnulla apud Matthaeum vel Lucam obvia, ad solos Iudaeos et inprimis ad Palaestinenses spectantia, aut horum cogitandi modo accommodata[15] v. c. Matth. 16, 2. 3. 19, 28. Luc. 4, 16-30. 23, 28-32. et

(9) parcior esset in allegandis Vet. Test. dictis, e. gr. Matth. 4, 14. 12, 17-21. 13, 14. 15. partim

(10) adderet illustrationis causa, quae suis lectoribus ad rectius intelligendam narrationem vel necessaria vel utilia putaret; e. gr. Marci 7, 3. 4. 8. 11, 13. 12, 42.

(11) persaepe quidem easdem formulas, phrasea et constructiones, quas Matthaeus et Lucas usurpassent, retineret, et inter has multas paullo inusitatiores; e. gr. Marc. 2, 10. λεγει τω παραλυτικω, 10, 22. ἠν γαρ ἐχων κτηματα πολλα. 12, 14. οὐ μελει σοι περι οὐδενος, οὐ γαρ βλεπεις εἰς προσωπον ἀνθρωπων, 13, 14. το βδελυγμα της ἐρημωσεως, et parentheticum illud ὁ ἀναγινωσκων νοειτω, et alibi saepe;

(12) attamen illorum libros neutiquam ad verbum exscriberet, sed *suo* modo, hoc est aliis formulis ac phrasibus, ea, quae legisset apud illos, narraret; imo haud raro

(13) παραφραστικως exprimeret ac planius et distinctius exponeret, quae illi brevius tradidissent, licet caeteroqui in seligendis rebus gestis et orationibus Christi, quas in commentarios suos quasi transplantare vellet, brevitatis studio duceretur, multasque ac nobiles utriusque Evangelii partes plane, ut vidimus, silentio praeteriret; (Paraphrasin agnosces v. c. Marc. 6, 17-29. 30. 31. 9, 14-29. 38-50. 11, 11-26.)

(14) adderet ad Matthaei et Lucae narrationes haud paucas περιστασεις singulares, quas suis lectoribus gratas esse futuras forte iudicasset, velut Marc. 2, 14. ὁ του ἀλφαιου. 5, 42. ἠν γαρ ἐτων δωδεκα. 6, 3. ὁ τεκτων. 6, 13. ἠλειφον ἐλαιω ἀρρωστους. 10, 46. υἱος τιμαιου βαρτιμαιος. 13, 3. πετρος και ἰακωβος και ἀνδρεας. 14, 51. 52. και εἰς τις νεανισκος ἠκολουθει αὐτω κ. τ. λ. 15, 21. πατερα ἀλεξανδρου και ρουφου. 15, 40. et 16. 1. και σαλωμη, et eiusdem fere generis innumera alia; tandem

(15) adiungeret narratiunculas quasdam, a Matthaeo aeque ac Luca praetermissas, sed pauculas et perbreves, (deinceps enumerandas) quas quo consilio adiecerit Marcus, lector attentus facile, dummodo curiose eas inter se conferre velit, coniicere poterit.

Sectio II

Ad confirmandam vindicandamve hanc sententiam nostram nolumus dicta ab aliis, qui nobiscum Matthaeum a Marco adhibitum esse statuunt, repetere, nec argumenta multa coacervabimus, sed *tribus* observationibus id quod volumus evicturos nos esse confidimus.

I. Marcus totum libellum suum, si viginti et quatuor circiter commata, quae de sua penu addidit, excipias, de quibus posthaec dicetur, e Matthaei et Lucae commentariis

370   (α) sic compilavit, ut nullo negotio monstrari queat, quid ex hoc, quid ex illo desumserit;

(β) ordinem a Matthaeo observatum ita retinuit, ut, sicubi ab eo recederet, Lucae vestigiis insisteret et hunc ordinemque narrationis eius κατα ποδα sequeretur, adeo ut

(γ) commata et vocabula, ubi a Matthaeo transit ad Lucam aut a Luca redit ad Matthaeum, non indicari tantum possint, sed

(δ) ratio etiam probabilis reddi plerumque possit, cur Matthaeum, licet hoc tanquam praecipuo duce uti statuisset, interdum deseruerit et Lucae sese adiunxerit, aut cur posthabito Luca ad Matthaeum suum iterum sese receperit, imo

(ε) intelligi etiam possit, quamobrem hoc praecise Matthaei loco, nec alio, filum quod antea, transiliens ad Lucam, abrupisset, rursum annectat. Paucis: veluti oculis cernere potes Marcum et Matthaei et Lucae volumina ad manus habentem, utraque perpetuo consulentem, ex utrisque quae suis lectoribus maxime profutura esse autumaret decerpentem, mox Matthaeum mox Lucam paullulum e manibus seponentem, semper vero ad eum ipsum utriuslibet locum, ubi divertere ab eo coepisset, redeuntem. Quod ut clarius appareat, rem in tabula, quam notulis nonnullis illustrabimus, *adspiciendam* exhibebimus.

	MAT.	MAR.	LUC.
371	[Cap. 1 et 2.][16]	——	
	3, 1 - 4, 22.[17]	1, 1 - 20.	
		1, 21 - 39.	4, 31 - 44.[18]
		——	[5, 1 - 11.][19]
		1, 40 - 3, 6.	5, 12 - 6, 11.
	12, 15. 16.[20]	3, 7 - 12.	
	[17 - 21]	——	
372		3, 13 - 19.	6, 12 - 16.[21]
	12, 22. 23.	3, 20. 21.	
	12, 24 - 32.[22]	3, 22 - 30.	
373	[12, 33 - 37.][23]	——	
	[12, 38 - 45.][24]	——	
	12, 46 - 50.	3, 31 - 35.	

	Mat.	Mar.	Luc.
	13, 1 - 23.	4, 1 - 20.	
		4, 21 - 25.[25]	8, 16 - 18.
4	[13, 24 - 30.][26]	4, 26 - 29.	
	13, 31. 32.	4, 30 - 32.	
	13, 34. 35.[27]	4, 33. 34.	
		——	[8, 19-21.][28]
5		4, 35 - 41.	8, 22 - 25.
		5, 1 - 43.[29]	8, 26 - 56.
	13, 53 - 58.[30]	6, 1 - 6.	
		6, 7 - 13.	9, 1 - 6.
	14, 1 - 2.	6, 14 - 16.	9, 7 - 9.
	14, 3 - 12.	6, 17 - 29.	
		6, 30. 31.	9, 10.
	14, 13 - 21.	6, 32 - 44.	9, 11 - 17.
	14, 22 - 16, 12.	6, 45 - 8, 21.	
	——	8, 22 - 26.[31]	
	16, 13 - 18, 9.	8, 27 - 9, 50.[32]	9, 18 - 51.
6	[18, 10 - 35.][33]	——	
		——	[9, 51 - 18, 14.][34]
	19, 1 - 12.	10, 1 - 12.	
	19, 13 - 23, 1.	10, 13 - 12, 38.[35]	18, 15 - 20, 45.
	[23, 1 - 39.][36]	——	
		12, 38 - 44.	20, 45 - 21, 4.[37]
	24, 1 - 36.	13, 1 - 32.	21, 5. sqq.
	[24, 37 - 25, 46.]	13, 33 - 36.[38]	
	26, 1 - 28, 8.	14, 1 - 16, 8.	
		16, 9.[39]	
7	[28, 9 - 15.][40]	——	
	[28, 16. 17.][41]	——	
		16, 10 - 13.	24, 10 - 35.
		16, 14.	24, 36 - 43.
	28, 18 - 20.	16, 15 - 18.	
		16, 19.	24, 50. 51.
		16, 20.	

Cum igitur, posita nostra sententia absque multarum hypothesium nimis artificiose excogitatarum adminiculo, planissime tum ostendi queat cur Marcus haec illa in suos commentarios retulerit, alia autem omiserit, tum etiam perspicue ratio reddi possit, cur quidque, ne unico quidem commate excepto, eo loco,[42] quo apud ipsum id legimus, positum sit: iam sic, quod volebamus, effecisse nos putamus. Sed idem alia adhuc ratione confirmari et evinci potest. Progredimur itaque ad alteram observationem nostram.

II. In tanta rerum memorabilium a I. C. gestarum multitudine sermonumque a Domino quotidie sive ad populum sive ad discipulos ac familiares suos habitorum incredibili varietate, casu utique fortuito non accidit, ut Marcus quod litteris consignaret haberet plane nihil, praeter id, quod Matthaeus aut Lucas similiter memoriae mandassent, vel cuius commemorandi saltim occasionem alteruter praebuisset. Lucas et Ioannes haud pauca tradiderunt, quae Matthaeus prorsus intacta reliquerat, et Evangelistae ipsi pluribus locis innuunt, multa in libris suis praetermissa esse gesta Christi illustria et mirifica, multosque praeteritos Domini sermones, quos Evangeliorum brevitas non caperet. Quid igitur causae est, cur ex tam immensa παραλειπομενων copia Marcus non proferat saltim nonnulla, sed eadem plane narret, quae ex amplissima scribendi materia Matthaeus etiam et Lucas decerpsere? Marcus, inquam, qui a matre sua Hierosolymis habitante, in cuius aedibus Apostoli caeterique Christiani suos conventus celebrare solebant, Act. 12, 12. permulta audire poterat, non omnibus nota; Marcus praeterea, qui aliquamdiu et Pauli et Petri minister ac comes fuerat, et ab his eorumque familiaribus procul dubio multa cum facta tum dicta Domini acceperat relatu sane non indigna; Marcus denique, qui Matthaei et Lucae narrationes tot singularibus περιστασεσι locupletavit, (vid. supra pag. 5. nr. 13 et 14.) ut nemo non videat, perbene cognitam eum habuisse Christi historiam, et longe plura, si voluisset, de Domino narrare potuisse; quid quaeso est, quod hic talis Marcus, praeter istas περιστασεις, iis quae Matthaeus et Lucas commentariis mandarunt nihil addiderit novi? Si quidem nobiscum statuas, propositum fuisse Marco, e Matthaei et Lucae Evangeliis seligere ea, quae iis quibus scribebat hominibus utilissima essent, eaque ita narrare, uti talibus lectoribus narrari deberent: plana sunt omnia et extricata. Sin contra proprio quod aiunt Marte et nullius adminiculis Marcum scripsisse sumas, prodigio simile est, in deligendo ex immensa materia libelli argumento non nisi eadem tractanda eum sibi sumsisse, quae Matthaeus etiam aut Lucas tractassent. Sin denique contendas, alios aut plures quam hos duumviros modo laudatos eum habuisse duces, scire velimus, qui factum sit, ut hi nihil aliud, si versus excipias circiter 24, ipsi suggererent, quam quod aeque e Matthaeo et Luca mutuari potuisset. *Nihil,* inquam, *praeter commata viginti quatuor.* Nam nec merae amplificationes paraphrasticae eorum, quae apud Matthaeum et Lucam leguntur, neque nonnullarum περιστάσεων additamenta paucis vocabulis comprehensa, qualia supra p. 5. (p. 368 sq.) nr. 10. 13. et 14. indicavimus, in censum hic venire possunt. Quare operam utique perderet, qui ad impugnandam thesin nostram provocare vellet ad Marc. 1, 2. 33. 2, 2. 3. 4. 27.[43] 3, 20. 21.[44] 10, 10. 11. 12. 12, 32. 33. 34. aut ad locos his similes. *Tres* tantum sunt *narratiunculae* de miraculis a Christo perpetratis, cap. 3, 7-12. cap. 7, 32-37. et cap. 8, 22-26. atque *duae parabolae*, cap. 4, 26-29. ac cap. 13, 33-36. quae forte Marco ita propriae videri possint, ut speciose opponi nobis queant.

Quod ad parabolas istas attinet, supra[45] iam ostendimus, utramque substitutam esse in locum alterius parabolae verbosioris sed similis argumenti, quae in eodem sermonis contextu apud Matthaeum legitur, et causam adeo vidimus, cur Marcus suas parabolas illis quas Matthaeus habet, praeferendas esse censuerit. Tantum igitur abest, ut ex his parabolis cogi possit, Marcum nullo, aut alio saltim quam Matthaeo, hic usum esse duce, ut potius manifestum sit, interserendarum harum parabolarum occasionem Marcum cepisse a Matthaeo. Eadem fere ratio est narrationis Marc. 3, 7-12. Nimirum Marcus scribit comm. 7. καὶ ὁ ἰησους μετα των μαθητων αὐτου ἀνεχωρησεν εἰς την θαλασσαν, και πολυ πληθος ἀπο της γαλιλαιας ἠκολουθησαν comm. 10. πολλους γαρ ἐθεραπευσεν comm. 12. και πολλα ἐπετιμα αὐτοις, ἰνα μη αὐτον φανερον ποιησωσιν. Matthaeus vero haec habet cap. 12, 15. 16. ὁ δε ἰησους γνους ἀνεχωρησεν ἐκειθεν και ἐθεραπευσεν αὐτους παντας, και ἐπετιμησεν αὐτοις, ἰνα μη φανερον αὐτον ποιησωσιν. Quis hic non videt, Marcum παραφραξειν textum Matthaei, et adiectis circumstantiis nonnullis amplificare tantum huius narrationem. Nam Marci, dum haec scriberet, oculis hunc ipsum Matthaei locum obversatum esse, e tabula quam supra exhibuimus et e nota (x)[46] apparet. Non igitur contra nostram sententiam, sed pro ea pugnat hic locus. Idem valet de narratione altera Marci 7, 32-37. Nam huius quoque hoc loco interserendae Matthaeus occasionem dedit. Matthaeus scilicet (cap. 15, 30. 31.) multos aegrotos a Christo sanatos fuisse tradit; Marcus vero unius ex ista turba sanationem, additis περιστασεσι nonnullis, quae notatu prae aliis dignae ipsi videbantur, curatius describit.

MAT. [15: 30, 31]

Και προσηλθον αὐτω ὀχλοι πολλοι
ἐχοντες μεθ' ἑαυτων...κωφους...
και ἐρριψαν αὐτους παρα τους ποδας του ἰησου,
και ἐθεραπευσεν αὐτους,
ὡστε τους ὀχλους θαυμασαι, βλεποντας κωφους λαλουντας...
και ἐδοξαζον τον θεον ισραηλ.

MAR. [7: 32, 35, 37]

Και φερουσιν αὐτω

κωφον μογιλαλον,
και παρακαλουσιν αὐτον,
ἱνα ἐπιθη αὐτω την χειρα...
και εὐθεως διηνοιχθησαν αὐτου αἱ ἀκοαι...
και ὑπερπερισσως ἐξεπλησσοντο,
λεγοντες · καλως παντα πεποιηκε.

Itaque *sola* superest historiola tertia Marc. 8, 22–26. Hanc fatemur
adiectam esse a Marco nec quidquam in Matthaeo vel Luca invenimus,
quod huic additamento h. 1. adponendo ansam praebere potuerit. Utut
est, si hancce historiolam cum duabus aliis, de quibus modo disserebamus,
curiosius comparamus, mirum inter eas consensum deprehendimus, atque
383 sic prona coniectura non solum causam assequimur, cur haec coeci cuiusdam hominis sanatio tanti momenti visa sit Marco, ut in ea narranda a
regula discederet, quam sibi praescripsit et constantissime, unico hoc loco
excepto, servavit, verum simul etiam rationem reddere possumus, cur duos
istos alios Matthaei locos mox indicatos (Matth. 12, 15. 16. et 15, 30. 31)
copiosiore rerum circumstantium enarratione illustrandos iudicaverit.
Nempe tribus istis historiolis commune hoc est, quod Iesus latere voluerit,
et iis quos sanasset, ne rem divulgarent, interdixerit. Nimirum Marc. 3, 12.
legimus: πολλα ἐπετιμα αὐτοις (daemoniacis) ἱνα μη αὐτον φανερον
ποιησωσιν. Marc. 7, 33. et 36. vero: ἀπολαβομενος αὐτον (τον κωφον
μογιλαλον) ἀπο του ὀχλου κατ ἰδιαν... και διεστειλατο αὐτοις, ἱνα μηδενι
εἰπωσιν. Tandem Marc. 8, 23. et 26. ἐξηγαγεν αὐτον (τον τυφλον) ἐξω
της κωμης...λεγων μηδε εἰς την κωμην εἰσελθης, μηδε εἰπης τινι ἐν
τη κωμη. Tribus his Marci locis addimus duos alios, eiusdem fere generis
additamento notabiles. Cap. 7, 24. narrat e Matthaeo, Iesum venisse in
confinia Tyri et Sidonis, atque *addit:* οὐδενα ἠθελε γνωναι, και οὐκ
ἠδυνηθη λαθειν. Cap. 9, 30. iterum Matthaeum secutus, Christum iter per
Galilaeam fecisse tradit, et itidem *addit:* και οὐκ ἠθελε, ἱνα τις γνω. Itaque
manifestum est, Marcum alias quidem *ubique* κατα ποδα vel Matthaeum
vel Lucam sequi, neque de suo (si curatiorem περιστασεων quarundam
enumerationem excipias) quidquam admiscere, *nisi* forte inveniret apud
Matthaeum vel Lucam historiolam, quae doceret, Iesum non captasse
384 populares acclamationes, sed plebi non raro ultro sese subtraxisse, imo
cavisse interdum sedulo, ne praeclare facta sua innotescerent multitudini;
non igitur vanae gloriae studio ductum eum fuisse, nec miracula eo patrasse
consilio, ut stupenti et otiosae plebi inusitatum praeberet spectaculum.
Hasce tales historiae Domini particulas copiosius pertractare solet, ac
sicubi Matthaeum et Lucam eiusmodi quid praetermisisse animadvertit,
supplere id satagit. Cur vero hoc narrationum genus prae reliquis omnibus

magni momenti esse et iis lectoribus, quibus libellum suum destinaverat, apprime utile futurum iudicaverit, non liquet. Non improbabiliter fortasse coniicere aliquis posset, doctores istarum regionum, charismate ἰαμάτων I Cor. 12, 9. instructos, simili fere modo interdum eo abusos esse, quo Corinthios nonnullos γλώσσαις temere usos fuisse scimus. Hos forte Marcus, proposito Domini exemplo, corrigere voluit.

III. Marcus, postquam alterutrius, sive Matthaei sive Lucae, vestigiis per longum velut tractum inhaesit, saepe repentino saltu ab altero ad alterum transsilit, mox vero ad priorem ducem redit; id quod fieri non potuisset, nisi utriusque commentarios simul inspexisset et inter se comparasset. Sic Marc. 3, 1-5. e Luca desumtum est; comma 6. autem, ad eandem narrationem pertinens, e Matthaeo. Praeterea Marcus cap. 5, 25. 26. 27. Luca utitur duce; comm. 28. Matthaeo; et comm. 29. seq. iterum Luca. Porro Marc. 8, 37. decerptum est e Matthaeo, et abest a Luca; comma 38. Lucae debetur, et desideratur apud Matthaeum; cap. 9, 1. 2. (μεθ᾽ ἡμέρας ἑξ) rursus e Matthaeo derivatum est. Tandem Marcus cap. 10, 22. 26. 27. imitatur Matthaeum; comm. 28. 29. [sic] cum Luca concordat et omittit quae Matthaeo propria sunt; sed comm. 20. [sic] transscribit e Matthaeo sententiam, quam hic solus habet. Denique cap. 13, 24. 25. Matthaei vestigia premit; commate 26. praetermittit quae Matthaeo peculiaria sunt et Lucam sequitur; comm. 27-32. autem in singulis paene verbis cum Matthaeo rursus concinit. Tacemus plura.

Sectio III

Declarata iam et, ut speramus, satis confirmata sententia nostra, progredimur ad examinandas, quae ad eam convellendam in medium a viris doctis prolatae sunt aut proferri forte possent, obiectiones. Neque tamen est, cur refutandis iis argumentis operam demus, quibus viri docti, Marcum non fuisse Matthaei epitomatorem, efficere studuerunt. Etsi enim Marcum multa quae Matthaeus habet praetermisisse ultro largimur, eundemque in conscribendo libello suo brevitati studuisse ipsi defendimus, tantum tamen abest ut, AUGUSTINO praeeunte, Matthaei breviatorem eum fuisse arbitremur, ut potius multa e Lucae Evangelio desumta, Matthaei narrationi interserta ac pleraque, quae ex Matthaeo in suum commentariolum transtulit, uberiore rerum circumstantium enarratione atque adeo interdum periphrasibus amplificata ab eo esse statuamus. Nec tela timemus, quae ad expugnandam nostram hypothesin ab ordine Marci, multum a Matthaei aeque ac Lucae ordine recedente, depromuntur, quibus nuperrime etiam Cel. EICHHORNIUS[47] usus est. Nam ordinis, quem in narrando Marcus tenuit, rationem abunde Sectione II. reddidimus. Verum aliae praeter has propositae fuerunt obiectiones, ad quas hoc loco respondendum est.

I. 'Si Marcus fere omnia debet Matthaeo et Luca, falsum est, scripsisse eum, ὡς Πετρος ὑφηγησατο αὐτω, et materiae, quam Petrus suppeditasse queat, paene nihil relinquitur. Atqui historica argumenta, quibus utuntur, qui Marcum Petro duce usum esse contendunt, labefactata nondum sunt, nec alia de causa reiicitur vetusta illa narratio, quam quod hypothesi repugnat, e sola libri Marci cum Matthaeo et Luca comparatione, sed nulla necessitate et evidentia, ductae.'[48] *Respondemus*: (a) utrum hypothesis nostra, trium Evangeliorum comparationi superstructa, evidentia destituatur et nulla necessitate sit ducta, iis iudicandum libenter permittimus, qui nulla praeconcepta opinione in videndo vero impediuntur. Nam viri docti, qui ante nos de Marci Evangelio alias hypotheses, nostra admissa ultro corruentes, publice proposuerant, utut sagacissimi verique amantissimi, tamen vix incorrupti satis iudices videntur. (b) Ingenue fatemur, vetustam illam narrationem, de Marco sub Petri auspiciis Evangelium suum exarante, iis a nobis annumerari commentis, qualia permulta apud scriptores antiquos occurrunt, a viris doctis plerisque hodie repudiata.[49] Nam (c) primus, qui Petro duce Marcum scripsisse tradit, Papias fuit, homo exiguae, ut omnes norunt, in rebus historicis auctoritatis. Eum secutus est, ut solet, IRENAEUS; huius narrationem repetierunt alii. (d) E PAPIAE verbis (apud EUSEB. III. 39.) apparet, duabus rebus deductum fuisse aut ipsum aut Ioannem presbyterum (quem narrationis suae testem laudat) in istam de Petro coniecturam. Primo quaerebatur, undenam res gestae et orationes Christi innotuerint Marco, qui Dominum, dum in his terris viveret, sectatus haud fuisset. Respondet PAPIAS, fuisse eum Petri discipulum et ἑρμηνευτην; Petrum autem passim in suis sermonibus, quos audiverit Marcus, res ad historiam Iesu pertinentes commemorasse. Deinde dubitabatur, cur apud Marcum res gestae et sermones Domini alio ordine legerentur, quam in aliis libris. PAPIAS, Marcum excusaturus, monet, Petrum in sermonibus suis res Domini non ordine accurato, sed ut ferret occasio, enarrasse, Marcum autem scripto eas consignasse, prout a Petro eas audivisset earumque nunc, dum scriberet, meminisset. Satis manifestum est, cuinam consilio commentum PAPIAE inservire debuerit. Sed hanc ipsam ob causam merito suspectum nobis est. (e) Valde improbabilis in se spectata Papiae est coniectura. Quis enim sibi persuadeat, Petrum in sermonibus suis historiolas de Christo sic uti apud Marcum (v. c. cap. 4, 35. 36. cap. 5, 1. 18. 21. cap. 10, 46-52. cap. 11, 4. 11-22.) eas legimus, hoc est cum minutissimis περιστασεσι, enarrasse? Aut quis credat, Petrum de resurrectione Domini nunquam alia et plura auditoribus suis tradidisse, quam quae habentur apud Marcum? Hoc vero, si Papiae fides est habenda, credere debemus. Ipso enim teste unice hoc propositum fuit Marco, *ne quidquam eorum, quae* (a Petro) *audivisset, omitteret,* nec narrationibus suis falsi

aliquid admisceret. (f) PAPIA auctore, Marcus quidem materiem, e qua
libellum suum construxit, e Petri sermonibus collegerat, Petrus vero
scribenti neutiquam adfuit aut opem tulit. Mendacii igitur Papias eos
arguit, qui dictante Petro Marcum scripsisse retulerunt. (g) Hac in re consentientem sibi habet *Irenaeum*, qui (Libr. III.I.) haec tantum habet:
'Post Petri et Pauli ἐξοδον Marcus discipulus et interpres Petri et ipse *quae
Petrus praedicaverat* per scripta nobis tradidit.' Sed idem Irenaeus (ibid.)
plane simillima de Luca quoque perhibet: 'Lucas, sectator Paulli, *quod ab
illo praedicabatur Evangelium* in libro condidit.' Posterius hoc falsum esse
et absonum,[50] fatentur paene omnes. Cur igitur prius illud ab Irenaeo
persuaderi nobis patiamur? (h) *Tertullianus* (adv. Marc. IV. 5.) similiter
utriusque fabulae meminit. 'Marcus', inquit, 'quod edidit Evangelium,
Petri *affirmatur*, cuius interpres Marcus. *Nam et* Lucae digestum Paullo
adscribere solent.' Capit magistrorum videri, quae discipuli promulgarint.
Quis non videt, haec non claris testimoniis aut certis documentis, sed vagis
rumoribus niti et parum firmis argumentationibus? Quia, quae discipuli
promulgant, magistris attribui possunt; *hinc* Marci Evangelium Petro et
Lucae libellum Paullo *adscribere solebant,* ne scilicet Marci et Lucae commentariis apostolica auctoritas deesse videretur. (i) *Iustinus Martyr* (dial.
c. Tryph. §. 106.) e *Petri* quidem ἀπομνημονευμασι refert, Iesum Zebedaei
filiis imposuisse cognomen βοανεργες, ὁ ἐστιν υἰοι βροντης: quod cum
apud solum Marcum (cap. 3, 17.) legatur, huius libellum Iustinus Petro
adscribere videtur. Sed primo, Iustini auctoritas in rebus historicis tantum
non est nulla. Deinde, nondum liquet, quod et quaenam e nostris Evangeliis
adhibuerit. Marco saltim alias nunquam usus est, nec alibi usquam ἀπομνημονευματων Πετρου meminit, sed constanter vel ἀπομνημονευματα simpli-
citer, vel ἀπομνημονευματα των ἀποστολων laudavit; quare mirum esset,
si unico hoc loco ἀπομνημονευματα Petri, tanquam diversa ab ἀπομνημονευμασι των ἀποστολων commemorasset. Praeterea, locus obscurior est,
quam ut certi aliquid effici ex eo queat. Posset ἀπομνημονευματα αὐτου
esse ἀπομ. χριστου. Posset etiam loco αὐτου legi αὐτων, scilicet των
ἀποστολων, ut alias Iustinus scribere solet. Tandem, si vel maxime con-
cedatur, Marci Evangelium isto loco indigitari et ἀπομνημονευματων
Πετρου nomine venire, dubium tamen manet, quam ob causam dicatur
Petri esse. Potuit quidem vagus et incertus ille rumor de Marco Petri interprete ut ad aliorum ita ad Iustini quoque aures pervenisse; sed potuit etiam
sub Petri nomine laudari libellus, quem hic Apostolus ecclesiis nonnullis
commendasse credebatur; quin potuerunt, quae alias Apostolorum ἀπομνημονευματα vocantur, Petri ἀπομνημονευματα appellari, quia hoc ipso
loco *primus* inter Apostolos Petrus dictus fuerat. Utcunque haec se habent,
Iustinus is non est, qui de Marci Evangelio certiora et veriora edocere nos

391 queat. (k) Aliorum narrationes novis additamentis exornatas repetiit
Clemens Alexandrinus. Retulit enim, (apud Euseb. II, 15. et VI. 14)
Marcum, utpote qui inde a longo tempore Petrum sectatus esset et magistri
dicta memoria teneret, *rogatum fuisse a Romanis*, ut doctrinam, quam ipsis
apostolus coram exposuisset, scripto comprehenderet.[51] Nec destitisse
Romanos, donec enixis suis precibus *tandem expugnassent Marcum*, ut
Evangelium suum scriberet. Petrum autem ea de re, revelante id ipsi Spiritu,
certiorem factum, *delectatum esse* propenso Romanorum studio, suaque
auctoritate librum *comprobasse, ut in ecclesiis legeretur.*[52] Sed ipse sibi
non satis constat *Clemens*. Nam apud *Eusebium* II, 15. Petrum delectatum
fuisse τη προθυμα Romanorum et Marci Evangelium comprobasse tradit;
contra vero apud Euseb. VI. 14. apostolum perhibet nec a proposito co-
hibuisse discipulum, *nec ad id exsequendum incitasse.* (l) Scriptores, quos
hactenus recensuimus, sumunt Marcum libelli sui argumentum decerpsisse

392 e sermonibus, quos Petrus *coram populo* habuisset. *Origines* vero (apud
Euseb. VI. 25.) e traditione didicisse se profitetur, Evangelium ordine
secundum a Marco (quem apostolus I Petr. 5, 12. filium suum appellet)
scriptum fuisse ὡς Πετρος ὑφηγησατο ΑΥΤΩι. (m) Tandem cunctis huiusmodi narratiunculis colophonem imposuerunt, qui, velut Auctor synopseos
Scripturae sacrae, de Evangelio nostro tradiderunt, ὁτι ὑπηγορευθη ὑπο
Πετρου ἐν 'Ρωμη ἐξεδοθη ὑπο Μαρκου, ἐκηρυχθη ὑπ' αὐτου ἐν Αλεξαν-
δρεια! (n) Ex his omnibus inter se collatis patet, famam quidem crevisse
eundo, sed antiquissimas etiam et simpliciores relationes *Papiae, Irenaei*
et *Tertulliani* pro meris habendas esse coniecturis. Quid eis excogitandis
ansam dederit, passim iam (lit. d. et h.) indigitavimus. Praeterea *interpretis
Petri* titulus, quo Marcus a *Papia, Irenaeo, Tertulliano, Hieronymo* et aliis
condecoratur, fingendis variis commentis occasionem praebuit. Primitus
quidem, ni fallimur, nomine isto indicabatur tantum, Marcum fuisse Petri
comitem, ministrum, ὑπηρετην, (Act. 13, 5.) internuntium, quem ad ex-
sequenda mandata sua, ubi opus esset, adhiberet.[53] Alii vero postea sic
intelligebant: Petrum, graeci sermonis non satis peritum, si cum Graecis
loqui aut ad eos scribere vellet, usum esse Marco *interprete.* Atque hinc alii

393 porro exsculpserunt, Marcum *etiam in conscribendo Evangelio suo* Petri
fuisse interpretem. Sic *Hieronymus* epist. ad Hedibiam cap. II. 'Paulus',
inquit, 'divinorum sensuum maiestatem digno non poterat graeci eloquii
explicare sermone. Habebat ergo Titum interpretem, sicut et beatus Petrus
Marcum, cuius *Evangelium Petro narrante et illo scribente compositum est.*
Denique et duae epistolae quae feruntur Petri, stilo inter se et charactere
discrepant: ex quo intelligimus, pro necessitate rerum diversis eum usum
interpretibus.' (o) Expendendis internis argumentis ex ipso Marci libro
petitis, quibus viri docti vetustam de Petro traditionem confirmari posse

autumarunt, Lectoribus molesti esse nolumus. Nempe si occurrunt apud
Marcum nonnulla ad Petrum pertinentia, quae non leguntur apud Matthaeum vel Lucam, e Petri dictamine haec profluxisse contendunt. Sin
contra in Marci libello quaedam huius generis desiderantur, quae apud
alios reperiuntur, Petri modestiae tribuendum id esse putant. Nostro vero
iudicio haec omnia precario sumuntur et ad probandum id, de quo quaeri-
tur, nihil valent.

II. 'Causa apparet nulla, cur Marcus novum conficeret rerum Christi
commentarium, si praeter tenue corollarium viginti et quatuor commatum,
Matthaei duntaxat Lucaeque libros compilasset.'[54] *Respondemus:* (a)
Causa procul dubio posita fuit in Christianorum nonnullorum, qui Marco
familiarius quam Matthaeo aut Luca usi fuerant, sive utilitate sive desiderio.
Horum commodis inservire voluit, ut alii aliis aliarum regionum Christianis
prodesse studuerant. (b) Neuter priorum Evangelistarum omnia complexus
erat, quae Marcus suis lectoribus utilia esse censebat. Hinc ex utroque, quae
amicis convenientissima putaret, selegit. (c) Utriusque Evangelistae commentarius continebat haud pauca, quae, utpote alii hominum generi scripta,
Marcus suis familiaribus minus necessaria esse iudicabat. Haec omittendo
effecit Marcus simul, ut amici haberent rerum gestarum Domini delineati-
onem multo breviorem atque adeo minori opere aut sumtu parabilem,
quam fuissent Matthaei et Lucae Evangelia in unum volumen coniuncta.

III. 'Conveniebat temporum rationi, novorumque Christianorum in cog-
noscenda suae religionis origine ardori atque studio, commentarios habere
de vita Iesu quam uberrimos et copiosissimos; conveniebat, quae a variis
hominibus narrata fuerant, scriptisque passim circumferebantur, rerum ab
eo gestarum fragmenta undique colligi, collecta in unum corpus coagmen-
tari, hocque novis, si quae occurrebant veraeque esse deprehendebantur,
narrationibus augeri et locupletari; non vero, quae iam collecta erant, et ab
Apostolo adeo collecta, denuo truncari epitomenque libri pro libro ipso
Christianis, nec singulis quidem his, sed universae cuidam ecclesiae, in manus tradi atque commendari.'[55] *Respondemus:* (a) Huiusmodi ratiocina-
tiones parum valebunt apud eos, qui secum reputaverint, quam anceps sit
de eo, quod certis temporibus, locis et hominibus conveniat, iudicium.
Quid? quod nescimus, utrum singulis Christianis an universae cuidam ecclesiae Marcus suum libellum destinaverit, multoque magis ignoramus, cuinam
ecclesiae in manus eum tradiderit. Quae enim veteres ea de re perhibuere,
merae sunt coniecturae et incertae traditiones. Quis igitur definire ausit,
quid ignotae nobis conditioni ecclesiae cuiusdam ignotae conveniens fuerit,
quid minus? Marcus recte diiudicare hoc potuit; nos non item. (b) Perperam
sumitur, haud licuisse Marco quidquam omittere eorum, quae de Iesu historia ipsi nota essent, sed debuisse eum novis potius augmentis aliorum

narrationes locupletare. Certe de nativitate Iesu ne unicum quidem verbulum protulit, quamvis quasdam saltim eius rei περιστασεις non potuerit non scire, qui tum Hierosolymis in matris suae domo, tum alibi in comitatu Petri Paulique cum tot familiaribus Domini conversatus fuerat. Ac eius generis plura silentio praeteriit, quae eum (si vel maxime Matthaeum ac Lucam nunquam legisset) latere non poterant.

IV. 'Probabile est, brevius Evangelium tempore fuisse prius, copiosiora autem, in quibus supplebantur et amplificabantur omissa aut nimis succincte tradita in illo, seriori tempore esse exarata.' *Respondemus:* Ab auctoris consilio unice pendet, utrum iis, quae alii ante ipsum scripsere, addere aliquid, an demere ab illis nonnulla satius sit.

V. 'Si Marcus, quae cel. Storrii est sententia, primus scripsit et a Matthaeo Lucaque lectus et adhibitus fuit, ratio facillime reddi potest eorum, quae tria Evangelia curiosius inter se comparanti non possunt non mira videri, et quae excogitandis tot de Marci Evangelio hypothesibus occasionem praebuerunt. Nempe Matthaeus et Lucas (a) non raro iisdem, quibus Marcus, verbis usi sunt; quia huius libellum ante oculos positum habebant; (β) orationem hic ibi variarunt multaque suo quisque modo, hoc est aliter quam Marcus, narrarunt; quia non locupletiorem Marci editionem, sed novos de rebus Christi commentarios concinnare sibi proposuerant; (γ) creberrime quidem easdem ipsas res, quas literis consignaverat Marcus, memoriae prodiderunt, attamen, quod in immensa illa παραλειπομενων copia exspectare licebat, nova etiam complurima, alius alia, de suo, ne actum agerent, addiderunt.'[56] *Respondemus:* Hypothesi huic, quae Matthaeum et Lucam usos esse Marci Evangelio sumit, plura officere videntur, e quibus ea tantum hic attingemus, quae prae caeteris ad vindicandam *nostram* sententiam pertinent, et ex hactenus disputatis nullo negotio intelligi possunt, nec verbosa declaratione indigent. Nimirum (a) credibile non est, Matthaeum, testem oculatum, ducem sibi elegisse in tradenda Christi historia scriptorem, qui rebus gestis haud interfuerat. (b) Marcus perspicua et definita rerum expositione Matthaeum antecellit, imo nonnunquam, ut exemplis postea docebitur, accuratior est et propius ad rerum gestarum veritatem accedit. Cur igitur Matthaeus his in locis recessit ab eo, si alias vestigia eius premere solet? (c) Marcus, cum multas rerum περιστασεις, tum etiam integras narratiunculas quasdam habet, vel a Matthaeo vel a Luca vel ab utroque neglectas. Has quoque cur fastidiverunt duumviri illi, si reliqua in suos usus convertere haud dedignati sunt? Autumat quidem Cel. *Storrius,*[57] 'Matthaeam et Lucam passim, *ut novis additamentis locum facerent*, Marci orationem circumcidere et contrahere potuisse, maxime cum narrationes omissarum similes de suo addidissent.' Verum enim vero nec in Matthaei neque in Lucae commentario tale brevitatis studium se prodit, quod deterrere hosce auctores potuisset a retinendis istis Marci particulis, quas si una cum caeteris servassent, parum molis addidissent suis libris. Atque praeterea mirari licet, quid sit quod uterque quinquies, ut supra notavimus, omiserit vel saltim breviaverit narratiunculas, e quibus discimus, noluisse Iesum stupenda facta sua divulgari. Cur haec tam studiose toties resecarentur, ratio probabilis adfuit nulla, multoque est verisimilius, certas ob causas adiecta ea esse a Marco ad narrationes Matthaei et Lucae, quam ab his temere fuisse iugulata. (d) Matthaeus, fatente ipso Ven. *Storrio*, chronologico ordine posthabito, saepe res, quarum memoriam prodere posteris vellet, ita disposuit, uti affinitate quadam inter se coniunctae essent. Si primus Christi historiam scripsit, facile arridere ei talis methodus potuit. Sin vero ducem habuit Marcum, ab artificiosiore hac ratione alienum, vix erat cur in effingendo novo ordine elaboraret, nisi ad temporis leges curatius omnia redigere vellet, id quod certe propositum ei haud fuit. (e) Quae de ordine, quo apud Marcum narrationes sese excipiunt, et de crebris ac subitaneis Marci transitionibus a Matthaeo ad Lucam et vicissim a Luca ad Matthaeum supra observata a nobis sunt, abunde docent, Marcum scripsisse post Matthaeum et Lucam, horumque commentarios inspectos ab ipso fuisse. Cur Marcus e. gr. Matth. 5, 1. Matthaeum, Luc. 6, 20. Lucam, Matth. 13, 36. iterum Matthaeum de manibus posuerit; item, cur a Matth. 4, 22. ad Luc. 4, 31. ac a Luca 6, 11. ad Matth. 12, 15. atque a Matth. 13, 35. ad Luc. 8, 22 transsilierit, nostra admissa hypothesi planissime patet. Sed si statuas, Marcum consultum fuisse a Matthaeo et Luca, obscurum manet, cur v. c. Matthaeus ea, quae habentur Marc. 1, 21 – 3, 6. partim omiserit, partim in alium ordinem redegerit. Sed nolumus addere plura, quae quilibet ex iis, quae supra Sectione II. disputavimus, petere potest. Neque enim evertendis aliorum hypothesibus, sed nostrae stabiliendae et ab obiectionibus vindicandae operam hic damus.

VI. 'Non in Matthaeo solum, sed in Marco etiam et Luca multa occurrunt indicia, e quibus colligi potest, tres illos libellos profluxisse ex *uno* fonte, eodemque non graeco sed *ebraico*. Reperiuntur enim in Evangeliis nostris nonnullae narrationum discrepantiae, ortae ex erroribus, quibus ansam dedit vocabulorum ebraicorum ambiguitas, aut vocum in Ebraeorum sermone consimilium et facile confundendarum permutatio. Praeterea universus habitus narrationis Evangelistae cuiusque in pericopis, quae duobus aut tribus communes sunt, plane sic comparatus est, uti versio quaeque habere se solet ad alias eiusdem archetypi versiones. Hinc collaturus tres Evangelistas inter se, quavis fere pagina deprehendet v. c. voces, phrases et orationis structuras, diversas quidem sed idem significantes et uni eidemque ebraicae loquendi formulae respondentes. Huius vero rei probabilis ratio reddi nequit, praeter hanc: tres Evangelistas usos esse eodem archetypo ebraico, quem suo quisque modo in graecum sermonem converterit, et cui nonnulla ex propria penu passim adsperserit. Hoc posito, omnes evanescunt difficultates. Contra vero, si alterius Evangelistae commentarium ab altero adhibitum et particulatim exscriptum esse sumas, concedere debebis, *vel* studiose celare voluisse posteriores Evangelistas fontem unde sua depromserint, eamque ob causam synonymas phrases substituisse in locum earum, quibus anterior scriptor usus fuerat; id quod vehementer abhorret ab horum auctorum simplicitate et integritate, *vel* phrasibus variandis puerilem ipsos operam impendisse; quod viri gravis persona vix dignum videtur.'[58] *Respondemus:* (a) nullum nobis adhuc innotuit documentum indubium, e quo probari queat, interpretes in convertendo archetypo ebraico lapsos errore esse; sed loci omnes, ad quos provocatur, absque hac hypothesi explicari et ab opinata difficultate liberari possunt. Demonstraturi hoc essemus singulos percurrendo locos, si huius commentationis limites id permitterent. Monuisse sufficiat, multos viros doctos similiter visos sibi esse in epistola ad Ebraeos deprehendisse varios graeci interpretis errores. Sed satis iam constat, vanas fuisse istas suspiciones, epistolamque graece esse ab auctore scriptam. (b) Errorum quos aiunt, exempla pleraque saltim notabiliora, e Matthaeo conquisita sunt. Quae enim e Marco et Luca proferuntur, et pauciora sunt et leviora. Atqui salva hypothesi nostra largiri possemus, Matthaeum scripsisse ebraice. Quid enim obstat, quominus Marcus ebraicos Matthaei et graecos Lucae commentarios inspicere inque suos usus convertere potuerit? Ac, si forte rationem simul reddere velis crebri concentus inter Matthaeum nostrum et Marcum in graeca adeo phrasi, sumere tibi licebit, cum ebraicum archetypum Matthaei tum graecam eiusdem versionem praesto fuisse Marco, eumque mox hanc, mox illum, mox utrumque, praeter Lucae libellum, consuluisse. Mallemus sane, nisi alius superesset ex his tricis nos expediendi modus, huic coniecturae calculum adiicere nostrum, quam nimis artificiose compositae et tum chronologicis rationibus, tum iis, quae Sectione II, scripsimus, repugnanti hypothesi adsentiri, statuenti plures archetypi recensiones, easque varie iam inter se permixtas, et graecas earum versiones plures. (c) E phrasium synonymarum et grammaticae structurae permutationibus, in tribus Evangeliis obviis, nihil contra nostram sententiam efficitur. Evangelistas nec fontem unde hauserunt dissimulare voluisse, nec variandis phrasibus puerorum more insudasse, ultro largimur, quin si alterutrum necessario esset concedendum, lubenter hypothesin nostram abiiceremus. Sed ad neutrum illorum admittendum cogimur, quia, ut cum dialecticis loquamur, *datur tertium*. Quis nescit, posse scriptorem, quae apud alium legit, *suo* modo *suisque* verbis repetere? Et quis tam severus est et inhumanus, ut talem auctorem, nisi aliae subsint suspicionis causae, vel dissimulationis

parum ingenuae accuset, vel pueriliter in phrasibus lusisse contendat?
Quemadmodum igitur historici, ex aliorum commentariis velut e fontibus
narrationum suarum argumenta derivantes, non hanc sibi legem scribunt,
ut superstitiose iisdem vocibus et formulis sese adstringant, quas ab illis
adhibitas cernunt: ita Marcus quoque Matthaei et Lucae libros utique con-
sulere potuit, neque tamen horum narrationes *ad verbum* exscribere debuit.
Nempe perlecta pericopa quadam apud Matthaeum vel Lucam vel utrumque, ad scribendum sese adcinxit et quae apud illos legerat ita enarravit,
prout ea memoria teneret. Sicubi ipsorum Matthaei aut Lucae verborum
meminit, haec retinuit, nec de varianda oratione sollicitus fuit; ubi vero
illa exciderant, alia in eorum locum substituit. Nonnunquam fortasse
Matthaei Lucaeve commentarios denuo, dum scriberet, inspexit; neque
tamen semper hoc necesse esse putavit, quia non illorum libres exscribere
aut in epitomen redigere, sed ad eorum ductum *novam* narrationem, suorum lectorum usibus accommodatam, componere decreverat. Hoc posito,
intelligitur, unde non solum in verbis et phrasibus, sed etiam in narrationum quarundam conformatione universa (e. gr. Marc. 7, 6–13. coll. Matth.
15, 3–9. coll. Matth. 19, 3–8.) diversitas quaedam orta sit. Interdum quidem de consulto Marcus immutasse nonnulla videtur; sed plerumque casui
debentur eiusmodi discrepantiae.

VII. 'Omisit Marcus non pauca, quae vel Matthaeus habet vel Lucas,
egregia notatuque dignissima. Qui vero neglexisset res a Christo gestas tanti
momenti et sermones Domini longe utilissimos iucundissimosque, a Matthaeo aut Luca literis mandatos, si horum Evangelia suis oculis, dum scriberet,
usurpasset et pleraque, ac in his etiam nonnulla minoris momenti, ex iis
transscripsisset? Qui passim silentio praeterire potuisset rerum a se narrata-
rum περιστασεις quasdam, a Matthaeo et Luca commemoratas et iis, quae
ipse in literas retulerat, haud parum lucis afferentes, has, inquam, quomodo
aspernari potuisset, si duumvirorum illorum libelli praesto ipsi fuissent?
Huiusmodi omissiones, narrationem reddentes impeditam et imperfectam,
excusare haud poteris, nisi vel nullum Evangelistam alterius scripta ad
manus habuisse contendas, vel Marci Evangelium caeteris prius exaratum
fuisse statuas. Saltim, Cel. *Storrio* iudice, causa cur Matthaeus et Lucas
tam multa narraverint, quae apud Marcum non leguntur, multo facilius
perspicitur, si Marcus prior scripserit, quam si Matthaeus et Lucas scribenti
ad manus fuerint. Posteriores enim auctores, ne actum agerent, res a superi-
ore scriptore narratas augere et amplificare debuerunt.'[59] *Respondemus:*
Ex iis, quae huius commentationis Sectione I, nr. 4. 5. 6. 8. 9 et passim in
notis ad eam, inde a nota 15 p. 366., monuimus, satis patere confidimus,
pleraque a Marco praetermissa consulto intacta esse relicta. Praeterea a
Marci commentariis non abesse non poterant, quae vel in iis Matthaei locis

leguntur, quos ille, Luca duce tum usus, transsilierat, vel in iis Lucae capiti-
bus occurrunt, quae Noster, dum Matthaei vestigia premeret, vix obiter
404 consuluerat. Vide verbi causa loc. cit. notam 22 p. 372. Tandem usu venire
potest facile, ut verae causae, cur Marcus nonnulla praeteriverit, nos lateant,
cum de libri auctore perparum, de lectoribus in quorum gratiam scripsit
horumque conditione paene nihil sciamus, ac de consilio scribentis coniec-
tando vix paucula assequi valeamus.[60] Quae omnia si reputare secum velint
arbitri haud iniqui, fatebuntur sine dubio, inconcussam manere hypothesin
nostram, si vel plura Marcus intacta praeterivisset. Interim omissionibus
nonnullis tantum ponderis inesse opinati sunt viri perdocti, ut horum iudicio non tantum, quantum omnino par est, tribuere videri possemus, si eas
silentio praetermitteremus, nec causam, cur ad convellendam sententiam
nostram eas non satis idoneas esse censeamus, exponeremus. Atque ex his,
quas attingemus, de reliquis iudicari poterit. Itaque

(1) Colloquium Iesu cum Ioanne de baptismo in se etiam suscipiendo
Matth. 3, 14. 15. omisit Marcus quanquam in antecedentibus et sequentibus
405 cum Matthaeo concinat. *Resp.* Duo continentur his commatibus: primo,
Ioannem agnovisse, inferiorem esse se suumque baptismum Domini persona
ac baptismo; deinde, ideo Iesum voluisse sacro fonte lavari a Ioanne, quia
πρεπον ἐστι πληρωσαι πασαν δικαιοσυνην. Prius praetermitti poterat, quia
proxime praecesserat apud Marcum (cap. 1, 7. 8.) aliud Baptistae testimo-
nium de Iesu dignitate suam longe superante. Posterius silentio forte prae-
tereundum esse, fervente iam de legis mosaicae valore perpetuo contro-
versia, Marcus censuit, ne Iudaizantes abuterentur isto Domini effato ad
inculcandam Christianis rituum iudaicorum observationem, velut prae-
cipuam δικαιοσυνης, quam πληρωσαι debeant, partem. Praeterea Lucas
etiam intacta haec reliquit. In pericopis autem Matthaeo et Lucae com-
munibus, eas particulas textus Matthaei transsilire fere solet Marcus, quas
a Luca abesse cerneret.

(2) In tentationis historia Matth. 4, 1-11. Luc. 4, 1-13. Marcus brevis-
sime tantum rei summam attigit cap. 1, 12. 13., modos autem, quibus
Dominus tentatus restitit vicitque, reticuit. Cum vero a Marci ingenio ab-
horreat narrationis uberioris breviatio et περιστασεων ipsi notarum omis-
sio, credibile est, pleniorem descriptionem, quae apud Matthaeum et Lucam
extat, cognitam ei non fuisse. *Resp.* Duo erant, quibus Marcus deterreri
poterat, ne copiosiorem narrationem suo libello insereret. (a) Forma narrationis iudaicum cogitandi cogitataque explicandi modum redolens, ingenio
lectorum, quibus Marcus Evangelium suum destinabat, minus adaptata vide-
406 batur. (b) In colloquio Servatoris cum tentatore *quater* Veteris Testamenti
oracula laudantur. Marcus autem huiusmodi allegationes resecare solet.
Vid. Sect. I. nr. 9. Iam, si quatuor illa carmina omittenda censebat, narra-

tionem (nisi totam praeterire vellet) vel penitus immutare, vel rei tantum summam, missis circumstantiis omnibus, attingere debebat. Posterius placuit Nostro.

(3) Cel. *Storrio* iudice,[61] a veri specie omnino abhorrent, quae supra Sect. II. not. 17 p. 371 not. 21 et 22 p. 372 et sq. de omissa a Marco oratione montana diximus. Incredibile Viro doctissimo videtur, Marcum insignem hunc sermonem ita refugisse, ut non solum Matthaei librum, simulac ad hunc locum (Matth. 5) pervenisset, seponeret, sed Lucam quoque, ad quem novum ducem transiisset, ut primum (Luc. 6, 20-49.) in similia dicta (licet breviora et ab ipso Luca non Palaestinensibus, verum exteris, tradita) incidisset, pariter desereret et ad Matthaeum se reciperet, imo vel pauculos versiculos Matth. 12, 33-37. hac una de causa, quod sententias his similes in oratione montana legisset, a suo libro reiiceret. *Resp.* (a) Oratio, quae apud Lucam legitur, brevior quidem est ea, quam Matthaeus exhibuit; at in se spectata satis est verbosa et per *triginta* versiculos protenditur. Sermones tam longos fere semper Marcus transsilit. Nec doceri potest, *debuisse* eum hancce orationem, si ea ipsi nota erat, omnino retinere. (b) Quod ad Matth. 12, 33-37 attinet, iis quae supra nota 23 p. 373 monuimus, addere hic licebit, praecessisse apud Matthaeum (comm. 25-32.) aliam orationem, quae in Marci quoque Evangelio legitur, et rursus sequi aliam, vs. 39-45. Cum igitur Marcus plures a Matthaeo sermones Domini coacervatos esse videret, ipse, ne in nimiam molem excresceret libellus suus, eam tantum orationis partem, quae apud Matthaeum comm. 25-32. extat, retinuit saltuque facto a commate 32. statim ad comma 46 transivit, praetermissis non solum commatibus 33-37. (quae contra nos urgentur) sed etiam comm. 38-45.

(4) Quae Matth. 8, 5-13. et Luc. 7, 1-10. legitur historia de centurionis Capernaitici puero a Christo sanato, memorabilis in primis visa nonnullis tum propter singularis plane fiduciae a centurione in Christo positae exemplum, tum quia ex hac narratione patebat, Iesum aegrotis adeo absentibus integram valetudinem reddere potuisse, abest a Marco. *Resp.* (a) Marcus cap. 7, 29. 30. aliam exhibet historiam, quae Dominum absentes etiam sanasse docet; illa igitur altera carere ipsius lectores facile poterant. (b) Tabula, quam Sectione II. cum Lectoribus communicavimus, ostendit, Marcum a Matthaei cap. 4, 21. transiliisse ad cap. 12, 15. et a Lucae cap. 6, 16. ad cap. 8, 16. Quare, cum historia illa apud Matthaeum legatur capite 8 et apud Lucam capite 7, neglecta fuit a Marco una cum aliis in utroque Evangelista eam et praecedentibus et consequentibus.

(5) Matth. 11, 2-19. et Luc. 7, 18-35. Responsio a Domino data Ioannis baptistae legatis, quaerentibus ex ipso, num sit ὁ ἐρχόμενος, praetermissa est a Marco eandem ob causam, quam modo afferebamus. Nimirum Mattha-

eus alio loco et ordine haec narrat, quam Lucas. Marcus vero eo loco, quo
Matthaeus haec habet, secutus est Lucam, et contra illo loco, quo apud
Lucam occurrunt, non hoc sed Matthaeo usus duce est, uti e tabula mox
laudata apparet; hinc utroque loco omisit.

(6) Matthaeus cap. 14, 28-31. Petrum super undis lacus Gennesaret procella agitatis ambulasse perhibet. Marcus autem, *Petri* discipulus et interpres, in antecedentibus et sequentibus plane quidem consentit cum Matthaeo; haec vero commata, rem ad *Petrum* spectantem tam singularem et
inauditam narrantia, silentio praeterit. *Resp.* Causam, cur Marcus hanc
narrationis partem a suo Evangelio abesse voluerit, quae multiplex et varia
esse potuit, ignorari fatemur. Verum cum tam multa alia, quae apud Matthaeum leguntur, praetermissa sint a Marco, hancce nominatim omissionem
ii tantum mirabuntur aut contra nos urgebunt, qui Evangelistam, Petro nisi
dictante saltim moderante, libellum suum exarasse autumant; quam opini-
onem, vetustam quidem, sed iis omnibus quae in antecedentibus evicisse
nobis videmùr repugnantem, commentis annumerare nulli dubitamus.

(7) Matth. 19, 27. Apostolis promittitur, sessuros eos esse in duodecim
409 tribunalibus iudicaturosque duodecim tribus Israelis, et cap. 20, 1-16.
parabola de operariis, in vineam diverso tempore ablegatis, illustratur
gnoma: πολλοι ἐσονται πρωτοι ἐσχατοι, και ἐσχατοι πρωτοι. Tam pro-
missioni quam gnomae cum parabola occasionem dederat quaestio a Petro
prolata: Ἡμεις παντα ἀφηκαμεν και ἠκολουθησαμεν σοι. τι ἀρα ἐσται
ἡμιν; Quaestio haec (omissis tantum verbis τι ἀρα ἐσται ἡμιν; quae sensu
manente eodem, abesse poterant) una cum gnoma illa et ea responsionis
parte, quae apud Matthaeum legitur com. 29. extat apud Marcum; sed
desideratur cum promissio, quae com. 28 continetur, tum parabola. *Resp.*
Utraque desideratur etiam apud Lucam, cap. 18, 28-30. Huius igitur vestigiis hoc loco insistit Marcus, et a Matthaeo gnomam tantum illam brevissimam et paradoxam mutuatus est. Parabola vero, illustrationis causa adiecta, nimis verbosa procul dubio visa est auctori, brevitatis studio longiores
orationes plerumque omittenti. Eandemque ob causam praeteriit etiam
quae Matth. 22, 1-14. 23, 2-39 et cap. 25. leguntur. Atque haec omnia
etiam a Luca absunt.

(8) Marcus cap. 14, 28 et cap. 16, 7. mentionem bis iniicit promissi, discipulos Christum e sepulcro suscitatum visuros esse in Galilaea. Matthaeus
cap. 28, 16. 17. hoc revera evenisse narrat. Marcus autem de itinere in
Galilaeam instituto et de viso ibi a discipulis Christo, ne verbulo quidem
admonet lectores, sed incertos eos relinquit, utrum promissum illud, cuius
410 ipse bis meminerat, impletum fuerit nec ne. Quod quomodo fieri potuerit,
si ista Matthaei commata oculis ipsius obversata essent, nemo facile dixerit.
Resp. (a) Si ultima Marci commata, a nono inde usque ad vicesimum,

genuina essent, aut Marcus commate iam octavo finem libello suo imposuisset, illius omissionis ratio probabilis reddi vix posset. Sed deesse ista commata in codice pereximio vaticano et abfuisse olim a multis libris manuscriptis, scimus. Attamen omni veri specie caret, Marcum commate octavo verbis ἐφοβοῦντο γαρ librum finivisse. Itaque coniicere licet, genuinam Evangelii clausulam, in qua procul dubio itineris in Galilaeam mentio facta erat, casu periisse, et seculo primo finiente aut secundo ineunte ab ignoto homine utcunque suppletam esse; quo posito, non erit profecto, cur istam omissionem miremur. Atque huic coniecturae, si quid iudicamus, non omnino nihil novi ponderis hac ipsa observatione, de itinere illo a Marco praetermisso, accedit.

(b) Utut haec se habent, (neque enim huius loci est examen accuratius authentiae ultimorum Marci commatum,) omissa itineris galilaei mentio hypothesin nostram labefactare non potest. Quamcunque enim de fontibus a Marco adhibitis sententiam amplectaris, difficultas e silentio de isto itinere orta prorsus eadem manet. Ponamus, clausulam Evangelii esse genuinam, et demus paullisper, Matthaei commentarios minime inspectos fuisse a Marco, tamen non mirari non possumus, quid sit, quod hic reticuerit, utrum et quomodo Dominus steterit promissis, quae data esse discipulis Marcus in antecedentibus bis commemoraverat. Certe Matthaeo monitore opus non habeat Marcus, e cuius memoria elapsa esse nondum poterant, quae paucis στιχοις interiectis scripserat.

(9) Tandem plures etiam narrationes de rebus gestis Domini et orationes eius haud paucas, easque notatu admodum dignas, apud *Lucam* occurrentes, in Marci commentariolo desiderari monuerunt viri docti, et consequi inde existimarunt, Marcum in conficiendo suo libello neutiquam Lucae Evangelio usum esse. Verum quae in priore commentationis huius Sectione disputavimus et in notis ad tabulam, quam ibi exhibuimus, de locis singulis diximus, ad obiectionem hanc confutandam sufficere videntur. Conferri nominatim potest de omissa pericopa Luc. 7, 35–8, 9. nota 21 et 22; p. 372 et de loco Lucae 19, 1–27. p. 376. nota 35.

Paucula tamen hic addimus ad ipsum initium Evangelii Marci spectantia. Nempe Lucas historiam publici muneris a Iesu suscepti orditur cap. 3, 1. a diligenti notatione temporis, quo Dominus docere coepit; Marcus autem omissis istis omnibus narrationem suam absque ullo chronologico iudicio inchoat. Verum praeterire haec potuit velut *suis* lectoribus minus utilia. Homines enim a Palaestina remoti (Sect. I. nr. 7.) nomina tetrarcharum, qui ante viginti vel triginta annos Galilaeae, Ituraeae, Trachonitidi et Abilenae praefuerant, pontificumque iudaicorum successiones vix noverant; imo dubitare licet, utrum seriem et chronologiam procuratorum Iudaeae accurate cognitam habuerint. Itaque restabat tantum nota temporis ab annis Tiberii desumta. Hanc vero Marcus *una cum caeteris* praetermisit, quia eo quo nostrum Evangelium prodiit tempore inter Christianos esset nemo, qui imperante Tiberio Iesum claruisse nesciret; quoto autem Imperatoris huius anno doctoris provinciam in se susceperit, id vix magni momenti esse videbatur. Nobis quidem pergrata est diligentia a Luca adhibita; sed primi Evangeliorum lectores talem ἀκρίβειαν haud postulabant, nec necessaria ea erat ad obtinendum finem, quem Marcus sibi videtur proposuisse.

VIII. 'Marci Evangelium in locis haud paucis cum narrationibus Matthaei aut Lucae aperte pugnare videtur. Hinc apparet neutrum a Marco fuisse consultum. Istas enim ἐναντιοφανείας evitare potuisset, ac studiose evitasset procul dubio, si priorum Evangelistarum commentarios evolvere ei licuisset.' *Respondemus:* (a) Marco in mentem non venit, fore, ut interpretes suum librum cum Matthaei et Lucae Evangeliis anxie comparent, locos qui inter se pugnare videantur sedulo notent, in componendis his Evangelistarum dissidiis desudent, et unum e tribus quatuorve libris conflare satagant. Id enim si vel levi coniectura prospexisset, facillimo negotio ad caeterorum Evangelistarum narrationes suam conformare, vel dissensus sui causas unico addito verbo indigitare potuisset. Sed minuta hac diligentia supersedere se posse existimavit. Minutam dicimus, quia dissensus nunquam in rei summa sed in singulorum eventuum singulis circumstantiis cernitur. Huius generis ἐναντιοφανείας auctor, ad scholae legem neutiquam edoctus et libellum ad vulgarem popularemque sensum accommodatum conscribens, nullius momenti esse censuit. (b) Interdum Marcus discrepat a Matthaeo, quia illo loco non hunc, sed Lucam secutus est ducem. (c) Nonnunquam consulto discedit paullulum a prioribus Evangelistis, et eventus, quos penitius cognitos habebat, accuratius quam ab illis factum erat enarrare studet. Sed age, ἐναντιοφανείων istarum veram indolem exemplis nonnullis, verum propter spatii angustiam paucis, ob oculos Lectoribus ponamus.

(1) Marcus cap. 2, 14. portitorem a Iesu a τελωνίῳ avocatum Levin appellat, Matthaeus autem cap. 9, 9. Matthaeum h. e. se ipsum tunc vocatum esse tradit. *Resp.* Cum Marco consentit etiam Lucas, cap. 5, 27. Et Marco plura de isto Levi nota erant, quam vel ipsi Lucae. Narrat enim, Alphaei filium eum fuisse. Atque hinc porro augurari forte licet, Marci lectoribus sive Levin sive Alphaeum propius cognitum fuisse, eamque ob causam satius duxisse Marcum praeeunte Luca, Levis commemorare vocationem, quam Matthaei, hominibus istis fortasse ignoti. Caeterum utrumque, et Matthaeum et Levin, eodem tempore in numerum discipulorum Christi fuisse cooptatum probabile est.

(2) Cap. 2, 27. omittit Marcus sententias nonnullas, quae apud Matthaeum cap. 12, 5. 6. 7. habentur, et in eorum locum substituit aliam: τὸ σαβ-

βατον δια τον ἀνθρωπον ἐγενετο, οὐχ ὁ ἀνθρωπος δια το σαββατον, quo
ipso additamento sensus sequentis sententiae, κυριος ἐστιν ὁ υἱος του
ἀνθρωπον και του σαββατου contra Matthaeum prorsus immutatur. *Resp.*
(a) Quae apud Matthaeum leguntur praetermissa sunt, quia hoc loco Marcus seposito Matthaeo ad Lucam sese converterat, ut patet e tabula, quam
Sectione I. [sic] exhibuimus, et e consensu in formula: και ἐλεγεν αὐτοις,
(b) Additamentum textui Lucae a Marco adiectum neutiquam sententiae
sequentis sensum immutat, qui hic est: Si sabbatum institutum est propter
hominum utilitatem, atque legibus de sabbato nemo ita tenetur, ut per eas
a promovenda sua aliorumque felicitate prohibeatur; sequitur, multo minus
Messiam istis legibus sic esse adstrictum, ut licitum ei non sit ab earum
praescripto recedere, aut eis solvere discipulos suos.

(3) Si duodecim discipulorum delectus eo tempore contigit, quo Marcus
cap. 3, 7-19 eius mentionem iniecit, antecessit orationem in monte habitam; hoc vero repugnat Matthaeo quoad id, quod occasionem praebuit
pharisaeorum calumniae, de foedere Christi cum Beelzebul inito. *Resp.*
Confer de utroque loco Sect. II. notam 22 p. 372. ubi causas exposuimus,
cur Marcus duas illas narrationes hoc ipso loco exhibeat, quo eas apud
415 ipsum legimus. Ad ista observata nostra si velis attendere, evanescet
repugnantiae species.

(4) Marc. 4, 35. coll. cap. 1, 35. ita discrepat a Matth. 8, 18. coll. cap.
13, 54 et cap. 14, 22. ut vix uterque historiographus vera narrasse possit,
sed alter alterum erroris convincere videatur; quod profecto non accidisset,
si Marcus, dum suum libellum exararet, ad manus habuisset Matthaei commentarios. Secundum Matthaeum, in discipulorum numerum allectis Petro,
Andrea, Iacobo et Ioanne, cap. 4, 18. *post habitam orationem montanam*
cap. 5. 6. et 7. Christus statim sanat leprosum, cap. 8, 1. 2. quem ad sacerdotes ablegat, et mox, Capernaum ingressus, centurionis servulum comm.
5. et Petri socrum comm. 14. a morbo liberat, ac, concurrente ingenti
populi multitudine, *lacum Gennesaret traiicit*, comm. 18, 23. et postquam
cum discipulis violentam tempestatem subiisset, hancque verbo sedasset,
in regionem Gergesenorum pervenit. comm. 28. Deinceps alio tempore
daemoniacum coecum et mutum sanat, cap. 12, 22. quo egregio facinore
perculsus populus eum rogitare inciperet, numne Messias ipse sit, comm.
23. Pharisaeorum alii Beelzebulis ope daemonia eum abigere criminati
sunt, comm. 24, alii signum e coelo poposcerunt, comm. 38. Quibus cum
adhuc responderet, mater eius et cognati advenere, colloqui cum ipso cupi-
entes. comm. 46. Ea die, (ἐν τη ἡμερα ἐκεινη) egressus e domo, cap. 13, 1.
navem conscendit, et populum in littore stantem edocuit *de regni coelestis*
416 *indole*, quam copioso sermone multisque *parabolis* coacervatis graphice
delineavit, comm. 3. Postea comm. 53. in patriae urbis synagoga comm.

54. verba ad populum fecit, et auditores in admirationem rapuit. Illo tempore (ἐν ἐκεινῳ τῷ καιρῳ) cap. 14, 1. insidias metuens Herodis, com. 1. 2. [sic] et 13. qui baptistam etiam occiderat, comm. 3. discessit illinc in navi in *desertum locum*, comm. 13. ubi quinque panibus virorum quinque millia saturavit, comm. 15. et nocte sequente redeuntibus in navi discipulis, turbine iactatis, in aqua ambulans subvenit, comm. 22.... Iam cum Matthaeo Marci comparemus narrationem. Hoc igitur auctore, Christus, Petro, Andrea, Iacobo et Ioanne vocatis, cap. 1, 16. (coll. Matth. 4, 18–22)[62] Capernaum venit comm. 21. (coll. Luc. 4, 31.) et, sanato in synagoga daemoniaco, comm. 23. (coll. Luc. 4, 33.) eodem die Petri socrum sanitati restituit, comm. 29. (coll. Luc. 4, 38) ac confluente sub vesperum tota civitate ad fores, comm. 32. (coll. Luc. 4, 40.) proximo mane *in locum desertum* secessit, comm. 35. (coll. Luc. 4, 42.) posteaque universam Galilaeam peragravit, comm. 39. (coll. Luc. 4, 44.)[63] et leproso sanitatem reddidit, quem sacerdotes adire iussit. comm. 40. (coll. Luc. 5, 12.) Deinde alio tempore ascendit in montem, cap. 3, 13. (coll. Luc. 6, 12.)

417 et duodecim elegit apostolos, comm. 14. (coll. Luc. 6, 13.). Hic Lucas comm. 20. montanam orationem inseruit.[64] Domum reversus, comm. 20. [sic] ab accurrente populi turba ita fatigabatur, ut οἱ παρ' ἀυτου exirent κρατησαι αὐτον, quia dicebant, ὁτι ἐξεστη comm. 21.[65] Scribae autem hierosolymitani calumniabantur, Beelzebule opem ferente daemonia eum expellere, comm. 22. (coll. Matth. 12, 24.[66]). Hos cum confutaret, mater eius et cognati foris stabant et admitti cupiebant, comm. 31. (coll. Matth. 12, 46.) Porro Iesus, progressus ad lacum Gennesaret, populo in littore stanti *regni coelestis indolem* exposuit, variis usus *parabolis*, cap. 4, 1. coll. Matth. 13, 1.). Qua oratione finita, mox, ὡς ἠν ἐν τῳ πλοιῳ, *lacum Gennesaret traiecit*, comm. 35. 36. (coll. Luc. 8, 22.[67]) et postquam cum discipulis vehementi procella agitatus esset hancque verbo compescuisset, in Gadarenorum regionem venit, cap. 5, 1. (coll. Luc. 8, 26.)... Hic non solum universus narrationis ordo, quem sequitur Marcus, differt ab eo,

418 quem Matthaeus praeivit, sed hic etiam cum illo pugnare videtur. Nam, Matthaeo teste, Iesus post habitam orationem montanam sanatamque Petri socrum, lacum Gennesaret, tempestate agitatum, traiecit, et in Gergesenorum (seu Gadarenorum) regionem venit; deinde autem post traditas parabolas de regno Dei, secessit in locum desertum. Contra vero, si Marcum audias, locum desertum petiit mox post sanatam Petri socrum; lacum vero Gennesaret, ventorum vi turbatum, traiecit et in Gadarenorum terra appulit, postquam parabolas de regno coelesti proposuisset...*Resp.* Difficultates omnes evanescent, si, missis opinionibus praeiudicatis de ordine chronologico ab Evangelistis anxie servato, attendere velimus, *ubi* et *cur* Marcus a Matthaeo transeat ad Lucam, ab hoc redeat ad Matthaeum,

et hoc iterum seposito denuo revertatur ad Lucam. Qua de re cum affatim dictum sit Sectione II., quo etiam Lectores in notis antecedenti paginae subiectis ablegabamus, non est cur multa hic addamus. Manifestum enim esse censemus, ἐναντιοφανειας omnes inde oriri, quod Marcus, de rerum gestarum ordine chronologico nequaquam sollicitus, non unum eundemque ducem, sed mox hunc mox illum, secutus sit. Itaque res eo redit, ut inquiratur, qui factum sit, ut *Lucas* narrationis partes aliter disponeret quam Matthaeus? cuius rei investigatio huius loci, ubi de Marco disputamus, non est. Verbo monere licebit, Lucam minus recessisse a vera eventuum serie, quam Matthaeum. Saltim quae Matthaeus habet cap. 14, 1. 3. et comm. 13. 14.

419   isto ordine neutiquam evenisse videntur.

(5) Marcus cap. 5, 23. archisynagogum sic loquentem inducit: το θυγατριον μου ἐσχατως ἐχει. Matthaeo autem teste, (cap. 9, 18.) puella ἀρτι ἐτελευτησεν, quocum Lucas (cap. 8, 42.) consentire videtur, inquiens: αὐτη ἀπεθνησκεν. *Resp.* Si Marcus h. l. Matthaeo duce usus est, mirum videri non debet, posteriorem scriptorem plenius, accuratius ac rectius totam rem enarrasse, quam a priore scriptore tractata esset. Sed e Luca potius haec omnia desumsit Marcus (cf. p. 375 not. 29). Iam vero apud Lucam commate quidem 42. legitur: αὐτη ἀπεθνησκεν. At e commate 49. manifestum est, puellam tum mortuam nondum fuisse. Marcus igitur, collata interpretatione authentica ab auctore commate 49. suppeditata, phrasin ambiguam commatis 42. rectissime et menti Lucae convenientissime permutavit cum alia clariore. Atque hinc patet simul, omni fundamento destitutam esse eorum persuasionem, qui hunc locum iis annumerant, e quibus probari posse putant, tres Evangelistas usos esse ebraico archetypo, cuius ambiguitate decepti phrasin ebraicam eandem diversis modis, nec facile conciliandis, interpretati sint. Optime convenit inter Marcum et Lucam, dummodo Lucae comma 42. e commate 49. explicetur. Sed nec Matthaeus dissentit. Hic enim quia ea omisit, quae apud Lucam commate 49. de morte puellae leguntur, statim ab initio brevioris suae

420   narrationis, ubi Lucas et Marcus animam egisse puellam perhibent, mortuam esse tradere *debuit*.

(6) Marcus cap. 10, 46–52. de coeco prope Hierichuntem sanato talia refert, quae a Matthaei aeque atque a Lucae narratione (Matth. 20, 29–34. Luc. 18, 35–43.) discordant. *Resp.* Cuilibet tres Evangelistas inter se comparanti et ad περιστασεις singulares a Marco solo commemoratas animum advertenti, manifestum erit, Marcum accuratissime de hoc eventu fuisse edoctum. Ubi igitur ab aliis discedit, tacite corrigere hos voluisse censendus est.

(7) Quae Marc. 11, 11–27. leguntur, occurrunt etiam Matth. 21, 10–23. Sed alio et quidem probabiliore ordine narrationis partes apud Matthaeum

sese excipiunt, quam apud Marcum. Matthaeo auctore Christus *eodem* die, quo magna ovantis populi stipatus caterva Hierosolymam ingressus est, e templo profanato eiecit vendentes et ementes. Nam his expulsis aderant adhuc pueri Hosanna filio Davidis acclamantes, Matth. 21, 15. qui procul dubio una cum reliqua turba, Hosanna Iesu occinente, templum intraverant. Secundum Marcum autem Christus templi profanatores exire coegit *postridie*, quam urbem ingressus erat. Atqui, cum populari favore nil sit inconstantius, veri similius est, Christum, utpote virum prudentissimum, mox post introitum in urbem et templum eo ipso die, quo populus studium suum erga ipsum luculentissime significavisset, rem periculis plenam adortum esse, quam dilatam eam ab ipso fuisse in aliud tempus; nec credibile
421 est, eos qui boves et oves vendebant cum nummulariis tam facile loco fuisse cessuros, nisi populi velut in triumpho Iesum in templum deducentis iram metuissent. Praeterea, Matthaeo teste, Christus ficum sterilem exsecratus est die *sequente* postquam profanos e templo expulerat, et *statim* (παραχρημα) exaruit arbor; quo viso discipuli admirabundi protinus magistrum adeunt, et ab hoc de insigni vi πιστεως edocentur. Contra vero apud Marcum arbori male precatus est Christus *eo die* mane, quo postea templi profanationem ultus est; arefactam autem a radicibus esse arborem discipuli *postridie* demum observarunt, et Domino de fidei efficacia disserenti ansam praebuerunt. *Resp.* Plane persuasum nobis est, eo ordine et tempore rem universam evenisse, quo Marcus eam in suis commentariis collocavit. Sciens a Matthaeo recessit, quia accuratiorem, quam ex hoc peti potest, notitiam de universo isto negotio aliunde sibi comparaverat. Hinc comm. 11–14. et 20–26. copiosius, quae Matthaeus paucis indicaverat, enarrare, et comm. 16 περιστασεις nonnullas a Matthaeo praetermissas addere poterat. Praesertim temporis, quo quidque contigerat, momenta et intervalla penitus cognita habuit, eaque singulari plane studio distincte notavit. Vide comm. 11. 12. 15. 19. 20. 27. Etsi vero in tractanda hac historiae parte rectius et curatius quam Matthaeus versatus sit, hic tamen ab illo neutiquam falsitatis aut ignorantiae arguitur. Nam (a) Matthaeus nullibi disertis verbis affirmat, Christum eodem, quo urbem ingressus est, die profanam
422 turbam e templo eiecisse; nec e puerorum acclamatione colligi id potest; hi enim quae a caterva Christum comitante pridie audiverant, nova oblata occasione Matth. 21, 14 iam repetebant. (b) Noluit Matthaeus quae de ficu commemoranda erant in plures velut particulas dissecare, sed consulto exsecrationis mentionem paulisper distulit, dum eius effectum simul narrare posset.

Sectio IV

Superest, ut indicemus, quaenam ea sint, quae, admissa nostra hypothesi de origine Evangelii Marci, iusta consequentia derivari ex ea posse videantur. Potiora haec fere sunt:

I. Marcus Evangelium suum post scripsit quam Matthaeus et Lucas suos commentarios exaraverant. Mentiuntur igitur ὑπογραφαι singulis Evangeliis vulgo subiectae, quae Matthaeum octavo, Marcum decimo aut duodecimo, Lucam decimo quinto post reditum Christi in coelum anno scripsisse perhibent. Neque assentiri possumus Cel. *Storrio*, qui nuper Marci Evangelium primum omnium esse persuadere nobis voluit.

II. Quae *Papias* apud *Euseb. H. E.* libr. 3. cap. 39. de Marci Evangelio tradit, quamvis testem producit presbyterum Ioannem, figmenta sunt, multum a vero abhorrentia.

III. Patres antiquissimi, qui Petri auspiciis Marcum vitam Domini litteris consignasse tradiderunt, coniecturas suas, non historiam ex documentis fide dignis haustam, narraverunt, aut fallaci rumore decepti sunt. Corruunt igitur ea quoque omnia, quantumvis ingeniose excogitata et exornata, quae viri docti[68] huic hypothesi superstruxere. Unice hoc concedi forte potest, Marcum eas rerum περιστασεις, quibus passim Matthaei et Lucae narrationes locupletavit, a Petro accepisse; quamquam nec hoc satis certum sit; nam ex alio etiam fonte derivatae esse possunt.

IV. Fallitur etiam *Augustinus* de Consens, Evang. L. 1. C. 2. Matthaei breviatorem et pedissequum Marcum esse contendens.

V. Generatim omnes Patres de libris Novi Testamenti nil certi rescivisse videntur, praeterquam quod hic ille liber in hac illave ecclesia inde ab antiquissimis temporibus receptus, publice praelectus, et huic illive auctori attributus fuerit. Reliqua omnia, quae de tempore et loco scriptionis, occasione scribendi, consilio auctoris, fontibus, quibus usus sit etc. Patres tradunt, admodum incerta sunt.

VI. Etsi nostra de Marci Evangelio sententia non penitus eorum excludit hypothesin, qui Matthaeum ebraice scripsisse volunt, tamen, posita illa, haec valde improbabilis reperietur. Saltim Marcus graecum Matthaei exemplar omnino usurpasse videtur. Nam eaedem graecae formulae persaepe apud utrumque inveniuntur; ac si Marcus, graece scribens, partim ex ebraico Matthaei partim e graeco Lucae suum Evangelium compilasset, Matthaeo sine dubio praetulisset Lucam, et hunc potissimum secutus esset ducem. Hoc vero aliter se habere supra vidimus. Nuper quidem doctissimus Wahlius suspicatus est, e Matthaei ebraico et Lucae graeco Evangelio Marcum collegisse copticum. Sed haec coniectura, quae Nostrum aegyptiaca lingua scripsisse sumit, parum firmis superstructa est fundamentis, nec cum iis, quae de Evangelii Marci ortu et indole in antecedentibus disseruimus, conciliari facile poterit.

VII. A vero abhorret opinio nonnullorum, Evangelistas librorum, qui

sub ipsorum nominibus circumferuntur, veros auctores non esse, sed discipulos eorum scripto consignasse, quae ex Matthaei, Marci, Lucae etc. ore
olim audivissent.

VIII. Vero minime similis est, saltim quod ad Marci Evangelium attinet,
eorum coniectura, qui Evangelistas e commentariis, nescio quibus, dudum
deperditis, sive ebraicis sive graecis, libellos suos compilasse, et ea quae
notatu in primis digna aut suis lectoribus utilia viderentur, decerpsisse
statuunt, et hinc cum miram Evangelistarum consonantiam in verbis adeo
et loquendi formulis, tum etiam eorum inter se discrepantiam explicari
posse autumant.

IX. Marci Evangelium integrum superest et incorruptum, si postrema
ultimi capitis commata excipias, quae, ut diximus, deperdita et ab alia
manu suppleta esse, suspicari licet.

425   X. Iam Marci tempore Evangelia Matthaei et Lucae eadem eodem ordine
disposita continebant, quae hodie in iis leguntur, nec inde, quod Marcus
nonnulla omisit, consequitur, abfuisse ea primitus ab istis Evangeliis.

XI. Qui in concinnanda Evangeliorum harmonia operam suam collocare
volunt, in ea conficienda ad Marcum ne provocent, caveant. Hic enim de
ordine eventuum chronologico sollicitus plane non fuit, sed nulla temporis,
quo quidque evenerit, ratione habita a Matthaeo transit ad Lucam, et
vicissim. Hinc etiam patet, Apostolorum aetate necessarium neutiquam
visum esse, ut in narrandis rebus a Domino gestis temporis ordo servetur.
Atque inde porro suspicari licet, caeteris quoque Evangelistis propositum
non fuisse, annales seu diurnos scribere commentarios.

XII. Marcus de Evangeliorum scopo et usu longe aliter quam plerique
posteriorum seculorum theologi iudicavit. Ac si in animum induxisset,
Matthaeum iusto illustrare commentario, nae is admodum dissimilis
vulgaribus commentariis exstaturus fuisset. Lessingiis sine dubio placuis-
set iisque omnibus, qui optimarum litterarum studiis ingenium suum
acuere et perpolivere, et iustum tractandarum veterum historiarum
modum longo usu didicerunt; harmoniarum auctoribus et moleste sedulis
commentatoribus non item.

XIII. Qui Marcum scripsisse contendunt e theopneustia, satis exilem
informent necesse est.

6

A DEMONSTRATION THAT MARK WAS WRITTEN AFTER MATTHEW AND LUKE

(A translation of J. J. Griesbach's *Commentatio qua Marci Evangelium totum e Matthaei et Lucae commentariis decerptum esse monstratur*)

Bernard Orchard

[*Translator's note*: This is the first rendering into the English language of a Latin text which holds many subtleties of argumentation, but every endeavour has been made to remain faithful to the thought of the original. The translator has however deemed it necessary to introduce a certain number of sub-headings and also occasionally to insert a word to avoid ambiguity; all these additions are indicated by enclosure in square brackets. J. B. O.]

The Dissertation of J. J. Griesbach, Doctor of Theology and Principal Professor in the University of Jena, in which he demonstrates that the entire Gospel of Mark has been extracted from the Gospels of Matthew and Luke, written in the name of the University of Jena (1789–1790), now revised and furnished with many additions.[1]

[Introduction]

It is above all important to know the sources from which historical writers have drawn the things which they have put into their own commentaries, in order to interpret correctly their books, to evaluate justly the trustworthiness of the authors, and to perceive and judge skilfully the true nature of the events that they have recorded. Hence, on an earlier occasion,[2] we made a Dissertation about the sources from which the narratives of the Evangelists on Christ's Resurrection were derived. But at that time we were considering only that part of the Gospels which contains the account of Jesus' Resurrection, and we treated only Matthew, Luke and John in some detail, but with regard to Mark we gave our opinion only in passing and very briefly at that. Wherefore since the debate is particularly concerned with the question whence Mark drew his own material, and not merely with the sources of his resurrection account but also with those of the whole Gospel, and since many scholars, who have even very recently discussed it, seem almost to have neglected those arguments which in our opinion are especially suited to settle the debate, we shall now apply ourselves to clearing up this matter.

The most ancient writers, starting with Papias, have handed down, almost unanimously, that Mark committed to writing what he had heard from Peter, whose interpreter they name him. Augustine was, as we know, the first to state that Mark followed Matthew as a sort of abbreviator and close imitator.[3] From that time most scholars have been accustomed to hold both opinions, viz. that Mark derived his narrative partly from the Gospel of Matthew and partly from the mouth of Peter. But more recently some have shrewdly observed that the conformity of Mark with Luke is also so great that he [Mark] would seem to have had his [Luke's] Gospel at hand. On the other hand, however, Lardner[4] has tried to show by many arguments that Mark had not read Matthew. To these arguments J. B. Koppe[5] added more in the effort at least to prove that Mark was not the abbreviator of Matthew. By these clearly specious arguments, even Michaelis, previously a defender of the common view, was induced in the latest edition of his introduction to the N.T. books to reconsider this opinion and to deny that the book of Matthew was available to Mark when he wrote. And though the conformity between Matthew and Mark is so great (not only in content but also in words and phrases) that nobody can deny it, those who do deny that Mark used the Gospel of Matthew have gone to great pains to explain in various ways the origin and meaning of so great a harmony.

G. S. Storr[6] has been at pains to construct an hypothesis diametrically opposed to the accepted one: that is, that Mark wrote his Gospel during the period mentioned in Acts 11: 17–30; that after him Luke prepared his own works, carefully consulting the volume of Mark; and finally that Matthew decided to write the 'memorials' of Jesus Christ and transferred many things from the Gospel of Mark into his own. Koppe thought that there had once existed many documents now lost on the subject of Jesus, longer or shorter, written in Hebrew and Greek, documents from which Matthew, Mark and Luke compiled their own books; and hence he thought it was easy to understand not only why Mark generally agrees with Matthew, but also why one occasionally disagrees with the other in words and sentences and order, and on the one hand, why Mark omits many things worthy of note which Matthew recounts, and why on the contrary he also has some things omitted by Matthew. Obviously where they narrate the same things in the same way, they are regarded as having utilized the same source; but where by reason of additions or omissions or a different version of the matter they disagree with one another, they prove that they have used different and more ancient books. Recently, J. G. Eichhorn[7] has cleverly developed, refined and endeavoured to confirm and commend this theory by means of a great number of new observations drawn from a comparison of the Gospels among themselves. Indeed, this learned scholar assumes that in the very earliest times there existed a primitive Gospel, written in Hebrew or Syro-Chaldee, which comprised most of the material common to our Evangelists. And so a probable conjecture can be made about its content and nature from the sections of our Gospels that are in agreement; that it was written in Hebrew and then in various ways translated more or less accurately into Greek by several people; that these versions of the Primeval Book were quite often transcribed[8] and glossed throughout with many and various additions by various translators, copyists and readers, and that these glosses may have found their way into the Hebrew original before it was translated into Greek; moreover the additions found in many copies were conflated into one by those who were anxious to have a copy as far as possible absolutely complete.[9]

Copies of this sort, therefore, of three versions of the Primeval Script (versions that were not untouched but already mixed in various ways and interpolated with many additions and augmentations) had then come both into the hands of our three Evangelists,[10] who made fresh additions from their own store – and into the hands too of other authors of similar books about the life of Christ.

This hypothesis of Eichhorn was principally constructed on these arguments: that Matthew did not use either Mark or Luke; that Mark did not use either Matthew or Luke; and that Luke did not use either Matthew or Mark. The reason for their agreement is therefore to be sought from some common source, from which they all drew; that many indications suggest that this source was Hebraic (these will be dealt with by us later); nevertheless our Gospels, though indeed in many verses they very often agree in the Greek wording, do not seem to have issued immediately from this Hebrew text;[11] and therefore, before our Gospels were written the Hebrew archetype had already been translated into Greek; but there must have been many versions in existence, because the Evangelists, even when narrating the same thing in the same order, still often use different phrases; nevertheless we are forced to conclude that both the Hebrew and the Greek exemplars were carefully augmented at a later date; we may gather this from the fact that the additions which were originally lacking in the Hebrew archetype, now uniformly turn up sometimes in Matthew and Mark, sometimes in Matthew and Luke, sometimes in Luke and Mark.[12]

Finally, omitting other views, an anonymous author[13] tried to persuade us that the Gospel of the Hebrews was the first to be written; that the Gospels of the Nazarenes and that of the Ebionites were different and less polished recensions of the former; that next appeared the Gospel used by Marcion and the Book of Mark; that then there followed the 'reminiscences of the apostles', praised by Justin Martyr, and the Gospel of Matthew; then the Gospel of Luke was published; it was not clear whether the Gospel of · John was later than all these, or prior to some of them.

We cannot but wonder at such extensive disagreement of these scholars, since in our judgement it is abundantly clear merely from the close comparison of the three Gospels with one another what degree of relationship binds them together. Now in order to make this plain to the reader we shall in Section I expound our view distinctly, in Section II prove it by a few select arguments, in Section III answer objections that can be brought against it, and in Section IV point out corollaries to be derived from our hypothesis.

Section I
[The thesis that Mark knew canonical Matthew and Luke]

This is a summary of the opinion we are defending: That Mark when writing his book had in front of his eyes not only Matthew but Luke as well, and that he extracted from them whatever he committed to writing of the deeds, speeches and sayings of the Saviour, in such a manner however that –

(1) he followed Matthew as his guide very closely and as a rule, but
(2) nevertheless at times, forsaking Matthew, he took Luke as his companion;
(3) where he stuck closely to Matthew, he nevertheless did not lose sight of Luke but matched him together with Matthew, and *vice versa*;
(4) he sought brevity, as one who wanted to write a book of small compass; and therefore
(5) he not only omitted things that did not pertain to the office of Teacher, which the Lord publicly exercised, i.e., Matt. 1 and 2; Luke 1 and 2, but
(6) he also passed over several of the longer sermons of Christ,[14] e.g., Matt. 5; 6; and 7; 10: 16–42; 11: 20–30; 12: 33–45; 13: 37–54; 18: 10–35; 20: 1–16; 22: 1–14; 23: 2–39; 24: 37–51; 25: 1–46; Luke 6: 17–49; 19: 11–28; and indeed Luke 10: 1 – 18: 14, where he has omitted almost an entire third part of Luke's Gospel, since it consists almost entirely of discourses of Christ. Thus in extracting from the Gospels of Matthew and Luke, he so acted that
(7) he took into consideration his readers, namely, men far removed from Palestine, for whom the rules and regulations of Palestinian Jews, especially of the Pharisees, were hardly known nor indeed necessary to know; and for this reason, *partly*,
(8) he cut out some things found in Matthew or Luke that concerned Jews

alone, especially Palestinian ones, or which were suited to their way of thinking,[15] e.g. Matt. 16: 2, 3; 19: 28; Luke 4: 16–30; 23: 28–32, and

(9) is more sparing in quoting O.T. texts, e.g. Matt. 4: 14; 12: 17–21; 13: 14, 15, partly,

(10) adds, for the sake of illustration, matters which he thinks either useful or necessary for better understanding the narrative, e.g. Mark 7: 3, 4, 8; 11: 13; 12: 42,

(11) retains very often the same formulas, phrases and constructions which Matthew and Luke have used, and among them many somewhat unusual ones, e.g. Mark 2: 10 'he says to the paralytic'; 10: 22 'for he was in possession of much wealth'; 12: 14 'you do not worry about anybody, for you do not regard the face of men'; 13: 14 'the abomination of desolation'; and that parenthetic 'let the reader understand'; and often elsewhere;

(12) nevertheless he in no wise copies their books word for word, but in *his own* way, i.e. he narrates what he has read in them, in other formulas and phrases,

(13) he expresses not infrequently by paraphrase and expounds more plainly and distinctly what they had handed down to him in a briefer form, though in other respects he was moved by the desire for brevity in selecting the actions and discourses of Christ that he wanted, it seems, to transplant into his own work; and clearly passed over in silence, as it seems to us, many noble passages of each Gospel (note paraphrases, for example, at Mark 6: 17–29, 30, 31; 9: 14–29, 38–50; 11: 11–26),

(14) he adds to the stories of Matthew and Luke many special details, which he thought would please his readers, such as Mark 2: 14 'the son of Alphaeus'; 5: 42 'for she was twelve years old'; 6: 3 'the carpenter'; 6: 13 'they anointed the sick with oil'; 10: 46 'Bartimaeus son of Timaeus'; 13: 3 'Peter and James and John and Andrew'; 14: 51, 52 'and a certain young man followed him etc.'; 15: 21 'father of Alexander and Rufus'; 15: 40 and 16: 1 'and Salome'; and countless others of a similar sort;

(15) finally, he adds some little stories, omitted by Matthew and Luke, very few and very brief (to be enumerated later), which were added by him for reasons the attentive reader can easily conjecture, provided he will go to the trouble of comparing them together.

Section II
[Three arguments for Mark's use of Matthew and Luke]

In order to confirm and justify this opinion of ours, we do not want to repeat the statements made by others who agree with us that Matthew has been used by Mark, nor shall we heap up many arguments, but we hope to carry our point with *three* observations.

The first observation
[*The argument from order*]

Mark compiled his whole work (apart from about twenty-four verses which he added from his own sources, of which we shall speak later) from the works of Matthew and Luke in such a manner that

(A) it can be easily shown what he took from the one and what he took from the other;

(B) he retained the order observed by Matthew in such a way, that wherever he forsakes it he sticks to the path of Luke and follows him and the order of his narrative step by step, to such an extent that

(C) the verses and words where he passes from Matthew to Luke or returns from Luke to Matthew can not only be pointed out, but also

(D) the probable reason can generally be given why at a given time he deserted Matthew (though he had set himself to use him as his chief guide) and attached himself to Luke, and why putting away Luke he once more attached himself to Matthew; and further

(E) it can also be understood why, precisely in *this* passage of Matthew and not in another, he again connects up the thread which he had previously broken by passing over to Luke.

Briefly, you can see, as with your own eyes, Mark having the volumes of Matthew and Luke at hand, continually consulting each, extracting from each whatever he thought would most benefit his readers, now laying aside Matthew, now Luke for a little, but always returning to the very same place of either one where he had begun to diverge from him. In order to show this more clearly, we shall show the whole thing for inspection in a table, which we will illustrate with some notes.

Matthew	Mark	Luke
(Chapters 1 and 2)[16]	——	
3: 1 – 4: 22[17]	1: 1–20	
	1: 21–39	4: 31–44[18]

Matthew	Mark	Luke
	——	(5: 1–11)[19]
	1: 40 – 3: 6	5: 12 – 6: 11
12: 15, 16[20]	3: 7–12	
(12: 17–21)		
	——	
	3: 13–19	6: 12–16[21]
12: 22, 23	3: 20, 21	
12: 24–32[22]	3: 22–30	
(12: 33–7)[23]	——	
(12: 38–45)[24]	——	
12: 46–50	3: 31–5	
13: 1–23	4: 1–20	
	4: 21–5[25]	8: 16–18
(13: 24–30)[26]	4: 26–9	
13: 31, 32	4: 30–2	
13: 34, 35[27]	4: 33, 34	
	——	(8: 19–21)[28]
	4: 35–41	8: 22–5
	5: 1–43[29]	8: 26–56
13: 53–8[30]	6: 1–6	
	6: 7–13	9: 1–6
14: 1–2	6: 14–16	9: 7–9
14: 3–12	6: 17–29	
	6: 30, 31	9: 10
14: 13–21	6: 32–44	9: 11–17
14: 22 – 16: 12	6: 45 – 8: 21	
——	8: 22–6[31]	
16: 13 – 18: 9	8: 27 – 9: 50[32]	9: 18–51
(18: 10–35)[33]	——	
	——	(9: 51 – 18: 14)[34]
19: 1–12	10: 1–12	
19: 13 – 23: 1	10: 13 – 12: 38[35]	18: 15 – 20: 45
(23: 1–39)[36]	——	
	12: 38–44	20: 45 – 21: 4[37]
24: 1–36	13: 1–32	21: 5ff.
(24: 37 – 25: 46)	13: 33–6[38]	
26: 1 – 28: 8	14: 1 – 16: 8	
	16: 9[39]	
(28: 9–15)[40]	——	
(28: 16–17)[41]	——	

Matthew	Mark	Luke
	16: 10–13	24: 10–35
	16: 14	24: 36–43
28: 18–20	16: 15–18	
	16: 19	24: 50, 51
	16: 20	

We have now set out our theory without [depending upon] the support of numerous hypotheses devised in a highly artificial manner. And accordingly we think that we have now done what we set out to do, namely, to have clearly shown exactly why Mark has related these particular things in his book and why he has omitted others; and we have also given clear reasons why everything – without excepting a single verse – is positioned in the very place in which we read it in Mark.[42]

But the same result can be confirmed and proved by yet another process of reasoning. We proceed therefore to our second observation.

The second observation
[*The argument from Mark being contained in Matthew and Luke*]

In the enormous number of memorable deeds performed by Jesus Christ, and in the incredible variety of the discourses given daily by the Lord, whether to the people or to his disciples and intimate circle, it surely did not happen by chance that Mark had literally nothing to put down in writing except what Matthew and Luke had recorded in a similar form or what one or the other had given him at least the occasion of noting down.

Luke and John handed on a number of things which Matthew had not touched at all, and the Evangelists themselves in several places hint that in their books they have passed over many wonderful and illustrious deeds of Christ and omitted numerous discourses of his which the brevity of the Gospels would not allow. How then did it happen that out of the enormous quantity of these omissions Mark in fact does not relate at least a few of them, but obviously relates the same items that Matthew and Luke took from the same ample source? Mark, I insist, was able to learn many things that could not have been known to everyone, because his mother lived in a house in Jerusalem, in which the apostles and other Christians used to hold their meetings (Acts 12: 12); moreover he had at one time been the servant and companion of both Peter and Paul and had without doubt learnt from them and their intimate friends many deeds and sayings of the Lord well worth relating; and lastly, it was Mark too who enriched the narratives of Matthew and Luke with so many special details (see above

Section I (13) and (14)), so that it was clear to all that he knew the story of Christ very well and could have told us a great many more anecdotes about him, if he had wished. Why is it then, I ask, that this same Mark added nothing new (except those details) to the books written by Matthew and Luke? If indeed you agree with us that Mark's purpose was to select from the Gospels of Matthew and Luke the items most useful for his intended readers, and to narrate them in the manner appropriate to them; then everything is clear and simple. If on the contrary you hold that Mark wrote without the aid of anyone and solely by his own efforts, it is almost a miracle that, in selecting the matter for his book from the enormous mass of material, he took over for treatment by himself the very same things that Matthew and Luke had treated. Finally, should you contend that he had other guides (or more guides) than these two Evangelists already mentioned, we should like to know how it happened that these persons suggested to him nothing other than what he could equally well have borrowed from Matthew and Luke, excepting only about twenty-four verses. *Nothing*, I say, *except twenty-four verses.*

For we cannot here add to this list either mere paraphrastic amplifications of items found in Matthew and Luke or some additional items consisting of a few words, such as we have pointed out in Section I (10), (13), and (14). Wherefore, it would be a waste of time for anyone who wished to attack our thesis, to appeal to Mark 1: 2, 33; 2: 2, 3, 4, 27;[43] 3: 20, 21;[44] 10: 10, 11, 12; 12: 32, 33, 34 and other similar passages. There are only *three short stories* of miracles wrought by Christ, 3: 7–12; 7: 32–7; 8: 22–6, and *two parables*, 4: 26–9, 13: 33–6, which can perhaps be seen to be so special to Mark as to appear to be real objections.

With respect to these parables [Seed Growing Secretly, Mark 4: 26–9, and the Householder on a Journey, Mark 13: 33–6], we have already shown[45] that both have been substituted for longer parables with similar content which are found in Matthew in the same context of the discourse, and we thus saw the reason why Mark considered his own parables preferable to Matthew's. So far, therefore, are we from being able to argue from these parables that Mark did not use anyone for a guide (or used someone other than Matthew), that on the contrary it is clear that Mark has accepted from Matthew the opportunity of interposing these parables.

Almost the same reasoning applies to Mark 3: 7–12. For Mark writes: (3: 7) 'And Jesus withdrew with his disciples to the sea, and a great multitude from Galilee followed... (3: 10) for he healed many... (3: 12) and he strictly ordered them not to make him known.' While Matthew (12: 15–16) has: 'Jesus, aware of this, withdrew from there. And many followed him, and he healed them all, and ordered them not to make him known.'

Who then does not see that Mark paraphrases the text of Matthew, and only amplifies the latter's story with some additional details. For it is clear from the table given above and an earlier note,[46] that Mark had this very passage of Matthew in front of his eyes while he was writing. Therefore this passage, far from weakening our view, gives it strong support.

The same applies to the other unit, Mark 7: 32-7; for again Matthew gave him the opportunity of inserting it in this place. That is to say, Matthew (15: 30, 31) relates that many sick were healed by Christ; but Mark describes with greater care the healing of one man out of this crowd, adding some details which seemed to him especially worth noting. Matthew (15: 30-1): 'And great crowds came to him, bringing with them... the dumb... and they cast them at Jesus' feet, and he healed them, so that the crowds wondered, when they saw the dumb speaking... and they glorified the God of Israel.' Mark (7: 32, 35, 37): 'And they bring to him a deaf-mute: and they beg him to lay his hand upon him... (verse 35) and immediately his ears were opened... (verse 37) And they were astonished beyond measure, saying, "He has done all things well."'

Thus there remains *only* the third little story, Mark 8: 22-6. We concede that this has been added by Mark, nor do we find anything in Matthew or Luke which can explain why this addition is found in this place. As it is, if we compare this unit more carefully with the two we have just been discussing, we discover a surprising agreement between them. Thus, by a likely conjecture, we ascertain not only the reason why this cure of a certain blind man seemed so important to Mark that, in narrating it, he departed from the rule he had made for himself, a rule that he kept consistently but for this single exception; but we are also able to understand why he thought that these two other instances already given (Matt. 12: 15, 16 and 15: 30, 31) ought to be illustrated by a fuller account of the surrounding circumstances. For it is common to these three units that Jesus wished to remain out of the public eye and that he forbade those he had healed to reveal what he had done. So in Mark 3: 12 we read: 'he rebuked the [demons] that they should not make him manifest', and in Mark 7: 33, 36: 'and taking him [the deaf mute] away from the crowd privately... and he ordered them to tell nobody.' Finally in Mark 8: 23, 26: 'And he led the [blind] man out of the village... saying, "Do not go into the village, and do not tell anyone in the village."'

To these three Marcan passages we add two more, notable for an addition of almost the same sort. Mark 7: 24 takes from Matthew that Jesus went into the district of Tyre and Sidon and *adds*: 'He did not want anybody to know, and he could not be hidden.' And in Mark 9: 30, again following Matthew, he relates that Christ made a journey through Galilee, and likewise *adds*: 'And he did not want anyone to know.' Therefore it is clear that *everywhere* else Mark follows either Matthew or Luke step by step nor does he add in anything of his own (apart from a certain number of details), *except* perhaps when he found in Matthew or Luke a short anecdote, which taught that Jesus did not seek popular acclaim, but often withdrew from the people and sometimes even hid himself carefully lest his deeds should give him away to the multitude; and that he had not been guided by a desire for vain glory, and that he had not worked miracles for the purpose of presenting a spectacle to a gaping and idle people. Mark has the habit of emphasizing more fully such details of the history of Jesus, and he takes care to supply them wherever he notes that Matthew and Luke have omitted something of this kind. But it is not clear why he considered this kind of story to be more important than all others and why it would be specially useful for his intended readers. Perhaps one might be able to conjecture with some probability, that teachers of those regions, possessing the gift of healing (I Cor. 12: 9), had sometimes abused it almost in the same way that we know some Corinthians used 'tongues' without discretion. Perhaps Mark wished to correct them, by putting forward the Lord's example.

The third observation
[*The argument from Mark's alternating agreement with Matthew and Luke*]

When Mark has closely adhered to either Matthew or Luke for a long stretch, he often passes with a sudden leap from one to the other, but soon returns to his former guide; and this could not have been done unless he had simultaneously seen and compared the works of each. Thus Mark 3: 1–5 is taken from Luke; Mark 3: 6, however, which pertains to the same story, is from Matthew.

Moreover in Mark 5: 25, 26, 27 he uses Luke as his guide; in verse 28, he uses Matthew; and again uses Luke in verses 29 and following.

Again, Mark 8: 37 has been culled from Matthew and is absent from Luke; verse 38 is owed to Luke and is missing in Matthew; Mark 9: 2 ('after six days') is again derived from Matthew.

Again, Mark 10: 22, 26, 27 imitates Matthew; in verses 28, 29*a* he agrees with Luke and omits material proper to Matthew; but in verse 29*b* he transcribes a sentence from Matthew that he alone has.

Finally, in Mark 13: 24, 25 he adheres strictly to Matthew; in verse 26 he omits what is peculiar to Matthew and follows Luke; but in verses 27–32 he agrees with Matthew almost word for word. Enough said!

Section III
[Objections to the thesis with replies]

[Introduction]

Having now explained, and as we hope, sufficiently proved our thesis, we turn to examine the objections which scholars have either brought forward publicly to overthrow it or which they perhaps could bring forward. There is no good reason why we should attempt to refute the arguments of those scholars who have tried to show that Mark is not the epitomizer of Matthew. For though we freely grant that Mark has passed over many things that Matthew has, and we ourselves maintain that he has aimed at brevity in writing his book, yet so far are we from thinking (as Augustine does) that he was the abbreviator of Matthew that we may rather assert that he has amplified, with greater abundance of detail and even at times with circumlocutions, much material taken from the Gospel of Luke, material spaced between the narrative of Matthew, and also a good deal that he has transferred from Matthew into his own treatise. Nor do we fear the arguments launched against our hypothesis, because the order of Mark very often forsakes the order of Matthew and Luke, arguments recently used by Eichhorn.[47] For we have amply explained the reasons for Mark's order in Section II. But the other objections, besides these, which have been put forward, we must deal with here.

[Specific objections and replies]

(1) *[Historical objections]*

[Objection:] 'If Mark owes almost everything to Matthew and Luke, it is untrue that he wrote "as Peter dictated to him", since almost nothing is left of the material which Peter might have supplied. But on the contrary the historical arguments used by those who maintain that Mark took Peter as his guide have not yet been disproved and this ancient testimony is rejected simply because it disagrees with the hypothesis put forward without any necessity or evidence, solely from the comparison of the book of Mark with Matthew and Luke.'[48]

[Reply:] Our answer is: (a) Whether our hypothesis, built up on the comparison of the three Gospels, lacks proof and compelling force, is a matter we gladly leave to the judgement of those who are not blinded by prejudice. For the scholars who, prior to us, had publicly propounded with regard to the Gospel of Mark other hypotheses which collapsed of their own accord when ours was put forward, though they are exceedingly clever and estimable persons, hardly seem to be unbiased judges.

(b) We candidly confess that this very ancient testimony about Mark producing his Gospel under the patronage of Peter is attributed by us to those fabrications of which many instances are found among ancient writers, and which are today rejected by most scholars.[49]

For, (c) the first to relate that Mark wrote under the guidance of Peter was Papias, universally recognized as a man of very little authority in historical matters. Irenaeus, as usual, followed him; others repeated his account.

(d) From the words of Papias (Euseb. *H. E.* III. 39) it appears that either he or John the presbyter (whom he quotes as a witness of his account) had been guided by two factors to this conjecture about Peter. First, there was the question of how Mark, who had never followed the Lord during his life on earth, had come to know about the actions and words of Christ. Papias replies that he had been the disciple and interpreter of Peter; and that Peter, throughout his discourses, which Mark would have heard, had recalled matters pertaining to the history of Jesus. Next, there was a doubt about why the actions and discourses of the Lord were read in Mark in an order different from the other books. Papias, trying to excuse Mark, declares that in his discourses Peter did not narrate the story of the Lord in accurate order, but as occasion required; and that Mark wrote them down just as he had heard them from Peter and as he now remembered them when writing them down. The purpose that Papias' fabrication was meant to serve is clear enough. But for this very reason it is rightly suspect for us.

(e) The conjecture of Papias is in itself exceedingly improbable. For who can be persuaded that Peter related in his discourses little stories about Christ such as we read in Mark (see 4: 35, 36; 5: 1, 18, 21; 10: 46–52; 11: 4, 11–22), that is to say, ones with most minute details? Or who would believe that Peter never related to his audience anything more about the resurrection of the Lord than what is found in Mark? This indeed we have to believe, if Papias is to be trusted. For he is our sole witness that Mark's purpose was *not to omit anything he had heard* (from Peter), and not to include anything untrue in his narratives.

(f) According to Papias, Mark had gathered the material he used for constructing his Gospel from the discourses of Peter, but Peter was not at hand when he wrote and did not offer his help. Papias therefore convicts of falsehood those who argue that Mark wrote at Peter's dictation.

(g) In this instance he (Papias) has the support of Irenaeus, who (*De Haeres.* III. 1) only has this to say: 'After the *exodos* [death] of Peter and Paul, Mark the disciple and interpreter of Peter also handed down to us in writing *what Peter had preached.*' But in the same passage Irenaeus himself makes an almost identical statement about Luke: 'Luke, the follower of Paul, wrote in a book *the Gospel preached by the latter.*' Subsequently, almost all agree that this is false and inconsistent.[50] Why therefore should we allow ourselves to be persuaded by the earlier statement of Irenaeus?

(h) Tertullian (*Adv. Marcion* IV, 5) likewise recorded each story. He says: 'The Gospel produced by Mark *is said* to be Peter's, whose interpreter Mark was; while the Gospel of Luke *is customarily ascribed to Paul*.' What the disciples published seems to be attributed to their teachers. Who cannot see that these assertions rely not on clear witnesses and reliable documents, but on vague rumours and arguments with little foundation? Since what the disciples publish can be attributed to the teachers, *therefore* the Gospel of Mark *was customarily attributed* to Peter and the book of Luke to Paul, evidently to make sure that the commentaries of Mark and Luke would not seem to lack apostolic authority.

(i) Justin Martyr (*Dial. Tryph.* § 106) quotes from 'the reminiscences *of Peter*', that Jesus imposed the surname 'Boanerges, that is Sons of Thunder', on the sons of Zebedee; and since this is found only in Mark 3: 17, Justin seems to ascribe this book to Peter. But in the first place, the authority of Justin in purely historical matters amounts to nothing. Secondly, it is not clear what and how much he has taken from our Gospels. At least he never used Mark elsewhere, nor did he elsewhere ever record 'the reminiscences of Peter' but either quoted simply 'the reminiscences' or 'the reminiscences of the apostles'; it would therefore be strange if in this one passage he had spoken of the 'reminiscences of Peter' as though they were a separate thing from 'the reminiscences of the apostles'. Moreover the passage is too obscure for us to draw anything certain from it. 'His reminiscences' could be 'the reminiscences of Christ'. Or instead of 'his', one could read 'their', i.e. 'of the apostles', as Justin usually writes elsewhere. Finally, even if one went so far as to concede that the Gospel of Mark is indicated in this passage and that 'the reminiscences of Peter' are intended, a doubt still remains over why they are said to be Peter's. Indeed that vague and unsubstantiated rumour about Mark being Peter's interpreter could have reached the ears of Justin as it did others; but the book, which this apostle was believed to have commended to several Churches, could also be quoted under the name of Peter, seeing that what are elsewhere referred to as 'the reminiscences of the apostles' could be named 'the reminiscences of Peter', because in this very place Peter is named *first* among the apostles. However it may be, Justin is not the man to give us more reliable and truthful information about the Gospel of Mark.

(k) Clement of Alexandria repeats the accounts of the others, elaborated with new details. For he related (Eus. *H.E.* II, 15, and VI, 14) that 'Mark, as one who had long followed Peter and remembered the words of his teacher, *had been asked by the Romans*, to put into writing the teaching which the apostle had publicly expounded to them;[51] and that the Romans did not desist until by their entreaties *they had persuaded Mark* to write his Gospel; that Peter, being informed of this by a special revelation of the Spirit, *was delighted* by the keen enthusiasm of the Romans, and *approved* the book on his own authority *for reading in the churches*.'[52] But Clement is not quite consistent with himself. For according to *H. E.* II, 15, he relates that Peter was pleased with 'the desire' of the Romans and approved the Gospel of Mark; but on the other hand, according to *H. E.* VI, 14, he says that the apostle did not restrain the disciple from his purpose, *nor did he urge him to carry it out.*

(l) The writers whom we have considered so far maintain that Mark has taken the subject-matter of his book from the discourses that Peter had given *in public*. But Origen (Eus. *H. E., VI. 25*) claims that he learnt from tradition that the Gospel second in order was written by Mark (whom the apostle in I Pet. 5: 12 calls his son) 'as Peter dictated to *him*'.

(m) Finally all these short narratives have been capped by those who, like the author of the Synopsis of Holy Scripture, related of our Gospel 'that it was publicly proclaimed by Peter in Rome, published by Mark, and proclaimed by him at Alexandria'!

(n) When you compare all these things with one another, it is clear indeed that even the more ancient and simple accounts of Papias, Irenaeus and Tertullian must be reckoned as mere conjectures. We have pointed out in many places already (see (d) and (h)) the reason for their being composed. Besides, the title 'interpreter of Peter' with which Mark is endowed by Papias, Irenaeus, Tertullian, Jerome and others, gave an opportunity for fashioning various falsehoods. Originally indeed, unless we are mistaken, the title only indicated that Mark had been Peter's companion, servant, assistant (*hupēretēs* Acts 13: 5), go-between, whom he had used, when required, to carry out his orders.[53] But others subsequently understood it in a different way; namely, that if Peter wanted to speak with Greeks or write to them, as he was not sufficiently versed in the language itself, he used Mark as his *interpreter*. And so others inferred from this that Mark had also been Peter's interpreter *when he wrote his Gospel*. Thus Jerome (*Letter to Hedibia*, chapter 2) writes,

'Paul was unable to explain the majesty of the divine meaning in discourse worthy of Greek eloquence. He therefore got Titus to be his interpreter, just as the blessed Peter had got Mark, whose *Gospel was composed by Peter narrating and Mark writing*. And further, the two epistles attributed to Peter also disagree with each other in style and character; from which we assume that he used different interpreters according to circumstances.'

(o) We do not wish to weary our readers by weighing the internal evidence drawn from Mark's Gospel, evidence by which scholars thought that the ancient tradition about Peter could be confirmed. For if some facts pertaining to Peter occur in Mark but not in Matthew or Luke, they assert that these have resulted from Peter's dictation. On the other hand, if some matters of this kind are found in the other Gospels but not in Mark, they think this omission must be attributed to the modesty of Peter. But in our judgement all these things are to be regarded as wishful thinking, and are of no value in proving the point for which they are alleged.

(2) [*Is Mark's Gospel unnecessary on this hypothesis?*]

[Objection:] 'There seems to be no reason for Mark to write a new account of the deeds of Christ, if, apart from the slim total of twenty-four verses, he has simply copied the Gospels of Matthew and Luke.'[54]

[Reply:] We reply: (a) Undoubtedly the reason was based on the need or desire of some Christians who had known Mark more intimately than Matthew or Luke. He wished to serve the requirements of these people, as the other Gospels had tried to benefit the Christians of other regions.

(b) Neither of the previous Evangelists had covered all the matters which Mark considered to be useful for his readers. Hence, he selected from both the things that he thought most suitable for his friends.

(c) The Gospels of both the other Evangelists contained many things which had been written for another audience and which Mark therefore considered to be unnecessary for his own friends. By omitting them Mark presented his friends with a much shorter outline of the Lord's actions, and consequently one realizable by correspondingly less effort and expense than by the Gospels of Matthew and Luke bound together in one volume.

(3) [*If Mark were totally dependent on Matthew and Luke, it could never have acquired full Gospel status.*]

[Objection:] 'It suited the nature of the times and the ardent zeal of the new Christians, in learning about the origin of their religion, to possess the richest and fullest accounts possible of the life of Jesus; and it was fitting that fragmentary accounts of his deeds, which had been narrated by various persons and were being circulated everywhere in written form, should be collected together; and it was fitting that such collections should be gathered into a single corpus and that this corpus itself should be increased and enriched by new stories as they came to hand and were deemed to be true. But it was not fitting that the assembled information, which had thus been collected by the apostle, should again be cut up and that an abridgement of a book, instead of the book itself, should be handed over and intrusted not just to individual Christians but to some universal Church.'[55]

[Reply:] We reply: (a) Such forms of reasoning will have little effect on those who are aware how ambiguous it is to judge what is fitting for a given age, place, or person. Why? Because we do not know whether Mark destined his book for individual Christians or for some universal Church, and we are still more ignorant of which church he handed it over to. For any pronouncements of the ancients on this matter are mere conjectures and unreliable traditions. Who therefore has dared to define what would have been fitting for a situation unknown to us of some unknown church and what would not? Mark could judge this accurately; but we cannot.

(b) It is wrong to assert that Mark should not have omitted anything about the history of Jesus that he himself knew, but that he himself would have been under an obligation to have filled up the narratives of others with new material. Certainly he did not produce even a single word on the nativity of Jesus, although it would have been impossible for him not to have known some details at least about this matter, since he had lived both in Jerusalem in his mother's house and then elsewhere in the company of Peter and Paul with so many acquaintances of the Lord. But he passed over in silence many things of this sort, things which could not have escaped him even if he had never by any chance read Matthew or Luke.

(4) [*Need the shorter Gospel be earlier than the longer?*]
[Objection:] 'It is more likely that the shorter Gospel was chronologically earlier; but the longer ones, in which the Evangelists supplied and amplified matters that had been either omitted or else related too concisely in the former, were composed at a later date.'
[Reply:] We reply: It depends entirely on the intention of the author whether it is preferable to add to, or to subtract from, what others wrote before him.

(5) [*Is the use of Mark by Matthew and Luke easier to account for?*]
[Objection:] 'If Mark – this is the opinion of Storr – wrote first and was both read and used by Matthew and Luke, it is very easy to account for those things which cannot but seem surprising to someone carefully comparing the three Gospels with one another, and which have given rise to so many hypotheses about the Gospel of Mark. For Matthew and Luke (a) often use the same words as Mark, because they had his book before their eyes; (b) varied the phraseology here and there and narrated much material, each one in his own individual way (i.e. differently from Mark); because· their plan was to create, not a fuller edition of Mark, but new commentaries

on matters pertaining to the life of Christ; (c) very frequently, it is true, they recorded the very same things that Mark had written; nevertheless, as one would rightly expect in view of the limitless amount of unrecorded material, they also added much that was new (each one something different from his own source), in order not to repeat what had been done before.[56]

[Reply:] We reply: Many things seem to oppose this hypothesis, which assumes that Matthew and Luke used the Gospel of Mark; but we shall only deal with those that closely concern the justification of *our* hypothesis, and which on account of our previous discussion can be understood without any difficulty and which do not require a lengthy explanation.

Now (a) it is inconceivable that Matthew, an eyewitness, chose as his guide for handing on the story of Christ a writer who had not been present at the events themselves.

(b) Mark surpasses Matthew in the clear and definite exposition of events; indeed he is sometimes more accurate (as we shall later show by examples) and comes closer to the truth of the events. Why therefore has Matthew receded from him in these passages, if he usually follows him closely elsewhere?

(c) Mark contains not only many details of events but also some complete short stories, that have been omitted either by Matthew or Luke or by both. Why have these two personages rejected them, if they did not refrain from turning the rest to their own uses?

Storr indeed considers[57] 'that *in order to make room for new additions* Matthew and Luke took pains in many places to cut down and abbreviate the story of Mark, especially since they were adding from their own sources stories similar to those left out'. But indeed in neither Matthew's nor Luke's Gospel does such a love of brevity betray itself as might have been able to deter these writers from retaining those details of Mark, which would have added little bulk to their books had they preserved them together with other matters. And moreover we are permitted to wonder why it is that each has omitted, or at least abbreviated, short stories on no less than five occasions (as we have noted above), from which we learn that Jesus did not want to make known his amazing deeds. No good reason exists why these [details] should be so carefully pruned on so many occasions; and so it is far more likely that these things were added by Mark for good reasons to the narratives of Matthew and Luke than rashly pruned by the latter.

(d) As Storr himself admits, Matthew, not esteeming chronological order, often arranged the materials he wished to hand on to posterity so as to connect them up with one another in a certain relationship. If he were the first to write the story of Christ, such a method could have been quite satisfactory for him. But if he had been guided by Mark, for whom this more complicated arrangement was foreign, there was hardly any reason why he should bother to create a new order unless he wanted to reduce everything more diligently according to the laws of time; and this certainly was not his purpose.

(e) We have previously observed the order in which Mark's stories follow one another, as well as his sudden and frequent transitions from Matthew to Luke and *vice versa*. These factors fully indicate that Mark wrote after Matthew and Luke and that he had studied both their books. On our hypothesis, it is entirely clear why Mark ceased to follow Matthew at Matt. 5: 1, Luke at Luke 6: 20, and Matthew again at Matt. 13: 36; and equally clear why Mark passed from Matt. 4: 22 to Luke 4: 31, from Luke 6: 11 to Matt. 12: 15; and from Matt. 13: 35 to Luke 8: 22. But if you say that Matthew and Luke used Mark, it remains obscure why Matthew for example partly omitted Mark 1: 21 - 3: 6 and partly transferred it to another sequence. But we do not want to repeat matters which can be found above in Section II. For we are not trying to overthrow the hypotheses of others, but to establish our own and overcome objections to it.

(6) [*Why not a common source or archetype?*]
[Objection:] 'Not only in Matthew but also in Mark and Luke there are many indications suggesting that these three books have all emerged from *one* source, namely a *Hebrew* and not a Greek one. For there exist in our Gospels some discrepancies in the narratives, arising from errors due to the ambiguity of Hebrew words or the interchange of sounds in Hebrew speech that are similar and easily confused. Besides, the whole nature of each Evangelist's narration in pericopes common to two or three has clearly been constructed so that each version is related to other versions of the same archetype. Hence a comparison of the three Evangelists together reveals for example on almost every page words, phrases and speech-structures which in spite of diversity mean the same and correspond to one and the same formula of Hebrew speech. The only likely explanation of this phenomenon is that the three Evangelists have used the same Hebrew archetype, which each in his own way has turned into Greek speech, and into which, at various junctures, each has scattered some material from his own store. Granted this, all difficulties vanish. But on the other hand, if you hold that the work of one Evangelist has been used and copied in detail by another, you will have to concede, *either* that later Evangelists deliberately wanted to conceal the source they had used and therefore substituted similar phrases for those which the earlier writer had used - a thing incompatible with the simplicity and integrity of these authors - *or* that they altered the phrases in a puerile fashion, which

hardly seems worthy of a responsible person.'[58]

[Reply:] To which we reply: (a) We know of no certain instance from which it can be proved that the translators have gone astray in converting the Hebrew archetype into Greek; but all the alleged instances can be explained without this hypothesis and freed from the supposed difficulty. We would demonstrate this by taking each instance in turn, if the limits of this essay would permit. Let it suffice to point out that many learned scholars have thought they saw various errors of the Greek translator in the Epistle to the Hebrews. But it is now generally agreed that these suspicions are groundless and that the Epistle was written by the author in Greek.

(b) Most of the examples of error mentioned, at least the more important ones, have been drawn from Matthew. Those selected from Mark and Luke are both fewer and less significant. But without damaging our hypothesis, we could grant that Matthew wrote in Hebrew. What then prevents Mark from having read the Hebrew work of Matthew and the Greek of Luke, and converted them for his own use? And if perchance you wish to take account of the frequent agreement between our Matthew and Mark even in the Greek text, you are entitled to hold that both the Hebrew archetype of Matthew and the Greek version of the same were available to Mark and that he consulted now the one, now the other and now both, in addition to the work of Luke. We would clearly prefer (unless there appeared some other way of freeing ourselves from these complexities) to add our own condemnation of this conjecture, which is entirely artificial and to be regarded as a repugnant hypothesis (both for chronological reasons and for the reasons given in Section II), because it proposes several archetypal recensions, each of them variously mixed up together, not to mention several Greek versions of them.

(c) From the permutations of parallel phrases and grammatical structure occurring in the three Gospels, nothing can be adduced against our hypothesis. We freely grant that the Evangelists neither wished to camouflage the source from which they drew, nor attempted to vary the phraseology in a puerile fashion; but we would not throw our hypothesis away willingly, should one or the other have necessarily to be conceded. However, we are not bound to admit either of them, because as the logicians would say, *there is a third way*. Who does not know that a writer can repeat in *his own* way and in *his own* words what he reads in another writer? And who is so strict and so lacking in human insight as to accuse such an author of deliberate dissimulation or to assert that he has indulged in a childish game of wordplay, unless there are other grounds for suspicion? For historians, when drawing material from the writings of others as if it were from the sources of their own narratives, do not make it a rule to bind themselves rigidly to the same words and formulas which they note the others have used. And so, in the same way, Mark too could surely have consulted the writings of Matthew and Luke without being obliged to copy out their narratives *word for word*. Undoubtedly, after reading any given pericope of Matthew or Luke or of both, he set about writing and recorded what he had read in them, just as he retained it in his memory. Wherever he remembered the actual words of Matthew and Luke, he retained them nor was he at pains to vary the phraseology; but where he had cut them out, he substituted others in their place. Sometimes, while he was writing, he may have taken perhaps a further look at the writings of Matthew and Luke; nevertheless, he need not always have thought this necessary, because his aim was to compose with their guidance a *new* narrative adapted to the needs of his own readers, and not to copy their books nor make a summary of them. This being so, it is understandable why some diversity may have arisen not only in words and phrases but also in the entire shaping of certain stories, e.g. Mark 7: 6-13, cf. Matt. 15: 3-9; 19: 3-8. Every now and then indeed, Mark seems to have changed something deliberately; but generally discrepancies of this sort are due to chance.

(7) [*The omissions of Mark*]

[Objection:] 'Mark has omitted many important and notable matters, which have been retained by either Matthew or Luke. But who would have neglected such important actions of Christ and the most useful and appealing discourses of the Lord, all put into writing by Matthew and Luke, if, as he wrote, he had had the benefit of these Gospels before his very eyes, and had actually copied a great deal from them including even things of lesser importance? Who could have so frequently passed over in silence certain details about matters he himself had narrated, details recorded by Matthew and Luke, and adding not a little light to what he himself had related – how, I ask, could he have disdained them if he had had the books of those two personages in his possession? You will scarcely be able to excuse such omissions as these, which make the narrative awkward and imperfect, unless you argue that no Evangelist had the work of the others at hand or claim that Mark was finished before the others. At least, as Storr would conclude, it is much easier to understand why Matthew and Luke narrated so many things not found in Mark, if Mark wrote earlier, than if Mark had Matthew and Luke at hand. For later writers are bound to augment and amplify the work of an earlier writer in order to justify writing at all.'[59]

[Reply:] We reply as follows: From what we have pointed out above in Section I (4), (5), (6), (8), (9) and in the notes thereto, and especially in note 15, we trust that it is clear enough that most of the things omitted by

Mark were left out on purpose. Besides there could not fail to be absent from Mark's book material which is found either in those passages of Matthew which Mark passed over when using Luke, or in those chapters of Luke which he had hardly consulted when following Matthew. See for example the passages cited in note 22. However it can easily happen in practice that the real reasons why Mark has omitted some things escape us, since we know so little about the author of the book, about the readers for whom he wrote and about their circumstances; and since we are able to arrive at very few conclusions when conjecturing the purpose of the writer.[60] On any fair judgement of the evidence one must admit that our hypothesis would remain unshaken, even if Mark had left out even more. However, some scholars think that so much weight is to be attached to certain omissions that, in their judgement, we would be failing to attribute as much importance to them as is right and proper, if we were to pass them over in silence and fail to explain why they are not strong enough to overthrow our thesis. From the cases we shall now consider, it will be possible to judge the remainder.

(a)

[Objection:] 'Mark omitted the dialogue of Jesus with John about his being baptized by him (Matt. 3: 14, 15), although Mark agrees with Matthew in what goes before and after.'

[Reply:] Two things are contained in these verses: first, that John acknowledged that he and his baptism were inferior to the person and baptism of the Lord; secondly, that Jesus willed to be baptized by John, because 'it was fitting to fulfil all righteousness'. The former could be omitted because in Mark (1: 7, 8) it is immediately preceded by another testimony of the Baptist about Jesus' worthiness far exceeding his own. As to the second, Mark thought that in view of the heated controversy then raging about the continuing value of the Mosaic Law, it ought perhaps to be passed over in silence; in this way he would prevent the Judaizers from misusing this saying of the Lord by insisting on Christians observing Jewish rites, as if such were a principal part of the 'righteousness' that they had to 'fulfil'. Moreover Luke also omits them. But in the pericopes common to Matthew and Luke, Mark has a habit of leaving out those details of Matthew's text which he found absent from Luke.

(b)

[Objection:] 'In the narrative of the Temptations (Matt. 4: 1-11 // Luke 4: 1-13) Mark only gives a brief summary of them (Mark 1: 12, 13) but remains silent on the ways in which the Lord resisted and overcame them. But since it is out of character for Mark to abbreviate a longer narrative and to omit circumstantial details known to him, one would have thought that he was not aware of the fuller description found both in Matthew and Luke.'

[Reply:] There were two reasons which might have deterred Mark from including the longer narrative in his book: (i) the form of the narrative, redolent of the Jewish mode of thought and expression, seemed unsuitable for the type of reader to whom Mark's Gospel was addressed; (ii) in the dialogue of the Saviour with the Tempter *four* Old Testament sayings of the Lord are mentioned. Mark however usually cuts out quotations of this sort. See Section I (9). Now if he thought he ought to omit these four sayings, without passing over the whole thing, he had either to change the entire narrative, or to give only a summary of it, omitting all details. Mark preferred the latter course.

(c)

[Objection:] 'According to the opinion of Storr,[61] what we said above in Section II, notes 17, 21, 22, about Mark's omission of the Sermon on the Mount, seems to be void of all appearance of truth. It seems incredible to this great scholar that Mark should have avoided this wonderful Sermon in such a manner that he not only set aside the Gospel of Matthew at the very moment he reached this passage in Matt. 5, but that he should likewise desert Luke, whom he had taken as his new guide. As soon as he came across Luke's version of the Sermon (Luke 6: 20–49, a shorter version it is true, and adapted by Luke himself for non-Palestinians), he deserted him in the same way and betook himself to Matthew, again rejecting from his Gospel even those few little verses, Matt. 12: 33–7, solely because he had read sayings similar to these in the Sermon on the Mount.'

[Reply:] (i) The Great Sermon in Luke is shorter than that in Matthew; but taken by itself, it is long enough and extends to *thirty* verses. Mark almost always omits such long discourses. Nor can it be proved that he was really *bound* to retain this discourse, even if he knew of it.

(ii) As regards Matt. 12: 33–7, we will add here to what we said above (see note 23), namely that in Matthew these verses are preceded by another discourse, viz. Matt. 12: 25–32, which is also found in the Gospel of Mark, and that again another one follows it at Matt. 12: 39–45. Since therefore Mark saw that Matthew had collected up many of the Lord's discourses, he retained only that part of the Sermon we find in Matt. 12: 25–32 in order to avoid his Gospel becoming too bulky; he then jumps at once from verse 32 to verse 46, omitting not only verses 33–7 (now quoted against us) but also verses 38–45.

(d)

[Objection:] 'Mark omits Matt. 8: 5–13 // Luke 7: 1–10, the story of the Healing of the Centurion's Servant at Capernaum – an event that some people regard as especially worthy of mention, both as an example of the unique faith of the Centurion in Christ and also as an instance of Jesus' power to restore the sick to health in their absence.'

[Reply:] (i) Mark 7: 29-30 gives another instance of the Lord healing at a distance; his readers could therefore easily do without this one.

(ii) The table which we gave our readers in Section II shows that Mark passed from Matt. 4: 21 to Matt. 12: 15 and from Luke 6: 16 to Luke 8: 16. Now since this pericope of the Centurion's Servant is read in Matt. 8 and Luke 7, it was passed over by Mark, together with other matters in each Gospel, both preceding and following it.

(e)

As regards the omission of Matt. 11: 2-19 // Luke 7: 18-35, the Lord's answer to the messengers of John the Baptist, when they asked him if he really was 'He who is to come', was passed over by Mark for the very reason we have just given. For Matthew relates the anecdote in another sequence and place from Luke. Now Mark was following Luke at the point where Matthew related it, but on the contrary at the point where Luke relates it, he is again using Matthew, not Luke, as his guide, as is clear from the previously mentioned table. Hence Mark omitted it in both places.

(f)

[Objection:] 'Matt. 14: 28-31 relates how Peter walked upon the storm-tossed waters of Lake Gennesaret. Mark, the disciple and interpreter of *Peter*, clearly agrees with Matthew in the passages that both precede and follow; nevertheless he passes over in silence these very verses which relate such a unique and unparalleled event that happened to *Peter*.'

[Reply:] We confess we do not know the reasons - they could be manifold and complicated - why Mark decided to omit this part of the story from his Gospel. But since Mark has passed over so many other things found in Matthew, this particular omission will only cause concern to, or provide an alleged argument for, those who think that the Evangelist Mark composed his book, if not at the dictation of Peter, at least under his guidance. But we do not hesitate to declare the complete falsehood of such a view, which, ancient though it be, is repugnant to everything which we seem to have proved in the preceding pages.

(g)

[Objection:] 'In Matt. 19: 27 Jesus promises the apostles that they will sit on twelve thrones judging the twelve tribes of Israel, and in 20: 1-16 the parable of the Workers sent off at different times to the Vineyard illustrates the saying: "Many that are first shall be last and the last first" (Matt. 19: 30). Now both the promise and the saying with the parable were occasioned by Peter's question: "We have left all things and followed you; what then shall we have?" This question ("What then shall we have?" is absent [from Mark 10: 28], but the sense remains the same) together with the saying and that part of the answer found in Matt. 19: 29, are also read in Mark, but he lacks both the promise contained in verse 28 and the parable.'

[Reply:] Both are also lacking in Luke 18: 28-30. Mark therefore sticks very closely to Luke in this passage, and has borrowed from Matthew only that very brief saying and paradox. But the parable, added [in Matthew] for the sake of illustration, seemed far too wordy for Mark, who generally omits longer speeches in the interest of brevity. And for the same reason he has also passed over Matt. 22: 1-14; 23: 2-39; and chapter 25. And all these are also missing from Luke.

(h)

[Objection:] 'Mark 14: 28 and 16: 7 each mentions the promise that the disciples will see Christ risen from the dead in Galilee. Matt. 28: 16, 17 narrates its fulfilment. But Mark gives his readers no hint of a journey into Galilee nor of Christ being seen there by the disciples, but leaves them uncertain whether the twice-mentioned promise was or was not fulfilled. But how can anyone properly explain this lapse if the Gospel of Matthew was really in front of his eyes?'

[Reply:] (i) If the last twelve verses of Mark (16: 9-20) were genuine, or if Mark had ended his Gospel at verse 8, it would be difficult to offer a feasible explanation for the omission. But we know that these verses are missing in the important Codex Vaticanus and were formerly lacking in many other ancient manuscripts. Nevertheless, it is very unlikely indeed that Mark ended his book at verse 8 with 'for they were afraid'. It is therefore reasonable to conjecture that the real ending of the Gospel (one that undoubtedly mentioned the journey into Galilee) was accidentally lost, and that another ending was supplied either at the end of the first century or at the beginning of the second century by some unknown person; and if this be so, there is surely no need to worry about this omission. Moreover, in our opinion, the following observation adds some new weight to this conjecture about Mark's omission of the Journey to Galilee.

(ii) However this may be explained (and there is no room here for a more accurate examination of the authenticity of Mark's last twelve verses), the omission of a mention of the Galilean journey cannot destroy our hypothesis. For whatever theory you hold about Mark's sources, the silence over this journey remains a problem. Let us suppose that the conclusion of the Gospel is genuine, and let us allow for the moment that the Gospel of Matthew had not been seen by Mark; all the same we should still be wondering why he remains silent over whether and in what manner the Lord had stood by the promises which Mark had earlier recorded to have been given to the disciples on two separate occasions. Certainly with Matthew as a reminder, Mark would not have any need to be silent, since he could not have forgotten what he had written about it only a few verses previously.

(i)

However scholars have noted that Mark has omitted many important stories of the Lord's deeds and not a few discourses that are found in Luke, and they have consequently thought Mark did not use Luke at all when composing his Gospel. However we think that what we argued in Section II and said in the notes to our table on each passage are sufficient to answer this objection. See particularly reference to Luke 7: 35 – 8: 9 (notes 21, 22) re the omitted pericope, and note 35 re Luke 19: 1-27.

All the same we add a few things here relating to the beginning of Mark's Gospel. Now Luke commences the history of Jesus' public ministry at Luke 3: 1ff. with a careful note of the time when the Lord began to teach; Mark however omits all this and begins his narrative without any chronological determination. But he could afford to omit all these as being of little importance to *his* readership. For men far distant from Palestine (Section I (7)) were not likely to know the names of the tetrarchs who had been ruling over Galilee, Iturea, Trachonitis, and Abilene twenty or thirty years before, or the succession of the Jewish high priests; indeed one may doubt whether they knew the exact sequence and chronology of the procurators of Judea. Thus there remained only the date taken from the years of Tiberius. But Mark omitted this *along with the others*, because at the time when our Gospel appeared every Christian knew that Jesus had lived in the reign of Tiberius; and it did not seem to him to be important to indicate in what year of this Emperor Jesus began his ministry as teacher. For us, however, Luke's accuracy is exceedingly gratifying; but the first readers of the Gospels did not demand such accuracy, nor was it necessary for the purpose which Mark seems to have had.

(8) [*Discrepancies that might argue for Marcan priority*]

[Objection:] 'In a number of places the Gospel of Mark seems to conflict openly with the stories of Matthew and Luke. Hence it would seem that he has consulted neither of them. For he could have avoided such discrepancies, and would certainly have done so if he had had the power to unroll the books of the earlier Evangelists.'

[Reply:] (i) Mark did not foresee that critics would carefully compare his Gospel with the other two, that they would diligently note passages which seemed to conflict with one another, that they would labour to settle these discrepancies of the Evangelists, and be at pains to harmonize one book out of three or four. For if he had foreseen it even a little, he

could easily have harmonized his Gospel with the others, or pointed out
the reasons for his disagreement by adding a single word. But he thought
that he could dispense with exercising such minute care. We say 'minute'
because the disagreement is never in the general drift but only in particular details of particular incidents. Our author, unfamiliar with the principles of scholarship and writing a book intended for popular consumption,
did not regard discrepancies of this sort as important.

(ii) Mark sometimes diverges from Matthew because in that place he is
following Luke instead.

(iii) Sometimes he deliberately departs a little from the earlier Evangelists, and takes pains to relate events of which he had a better knowledge
more accurately than the others had done. But come, let us set before our
readers' eyes the true nature of these discrepancies by giving some examples, though lack of space must limit their number:

(a) [Objection:] 'Mark 2: 14 names the tax-collector summoned by
Jesus from his place of work Levi, but Matt. 9: 9 says his name is Matthew.'

[Reply:] Luke 5: 27 agrees here with Mark. Mark indeed knew more
about this Levi than Luke, for he relates that he was the son of Alphaeus.
And hence it is perhaps legitimate to infer that either Levi or Alphaeus was
more familiar to the readers of Mark, and that for this reason Mark followed
the example of Luke in recording the calling of Levi rather than Matthew,
who was perhaps unknown to them. However, it is probable that both
Matthew and Levi were enrolled as disciples of Christ at the same time.

(b) [Objection:] 'At Mark 2: 23-7 Mark omits some sentences of Matthew, namely Matt. 12: 5, 6, 7, and in their place substitutes another:
"The Sabbath was made for man, not man for the Sabbath", by which
addition the meaning of the following sentence ("The Son of Man is also
Lord of the Sabbath") is completely altered in comparison with Matthew.'

[Reply:] (i) Matthew's words are omitted because at this point Mark
had turned from Matthew to Luke; this is clear from our table in Section
II and from their agreement over the formula: 'and he said to them'.

(ii) The addition made by Mark to Luke's text in no way alters the
meaning of the following sentence, which is: If the Sabbath has been insti-
tuted for man's benefit, and if nobody is so bound by the Sabbath-laws
that he is prevented by them from promoting his own or another's happi-
ness, it follows *a fortiori* that the Messiah cannot be so restricted by them
that he cannot abstain from them or free his disciples from them.

(c) [Objection:] 'If the selection of the Twelve Apostles happened at
the time when Mark 3: 7-19 speaks of it, it took place before the Sermon
on the Mount; but this conflicts with Matthew, in so far as it was the occasion of the calumny of the Pharisees who accused Jesus of forming an

alliance with Beelzebul.'

[Reply:] See in this connection Section II, note 22, where we have stated the reasons why Mark has both these pericopes at the same place in his Gospel. The discrepancy vanishes if you note what we observed there.

(d) [Objection:] 'Mark 4: 35 (cf. 1: 35) conflicts so much with Matt. 8: 18 (cf. 13: 54; 14: 22) that it scarcely seems possible for both writers to be telling the truth, but the one seems to prove the other's error; and this surely would not have happened if Mark had had the Gospel of Matthew at hand when composing his own Gospel. For according to Matthew, after the choosing of Peter, Andrew, James and John (4: 18-22) and *after the Sermon on the Mount* (chapters 5, 6, 7), Christ immediately heals a leper (8: 1-2), whom he sends off to the priests; then he enters Capernaum where he cures the Centurion's slave (8: 5) and Peter's mother-in-law (8: 14) of their illness; then when a great crowd of people gathers, *he crosses Lake Gennesaret* (verse 23); and after enduring the storm and stilling it with a word (verses 23-7), he comes to the Gergesene region (verse 28). Then at another time he heals a blind and dumb demoniac (12: 22f.), and as a result of this admirable deed the excited people begin to ask him if he is the Messiah (verse 23). Some of the Pharisees accused him of casting out devils with the aid of Beelzebul (verse 24), others demanded a sign from heaven (verse 38). And while he was still answering them, his mother and relations arrived wanting to speak with him (12: 46). 'On that very day' (13: 1), he left the house and got into the boat, and taught the people standing on the shore *about the nature of the heavenly kingdom*, which he illustrated vividly and at length with many *parables* (13: 3-52). Then he preached in the synagogue of his own city, to the wonder of his audience (13: 53-8). Then, 'at that time' (14: 1), fearing the machinations of Herod, who had already killed the Baptist (14: 3), he sailed to *a deserted place* (verse 13), where he fed the five thousand (14: 15-22). The following night, when the disciples, returning in the boat, were being tossed about by the winds and waves, he came to their assistance, walking on the water (14: 23-37)...

Now let us compare Mark's sequence with Matthew's. *With Mark*: After the calling of Peter, Andrew, James and John (1: 16 // Matt. 4: 18-22),[62] Christ entered Capernaum (1: 21 // Luke 4: 31), and having healed the demoniac in the synagogue (verse 23 // Luke 4: 33), cured Peter's mother-in-law on the same day (verse 29 // Luke 4: 38); and when the whole township came to the door, at eventide (verse 32 // Luke 4: 40), he withdrew early in the morning to *a deserted place* (verse 35 // Luke 4: 42); then he made a tour of Galilee (verse 39 // Luke 4: 44),[63] and healed the leper, commanding him to go to the priests (verse 40 // Luke 5: 12). Then at

another time he went up the mountain (3: 13 // Luke 6: 12) and chose the
Twelve Apostles (verse 14 // Luke 6: 13). At this point Luke inserted his
Sermon on the Mount.[64] Returning home (Mark 3: 20), he was so fatigued
by the bustling crowds that 'those with him' went out 'to seize him', saying
that 'he was beside himself' (verse 21).[65] Then the Scribes from Jerusalem
falsely accused him of casting out devils with the help of Beelzebul (Mark
3: 22 // Matt. 12: 24).[66] While he was refuting them, his mother and brethren came up and stood outside wanting to be admitted (verse 31 // Matt.
12: 46). Then Jesus went down to the Lake of Gennesaret and explained
to the people standing on the shore *the nature of the heavenly Kingdom*,
using various *parables* (Mark 4: 1ff. // Matt. 13: 1ff.). After this discourse,
'as he was in the boat', *he crossed the Lake of Gennesaret* (verses 35, 36 //
Luke 8: 22),[67] and after he and his disciples had been tossed by the storm
and he had stilled it by a word, he landed in the region of the Gadarenes
(Mark 5: 1 // Luke 8: 26)...

In the above, the whole sequence of Mark not only differs from that of
Matthew but also seems to conflict with it. For according to Matthew, after
the Sermon on the Mount and the healing of Peter's mother-in-law, Jesus
crossed the lake stirred by the storm, and entered the district of the Ger-
gesenes (or Gadarenes); then after relating the parables on the Kingdom of
God he withdrew to a deserted place. But on the other hand, according to
Mark, Jesus went to the desert immediately after curing Peter's mother-in-
law; but he crossed the Lake of Gennesaret, stirred by the storm, and came
to the Gadarene region only after he had delivered the parables on the
heavenly kingdom...'

[Reply:] All difficulties disappear if – putting away all prejudices about
the chronological order adopted by the Evangelists – we pay attention to
where and *why* Mark passes from Matthew to Luke, then returns from him
to Matthew, and then leaves him again for Luke. And since this matter was
fully dealt with in Section II (whither we directed our readers in the notes
attached to the foregoing pages), there is no reason to add any more here.
For we think it quite clear that all the discrepancies arise because Mark,
who is in no wise worried about the chronological order of events, has
followed now one and now the other, but never the same guide all the time.
Therefore, the question comes back to this: how did it happen that *Luke*
arranged parts of his narrative otherwise than Matthew? This is not the
place for examining the question, since we are dealing with Mark. We shall
only permit ourselves to note that Luke has departed less than Matthew
from the true sequence of events. At least what Matthew has got in 14: 1,
3, and 14: 13, 14 does not seem to have happened in that order at all.

(e) [Objection:] 'Mark 5: 23 relates the synagogue official as saying:

"My daughter is in extremity", whereas Matthew says (9: 18) the girl "has just died"; Luke seems to agree with this (8: 42) when he says "she was dying".'

[Reply:] If Mark here took Matthew as his guide, it should not appear strange that the later writer narrated the whole incident more fully, more accurately and more correctly than the earlier writer treated it. But Mark has taken all these things out of Luke (note 29). Now Luke (verse 42) reads: 'she was dying'. But from verse 49 it is clear that the girl was not yet dead. Mark therefore having compared the authentic interpretation furnished by Luke at verse 49, changed the ambiguous phrase of verse 42 for a clearer one in perfect conformity with Luke's thinking. And hence it is clear at the same time that there is no basis at all for the view of those who add this passage to those from which they think it can be proved that the three Evangelists used a Hebrew archetype and deceived by its ambiguity rendered the same Hebrew phrase in different ways not easily reconciled. There is perfect agreement between Mark and Luke provided Luke's verse 42 is explained by verse 49. Nor does Matthew disagree. For, since he omitted what we find in Luke's verse 49 about the death of the girl, Matthew *had* to refer to her as dead from the very start of his shorter narrative, where Luke and Mark relate that the spirit of the girl was still alive.

(f) [Objection:] 'Mark 10: 46–52 relates certain things about the blind man healed near Jericho which fail to agree with the narratives both of Matthew and Luke (Matt. 20: 29–34 // Luke 18: 35–43).'

[Reply:] Whoever compares the three Evangelists with each other, and notes the special details recorded only by Mark, will realize that Mark was very well informed about this event. Where therefore he departs from the others, he must be reckoned to have wanted to correct them unobtrusively.

(g) [Objection:] 'Mark 11: 11–27 corresponds to Matt. 21: 10–23. But the parts of the Matthean narrative follow one another in a different and more probable order than in Mark. For according to Matthew, Christ cast the buyers and sellers out of the Temple that they had profaned on the *same* day as he entered Jerusalem surrounded by a great crowd of enthusiastic people. For after they were driven out, there still remained children crying "Hosanna to the Son of David" (Matt. 21: 15), who had undoubtedly entered the Temple with the rest of the crowd hosanna-ing Jesus inauspiciously. According to Mark, however, Christ expelled the profaners of the Temple *on the next day after* he entered the city. But, since nothing is more fickle than popular favour, it is more likely that Christ, being a most prudent man, took this dangerous course immediately after his entry into the city, on the very day that the people had so clearly shown their feeling for him, rather than put it off to another time, nor is it credible that those who sold the oxen and sheep together with the money changers would so easily have given way unless they feared the anger of the people bringing Jesus in triumph into the Temple. Moreover, according to Matthew, Christ cursed the barren fig-tree on the *next* day after he had expelled the profaners from the Temple, and the tree withered *at once*; and when the disciples saw it, they immediately approached the master in amazement, and were instructed by him about the great power of "faith". But on the contrary, in Mark, Christ cursed the tree early in the morning of *the day on which* he later cleansed the Temple; and the disciples observed the tree withered to the root *on the following day* and gave the Lord the opportunity to instruct them on the power of faith.'

[Reply:] We are fully persuaded that the whole series of events happened in the order and time in which Mark has arranged them in his Gospel. He has deliberately chosen to differ from Matthew because he had acquired for himself from another source more accurate information about the whole affair than Matthew had. Thus he was able to expand in his verses 11–14 and 20–6 matters which Matthew had noted only briefly, and to add in verse 16 some details omitted by Matthew. He had especially noted the moments and intervals of time at which each event occurred, and then clearly recorded them with quite remarkable care. See verses 11, 12, 15, 19, 20, 27. But though in treating this part of the story, Mark handled the matter more correctly and carefully than Matthew, yet he in no way accuses him of ignorance or error. For (i) Matthew nowhere asserts in clear terms that Christ cast the profaning crowd out of the Temple on the same day that he entered the city; nor can this be affirmed from the acclamation of the children, who were simply repeating on another occasion (Matt. 21: 14) what they had heard said by the crowd who had accompanied Christ the day before. (ii) Matthew did not want to divide the story of the fig-tree up into several sections, but deliberately postponed the mention of its cursing for a few verses in order to narrate the result of the cursing at the same time.

Section IV
[Conclusions]

There remains for us to point out the correct corollaries that flow from the acceptance of our hypothesis concerning the origin of the Gospel of Mark. The more important are these:

I. Mark wrote his Gospel after Matthew and Luke had finished their respective works. False therefore are the ascriptions commonly attached to each Gospel which assert that Matthew was written in the eighth, Mark in the tenth or twelfth, and Luke in the fifteenth year after the Ascension of

Christ into heaven. Nor can we agree with Storr, who recently wanted to persuade us that Mark is the first Gospel of all.

II. The things that Papias (Eusebius *H.E.* III. 39) records about the Gospel of Mark are figments very far from the truth, although he produces the Presbyter John as a witness.

III. The most ancient Fathers, who recorded that Mark wrote the life of the Lord under the auspices of Peter, either narrated their own conjectures (not history drawn from trustworthy documents), or were deceived by false rumours. Furthermore, all those conclusions built up by scholars on this supposition also collapse, no matter how ingeniously conceived or elaborated.[68] This one thing can perhaps be conceded, namely that Mark received from Peter the circumstantial details, with which he enriched throughout the narratives of Luke and Matthew; although even this is not quite certain, for they could also be derived from another source.

IV. Augustine too in his *De Consens. Evang.* book 1, chapter 2, was wrong in holding that Mark was the abbreviator and copier of Matthew.

V. In general none of the Fathers seem to have known anything certain about the books of the New Testament, except that from very ancient times this or that book was received and publicly read in this or that church, and attributed to this or that author. All the rest that the Fathers record about the time and place of writing, the occasion for writing, the author's plan, the sources he used, and so on, remain quite uncertain.

VI. Although our judgement about the Gospel of Mark does not entirely exclude the hypothesis of those who think Matthew was written in Hebrew, yet, if you accept that view, this position will be found to be highly improbable. At all events Mark seems to have used the Greek exemplar of Matthew exclusively. For the same Greek formulae are very often found in both; and if Mark, writing in Greek, had compiled his Gospel partly from a Hebrew Matthew and partly from a Greek Luke he would undoubtedly have preferred Luke to Matthew and would surely have followed his guidance. But we have seen above that this is not the case at all. Recently indeed the learned C. A. Wahl suggested that Mark put together a Coptic [Gospel] from the Hebrew Matthew and the Greek Luke. But this conjecture which assumes that our [Mark] wrote in the Egyptian language, has very little foundation and cannot be easily reconciled with what we have already related about the origin and character of Mark.

VII. Very far from the truth is the opinion of some who think that the Evangelists are not the true authors of the books that are circulated under their names, but that their disciples consigned to writing what they at a former time had heard from the mouth of Matthew, Mark, Luke, and so on.

VIII. Also very unlikely is the conjecture (at least as regards the Gospel of Mark) of those who declare that the Evangelists compiled their Gospels from hypothetical documents either Greek or Hebrew, and now *lost*, and that they have culled from them the things that seemed particularly interesting or useful to their readers; and thus they think they are able to account both for the wonderful agreement of the Evangelists in words and formulas of speech, and for their disagreements with one another.

IX. The Gospel of Mark survives entire and incorrupt, save for the last verses of the final chapter, which, as we have said, one can justly conjecture to have been lost and then supplied by another hand.

X. Already in the time of Mark, the Gospels of Matthew and Luke contained the same things as are read in them today, and were arranged in the same order; nor does it follow that because Mark omitted some things they were originally lacking from these Gospels.

XI. Let those who wish to devote themselves to making a harmony of the Gospels, take care not to call upon Mark in constructing it. For he was clearly not interested in the chronological order of events, but passes from Matthew to Luke and back again, taking no account of the time at which each event occurred. Hence it is also clear that in the age of the apostles it seemed in no wise necessary to keep chronological order in narrating the deeds of the Lord. And thus one is entitled further to conjecture that it did not occur to the other Evangelists to write either annals or diaries.

XII. Mark understood the purpose and use of the Gospels quite differently from most theologians of later times. And if he had intended to illustrate Matthew by an accurate commentary, he would indeed have produced one quite unlike any of the customary commentaries. Undoubtedly such a work would have pleased the followers of Lessing and those who, by their study of *belles lettres*, have sharpened and polished their natural disposition and have learnt by long practice the right method of dealing with ancient literature; but it would not have pleased the authors of harmonies and tiresomely industrious commentators.

XIII. Those who argue that Mark wrote under the influence of divine inspiration must surely regard it as being a pretty meagre one!

7

GRIESBACH AND THE DEVELOPMENT OF TEXT CRITICISM

G. D. Kilpatrick

Introduction

'It is not that such a mode of conducting critical enquiries would not be very convenient, that Griesbach's theory is universally abandoned by modern scholars, but because there is no valid reason for believing it to be true.' So wrote Scrivener in his *Introduction to the Criticism of the New Testament.*[1]

This conclusion implies two judgements about Griesbach's theory, first, that it is fundamentally wrong and, secondly, that it had little or no effect on the subsequent development of the New Testament textual criticism. Both these judgements deserve further examination and it may be convenient for our purposes to take the second first.

I The lasting influence of Griesbach's text-critical theory

A. Preliminary remarks

Griesbach, building on the work of his teacher Semler, grouped his witnesses in three main classes, the Alexandrine, the Western and the Byzantine. This threefold division, as we shall see, had a great influence on subsequent textual criticism.

Before we examine the history of this influence we may notice two points which will require further consideration, the actual assignment of the witnesses to the several classes and the use made of these classes in the attempt to recover the original form of the text.

In Griesbach's assignments we may notice two features. First, several witnesses, whose evidence is available to us today, were then either inadequately known, such as B for example, or quite unknown, such as P[45, 66, 75] ℵ. Consequently, to that extent, Griesbach's lists of the numbers of the various classes were incomplete.

Secondly, Griesbach betrays some uncertainty in the assignment of some witnesses to the appropriate class. In this way he ascribes members of families 1 and 13 both to Alexandrine and Western classes. The definition of these two families was to be achieved much later and to be important for the development of the theory of a Caesarean class.

What use was to be made of this classification in the attempt to recover the original form of the text? There were at least two possibilities. A scholar could argue either that usually or always one class gave the original text or that he could take a vote and abide by the reading to be found in a majority of his classes. The first procedure was to become an effective instrument in the hands of Hort for disposing of the text and witnesses of his Syrian family. The second was to be the way followed by von Soden.

Griesbach himself did not follow either possibility rigorously. If we look at his discussion of the position of Rom. 16: 24-7, we find that he makes little obvious use of his classification in his argument that these verses originally belonged after Rom. 14: 23.[2] Instead he puts forward a theory of the composition of the last chapters of Romans which is intended to explain how the text of these chapters reached its present shape and, in particular, to defend his decision about 16: 24-7. Gabler points out that a large number of the Greek manuscripts known to Griesbach place these verses where Griesbach does, but Griesbach himself does not refer to this fact.

In general he does depart from the *Textus Receptus* (= T.R.) considerably but not so consistently as subsequent editors. For example, some fifty verses in the T.R. have been omitted or called in question by them. I have given the list of these verses most recently in *Scripture Bulletin*.[3] I repeat the list (see below) with indications of Griesbach's and Hort's practice.

	Griesbach	Hort
Matt. 9: 34	h	[ ]
12: 47	h	o
16: 2-3	h	[[ ]]
17: 21	h	o
18: 11	==	o
21: 44	+	[ ]
23: 14	o	o
Mark 9: 44, 46	+	o
11: 26	h	o
15: 28	==	o
16: 9-20	[ ]	[[ ]]
Luke 17: 36	o	o
22: 19-20	h	[[ ]]
22: 43-4	h	[[ ]]
22: 62	h	[ ]
23: 17	==	o
24: 12	h	[[ ]]
24: 40	h	[[ ]]
John 5: 4	[ ]	o
7: 53 - 8: 11	[ ]	[[ ]]

	Griesbach	Hort
John 12: 8	h	h
Acts 8: 37	o	o
15: 34	=	o
24: 6–8	=	o
28: 29	=	o
Rom. 16: 24	h	o
16: 25–7	after 14: 23	h

The signs in the Griesbach column have the following meaning:
h *means* has in the text without comment; + *means* a passage probably not
to be omitted; = *means* probably but not certainly to be omitted; [ ] *means*
not part of the true text; o *means* omits.
In the Hort column:
h *means* has; [ ] and [[ ]] *mean* puts in the corresponding brackets; o *means*
omits.

B. Hort

From this table we can see that Hort proceeded more rigorously than
Griesbach. The way in which he produced his edition encouraged this
rigour. Griesbach, with little variation, printed the T.R. and indicated the
readings he preferred in footnotes, but Hort printed his own text and so
had to make up his mind decisively at each point.

In passing we may note this possibility. Hort did much impressive work
in his day, but found it difficult to complete his undertakings. The result
was that after his death several works were published in incomplete form.
Westcott, on the other hand, was good at bringing his undertakings to completion, and we have from him, for example, several completed commentaries. We can detect in their Greek Testament some places where Westcott
and Hort were not agreed, and usually in these places Hort seems right and
Westcott wrong. We may suppose that had Hort been left to himself he
would have produced a better text, but his edition would never have been
completed. Thanks to Westcott it was finished, but it was not as good as it
might have been. Along his own lines Hort, left alone, would perhaps have
proceeded with even greater rigour.

Why was there this difference between Griesbach and Hort? First, there
was a large number of witnesses hitherto unknown or unreported which
were discovered and collated in the course of the nineteenth century. In
Tischendorf's and Tregelles' editions Hort had obviously superior collections of material. Secondly, Hort's classes or families were more clearly
defined. There is less uncertainty about where a witness belongs. This may
have been partly due to the greater amount of information available mentioned just above.

The greatest difference, however, was due to other developments, particularly in Classical scholarship. Lachmann had in his edition of Lucretius

given a good example of the genealogical method, and we must recognize that where the conditions are fulfilled it is a valid procedure. At the same time Classical scholars in editing their texts frequently picked out one manuscript which they followed sometimes through thick and thin and sometimes with more discretion.

Hort decided to follow both these practices, the use of the genealogical method and the cult of the best manuscript. His problem in doing so was to establish that the two practices really cohered. He did this by adjusting his genealogical pattern.

Hort inherited Griesbach's classes. He retained Griesbach's Western class under the same name, though it was already on the road to becoming a collection of miscellaneous items. Griesbach's Byzantine class he renamed Syrian, but he divided the Alexandrine class into two, Neutral and Alexandrine; B was pre-eminently the representative of the Neutral text with ℵ as runner-up. The others he retained in the Alexandrine class or family. Thus Hort was able to make use of both practices of Classical scholarship.

Together they enabled him to dethrone the Syrian text and with it the T.R. We see the extent of this achievement when we contrast it with the caution, we may be tempted to say, the timidity of Griesbach. We may be inclined now to think that Hort went too far in this direction in denying well-nigh all value to readings found only in his Syrian witnesses. He is, however, more cautious, for example, in dating his Syrian recension than some of his followers.

To many, Hort's distinction between Neutral and Alexandrine may seem artificial. If we find it unconvincing, then Hort's parade of the genealogical method may seem just so much window-dressing, fashionable to the extent that in general it has retained its place in scholarly esteem.

There is a piece of evidence which apparently supports this view. Hort, in expounding genealogy, draws up an hypothetical genealogy to illustrate his point, but he never himself draws up a genealogy of the actual New Testament manuscripts, though some of his followers had no compunction in doing so. If the genealogical method was to be used effectively in the way that Classical scholars used it, a family tree with all the relevant manuscripts given a precise relationship to each other was an essential.

Granted that Hort's genealogical theory is not an essential part of his argument, we can see behind his exposition a simple hypothesis. Of the three classes of witnesses which the traditional analysis presented to him, he discards two, the Syrian and the Western, on various grounds. He finds the main source for the original form of the text in the third class, the Alexandrine, and in particular in one or two manuscripts, which are its oldest representatives, namely B and ℵ. Even here a scholarly conscience moves him to recognize a failure to preserve the original text at all points. In a limited number of passages Hort goes outside his chosen few witnesses to discover the original form of the text elsewhere. It may be that he was more ready than Westcott to do this.

One reason why he was able to do this was that over the centuries there had been acquired a body of experience in dealing with textual problems. This experience was summarized in a series of maxims such as *lectio breuior potior* and *lectio difficilior praestat*, which provided an independent touchstone in considering variant readings. We see examples of this experience at work in some of the critical notes and references in the *apparatus* of Tischendorf and von Soden and in Hort's *Introduction*.

Here, the maxim *lectio breuior potior*, 'the shorter reading is preferable', is particularly important. It is one of the reasons why he preferred the text of D and its allies, for example at Luke 22: 19-20; 24: 3, 6, 12, 36, 40, 51, 52, against the vast majority of witnesses including B and, except for 24: 51, ℵ. We may agree that he was mistaken at 24: 51, but the important point is that Hort was prepared to depart from his obsequience toward ℵ B on occasion on intrinsic grounds, namely in part because these readings were shorter.

False gods have their uses. The maxim *lectio breuior potior* delivered Hort, on occasion, from idolatry, but is it true? When we consider the statement, 'the shorter reading is preferable', can we see any reason, apart from repetition and tradition, why it should be right or wrong? We can produce reasons for thinking sometimes that the longer text is right and sometimes that the shorter text is right, but that will not demonstrate our maxim.

Hort was on stronger grounds with the precept *lectio difficilior praestat*, but this has to be used with discretion. It is no excuse for preferring nonsense. Nonetheless it served to create a way of escape from the tyranny of the best manuscript.

When all is said and done, Hort has taken up the analysis of the witnesses which we owe to Semler and Griesbach. He has refined and developed it to become a more effective instrument of textual criticism than they had, and, if we may have second thoughts about some of his theses, we must recognize that he made substantial contributions to the textual criticism of the New Testament.

C. von Soden

Von Soden, in at least one direction, followed Griesbach more closely than did Hort. He renames his three classes of witnesses. Griesbach's Alexandrine becomes his Hesychian (= H), his Byzantine becomes von Soden's *Koine*

(= K) and his Western becomes von Soden's Jerusalem (= I). Hort's
Neutral is ignored. The I class becomes even more a collection of miscellaneous items than it was with Hort. Von Soden's analysis rests on a vast
collection of evidence, considerably greater than that assembled by
Tischendorf, though Tischendorf had made the more substantial discoveries.

In establishing his text, von Soden often followed the reading of two
of his classes against a third, thus choosing the other possibility than that
followed by Hort. He did not do this slavishly, allowing weight to internal
considerations as well as to attestation. His method had one commendable
consequence in that it took the evidence of the witnesses of the K class
seriously. This did not mean that von Soden tried to reinstate the T.R. in
its old position. Hort had done his work too well for that.

Again with von Soden we notice that intrinsic considerations influenced
his decisions. Some of the points made in his entries in his apparatus are
illuminating even today.

Thus far scholars had built on the Griesbach analysis by the First World
War. Of the possibilities mentioned earlier in our discussion, Hort in the
main pinned his faith to one class of witnesses and von Soden tended to
take a vote from all three. As far as construction of the text went, Hort
was the more influential and perhaps for two reasons. The first was that
he got in first and the second that von Soden presented his material and
arguments in an awkward and obscure manner made worse by the introduction of a new and unsatisfactory mass of symbols for his Greek manuscripts. Nonetheless he made a real contribution to the study of the text,
both in his massive apparatus and in his readiness to reconsider earlier
judgements.

D. Kirsopp Lake and Streeter

After the First World War, textual studies took a fresh start. There were
important discoveries of hitherto unknown manuscripts, new analyses of
the great body of material, and fresh attempts to arrive at the original
form of the New Testament text. All this assumed, and was built on, the
work of earlier scholars.

Kirsopp Lake (who had already before 1914 made an important contribution to these studies) and B. H. Streeter played an important part in
these developments. Between them they added another class or family of
manuscripts to those already recognized, the Caesarean. In his diagram
illustrating his theory of local texts,[4] Streeter has three primary divisions,
Alexandrian, Eastern and Western, and a revised text, the Byzantine. Each
of these is in two subdivisions, except the Byzantine text. The Caesarean

constitutes the principal subdivision of the Eastern type. While he was not committed to the details of Streeter's diagram, Kirsopp Lake, whose research did so much to establish the Caesarean as a type of text, would doubtless have agreed in its main features.

In it, unlike von Soden's hypothesis, the Byzantine text occupied a secondary position, so that Kirsopp Lake and Streeter agreed with Hort at this point.

Next Streeter, and, we may infer from the *Harvard Theological Review*,[5] Kirsopp Lake, had a view about the recovery of the original form of the text. As expounded by Streeter it runs:

'The ultimate aim of textual criticism is to get back behind the diverse local texts to a single text, viz. to that which the authors originally wrote. But the high road to that conclusion is first to recover the local texts of the great churches, and then to work back to a common original that will explain them all.'[6]

This statement leaves certain processes unexplained. How are we to recover or reconstruct the local texts from the readings of their witnesses? And how are we to work back to the common original from these local texts? We may not even be right in assuming that the same method is used in the two processes. In any case Streeter leaves us in the dark.

Kirsopp Lake is more informative. In the *Harvard Theological Review* he tells us:

'No single manuscript is as good as the quotations in the Demonstratio, but the group of manuscripts taken together represent very exactly the text which Eusebius used. Codex Theodorae (565), which is certainly the best of the group, has been corrected by an Ecclesiastical type of text in perhaps 20 or 30 per cent of variants, but in almost every case one or another codex of the group supports Eusebius, and a reconstruction based on the principle of eliminating Ecclesiastical readings in each manuscript would produce a text substantially true to type. This has been attempted in Excursus IV.'[7]

Excursus IV gives the reconstructed Caesarean text for Mark 1, 6 and 11. We may notice that no one witness is followed all the way, nor is a decision reached by any system of voting by the witnesses. Kirsopp Lake uses one intrinsic criterion, agreement with the Ecclesiastical or Syrian text. We may also suspect here and there the influence of Kirsopp Lake's own preferences as in the punctuation of Mark 1: 1–4.

It is interesting that Kirsopp Lake proceeded no further with his work of reconstructing the Caesarean text of Mark. We may suspect that he became less optimistic about it as time went on, but we have no clear evidence on this point.

How either Streeter or Kirsopp Lake would have chosen the text of the common original from the reconstructed local texts we have no means of knowing. Perhaps Streeter did not know.

We notice as a kind of footnote to the eliciting of the Caesarean text that later scholars, particularly in Spain, divided it into two, a pre-Caesarean and a Caesarean proper. This complication did not affect the basic analysis very much, nor did it, in matters of principle, take us far beyond the point reached by Kirsopp Lake and Streeter.

One important point has been raised by Streeter's statement about local texts and the common original. How do we decide between variant readings in working back from texts to a common original? It is at this point that the use of expressions like 'family' and 'genealogical method' becomes important.

We mentioned earlier on Lachmann's treatment of the manuscripts of Lucretius. He showed that the principal manuscripts of Lucretius had relationships between them which could be accurately described in a genealogy or family tree. This meant that at a number of points a decision could be made between variant readings with complete confidence, because the relationship of the manuscripts permitted only one reading to be that of the ancestor or archetype.

When we turn to the New Testament we find a different state of affairs. There are manuscripts which are related among themselves in such a way that their relationship can be expressed in terms of a family tree. Such are family 1 and family 13. We may add that the relationship between B and P^{75}, so ably explored by Dr Martini in Luke, can probably be expressed in genealogical terms. With a fair degree of confidence it is possible, for example, to reconstruct the text of the archetype of family 13 in many particulars, and this is possible just because we can state the relationships among themselves of the manuscripts composing the family with fair precision.

The majority of the New Testament manuscripts are in no such condition. They cannot be related in this way among themselves. Much less can any genealogical tree be constructed to cover the New Testament manuscripts as a whole. Consequently the rigorous arguments based on a genealogy such as that for the manuscripts of Lucretius cannot be made to apply, and the imprecise grouping of manuscripts in local texts or text-types, such as the Alexandrian, cannot be employed in this way.

E. An assessment of Griesbach's influence

Before we pursue this consideration further, we must bring the matter back to Griesbach and Scrivener's comment on his work. This review of much work on the text from Griesbach's day until the Second World War seems to belie, at any rate, the implications of Scrivener's statement 'that Griesbach's theory is universally abandoned by modern scholars'. It would be much to expect that subsequent scholars would maintain Griesbach's theory unchanged in all its details, but I have argued in the preceding pages that the scholars whose work we have considered built on the foundations laid by Semler and Griesbach. They had greater resources and they modified and developed their work in various directions, but they shared with them the observation that the bulk of the witnesses to the text of the New Testament fell into a few broadly discernible groups and that this grouping had some relevance to the attempt to recover the original form of the text.

We may notice that even today terms like Alexandrian, Western and Byzantine are current in the textbooks, though they do not appear to help us much toward the solution of our problem. If we have labelled a reading as Alexandrian or Western or Syrian, have we really discovered thereby that it is any more likely to be original? Nonetheless, in using these terms we bear witness to the influence of Griesbach's analysis until today.

Perhaps I should note here that I have not mentioned all the scholars who were indebted to Griesbach, but only those who have subsequently influenced textual studies. Scholz, for example, who did service in textual criticism in his own day, was influenced by Griesbach's theory about the classification of manuscripts.

II The validity of Griesbach's text-critical theory

A. Preliminary remarks

We have now to look at the other part of Scrivener's verdict on Griesbach's theory, namely, that 'there is no valid reason for believing it to be true'. If the theory was much more influential than Scrivener allowed, we may not rest content with his judgement about its truth.

Before we tackle this question we ought to consider how Scrivener came to make his judgement. In his survey of scholars who have worked on the text of the New Testament, in his *Introduction*, Scrivener pronounces on them severally according as they have approved or failed to approve the T.R. He writes of Griesbach:

'The joint testimony of two classes was, *ceteris paribus*, always to prevail; and since the very few documents which comprise the Alexandrian and Western recensions seldom agree with the Byzantine even when at variance with each other, the numerous codices which make up the third family would thus have about as much share in fixing the text of

Scripture, as the poor citizens whose host was included in one of Servius Tullius' lower classes possessed towards counterbalancing the votes of the wealthy few that composed his first or second.'[8]

Griesbach had failed to give to the T.R. the respect that was its due, and so, in Scrivener's eyes, Griesbach stands condemned. Beyond this, none of the scholars we have mentioned took over Griesbach's theory just as it stood. This appears to have been enough for Scrivener to have issued his condemnation. That he was so widely influential and that there was at least a core of truth in his theory counts for nothing against the perversity of his attitude to the T.R. Scrivener speaks with kindness and respect of Griesbach himself (he could hardly do otherwise) but this cannot conceal the sweeping condemnation of his judgement.

But was Scrivener right? Here we seem to be at an *impasse*. As we noticed earlier, the vast majority of our witnesses to the text of the New Testament seem to fall into a few broadly discernible groups, and the conviction that this grouping had some relevance to the attempt to recover the original form of the text has been widely held. On the other hand we must acknowledge that none of the attempts to use these groupings to this end have been successful, either in the more flexible form with which Griesbach himself operated, or in the more precisely formulated and more systematically practised forms that his successors used.

How are we to deal with this difficulty? We noticed earlier that alongside the theories of classes or families of manuscripts there had grown up a body of expertise which had come into being simply by practising the art. Examples are Hort's note on Matt. 13: 35 and on Luke 22: 19–20. Many other instances can be found up and down the 'Notes on Select Readings'.[9] This practical wisdom, if such we may call it for the moment, consisted in a series of maxims and principles which had only been formulated in a general sort of way and had not been fully developed into a theory of textual criticism. Nonetheless they were independent of any genealogical theory or any cult of a best manuscript and could, on occasion, lead to conclusions of real value. No one, however, had attempted to construct a text relying solely on such rules and principles. The Dutch scholar, Baljon, had here and there followed their indications in constructing his text, but in the main his procedure was more conventional.

B. The refinement of general principles

Meanwhile work in Germany and Great Britain was leading to a new development going beyond these rules and principles and amounting to a new way of handling the problem.

1 Wellhausen

In Germany Wellhausen, mainly in his commentaries on, and introduction
to, the Gospels was more systematic. He limited himself to a small number
of witnesses to the text, including D, and applied principally the criterion
of Semitic influence to the evidence. Other things being equal he preferred
the reading which reflected Semitic idiom to the reading which did not.
For the moment the important thing about this procedure is that it used
not a classification of the manuscripts but a linguistic criterion as the
means of eliciting the original form of the text.

2 Lietzmann

At the same time we may notice H. Lietzmann's judicious introduction to
the subject in his commentary 'An die Römer' in his *Handbuch zum Neuen
Testament*[10] and his discussion of particular passages such as Rom. 8: 24.

3 Burkitt

In Great Britain we may notice, first of all, the work of F. C. Burkitt. He
grew up in the shadow of Westcott and Hort in Cambridge, England, and
so it is the more remarkable that he showed such independence of judgement. An early indication of this is in his article on 'Text and Versions'
where he discusses a small group of readings in *Encyclopaedia Biblica*.[11]
Among them Matt. 6: 8; 11: 5; 21: 44; 22: 35; 25: 1; Luke 11: 33; John
12: 8; Acts 4: 6 deserve notice.

In his book *The Gospel History and its Transmission*,[12] Burkitt exam-
ined a number of passages in connection with the Ur-Markus hypothesis
and, on the basis of his solution of the Synoptic Problem, discussed the
text of Luke 8: 44; 18: 30; 22: 62. This discussion forms the core of the
comparable discussion by Streeter,[13] where more variant readings are
dealt with along the same lines.

Let me emphasize, by the way, that in citing these instances I am not
concerned to discuss at the moment where Burkitt and Streeter are right
or wrong in their views of the Synoptic Problem, but only to point out
that they too are not using the classification of manuscripts to decide on
readings but an hypothesis about the relations and composition of the
Synoptic Gospels. Thus they are moving outside the area of Griesbach's
principal hypothesis.

4 Turner

C. H. Turner provides another example. In earlier discussion he had treated
one or two texts such as Luke 17: 29, but his chief contribution came in a
series of studies in 'Marcan Usage' in the *Journal of Theological Studies*[14]

to which I can add one short unpublished paper.

His initial view of what he was doing can be stated in his own words: 'Dr. Hort, in the great *Introduction* to his edition of the Greek Testament, lays down as fundamental the principle that "Knowledge of documents should precede final judgement upon readings" (#38), using capitals in the text and italics in the table of contents to call special attention to the importance of the words. I want to enter a similar plea for what I conceive to be an even more important principle, namely that "Knowledge of an author's usage should precede final judgement", alike as to readings, as to exegesis, and – in this case – as to the mutual relations of the Synoptic Gospels. The studies that follow are intended to be a contribution to the textual criticism and the exegesis of St Mark, and also to the better understanding of that department of the Synoptic problem which is concerned with the agreements of Matthew and Luke against Mark.'[15]

Here Turner enunciates a principle, namely 'that the style of an author is a significant criterion for his text'.

Turner clearly hoped that the use of this criterion would help to clear up problems in the relation of the Synoptic Gospels and hints at issues like Ur-Markus and refers to the agreements in our texts between Matthew and Luke against Mark where they are closely parallel. He does not, however, claim to be using any hypothesis about the relations of the Synoptic Gospels as a means for determining their texts, even though his own sympathies are clear.

In the course of his investigations Turner adds another criterion, that of better and worse Greek. In the third of his investigations, that into εἰς and ἐν in Mark, he writes at the end of the study:

'These instances, taken together – even after allowance is made for the two, 2 and 10, where ἐν appears instead of εἰς, and another, 17, where εἰς has ousted ἐπὶ rather than ἐν – do seem to establish a definite tendency in Marcan usage for εἰς to encroach on ἐν. That encroachment is not peculiar to Mark, though among New Testament writings there is none where the encroachment is so marked as in his Gospel. The process which was commencing in the common speech of our Lord's time has ended in the complete supersession of ἐν in modern Greek. But it was still resented by scribes and scholars, or at any rate by some of them, in the first and second centuries A.D.'[16]

and a little further on:

'The evidence of undoubted cases like 1, 15, 18, 20, may fairly be used to turn the scale where the evidence is divided, and justifies the conclusion that the scribe of codex B or its ancestor, admirable as is his general fidelity, did not rise superior to the temptation of altering an incorrect idiom into accordance with the traditions of literary Greek.'[17]

We should not exaggerate the range of Turner's observations, important as they are. His studies of Marcan usage were pioneer work and left much still to be done. His views of what constituted literary and non-literary Greek are rudimentary and rarely documented. He did not apply his methods to the Syrian text as he seems to have accepted Hort's discussion of it as final. He did not take into account the influence of Semitic idiom. Lastly he did not have at his disposal the fuller apparatus of Legg's Mark.

Nonetheless, his work is of fundamental importance and has been a stimulus to subsequent scholars in that he presented a series of systematic explorations of the language of Mark, hitherto unparalleled. Except where Semitic influence was concerned, scholars, where they dissented from Westcott and Hort, had been content to discuss individual readings rather than whole classes of variants.

The consequences were greater than Turner realized. We can see this from his occasional comments on the leading manuscripts of Mark. In an article entitled 'A Textual Commentary on Mark i', he first wrote about the Western text:

'Now if all these types of so-called Western text are united against the Alexandrian or Neutral text, it is obvious that, whether we regard its age or its wide diffusion, it makes a very strong claim for consideration, and a claim that is stronger now, owing to fresh discoveries, than it was in the days of Dr Hort. But to speak in this sense of a Western text seems to me now so entirely misleading that I prefer to revert to Griesbach's usage, and mean by Western the authorities that are Western geographically. If the word is used in the other and wider sense, it is better to be careful to put it into inverted commas as "Western": it is better still, I think, to drop "Western" in this sense as far as possible, and to group these types of text, whether Western or Eastern, under the common heading "unrevised". Such a heading admittedly implies a contrast with a type of text that is revised, and I feel no doubt that the text contained in the codex Vaticanus is the fruit of a revision – a revision very carefully and very skilfully done, so that B stands out as our best witness to the text of the Gospels, but a revision for all that.'[18]

In similar terms he writes elsewhere:

'Here then are twenty-eight Western readings from the second half of the Gospel, selected more or less by chance, though it is hoped that a good many of the most important variants between the Alexandrian and the Western texts are included. In something like two-thirds of them I should myself judge the Western variation to represent more or less certainly what the Evangelist wrote: in nos. 2, 3, 5, 10, 20, 21, 26, 28 I should not put it higher than that the Western reading has the better claim of the two: in 16 and 18 the issue is doubtful – the balance may even incline the other way. But if these conclusions are anywhere near the mark, it is abundantly clear that the accepted results of the textual criticism of the Gospels need to be re-opened and re-examined. And, with that aim in view, some further precision both as to the causes which account for the depravation of the Marcan original in the Alexandrian tradition (reproduced in our critical texts), and also as to what seems *prima facie* to be the relative value in the cases before us of the different authorities or groups of authorities on the "Western" side, will not be out of place.'[19]

He then goes on to give examples of the shortcomings of the Alexandrian text as he sees them.

It is clear that Turner saw his studies as giving the textual criticism of Mark a new look, but did not see clearly how much the influence of the classification of manuscripts on the reconstruction of the text was going to be reduced by his researches. This was understandable. Hort had immensely impressed the young scholars of the next generation and it was hard for them to shake off the fascination that his work had upon them.

We may suspect that Turner's own interests had encouraged him to develop his research in the way he did. His work on Cyprian, the Latin versions of the *Shepherd* of Hermas, the Latin collections of Canons and other material had given him a great respect for the Latin versions and manuscripts. When he turned to Old Latin manuscripts of the Gospels he was equally impressed and could not easily believe that Hort's harsh judgement on the Old Latin New Testament was entirely justified.

His contribution advanced textual studies, but has suffered by surviving only in volumes of the *Journal of Theological Studies* to which not everyone has access. Wellhausen's work has likewise not had the influence among textual critics that it might. The result is that the text of Mark, for example, can be discussed from beginning to end without a mention of either of these scholars.

C. Progress in the development of criteria for text-critical decisions

Nonetheless considerable progress has been made in the use of linguistic criteria. First, the author's usage has been established as a major criterion. It should often indicate readings which conform and readings which are out of harmony with the author's style. Beyond this various kinds of alteration have been suggested, principally the avoidance of Semitic idiom where it was out of line with Greek and the substitution of more literary for less literary Greek.

One other criterion was brought into play. It was an old principle of New Testament textual criticism that readings which brought similar passages verbally closer to each other were less likely to be right than readings which made them more unlike. This principle of assimilation or harmonization was extended to include certain views about the relationships among the Synoptic Gospels. This was an *argumentum ad hominem*. If all participants in the discussion accept the theory, then among themselves they can make inferences from it about the text. Where the theory is not accepted, there the inferences from it will also probably not be accepted.

We may notice at this point one shortcoming in the practice of textual criticism, a tendency to follow one or two criteria in agreement. For example, there is the principle of harmonization or assimilation mentioned above, that the reading which makes similar passages less alike is more likely to be original than the reading which brings them closer together.

For example, at Mark 10: 7-8 we have a longer and a shorter text where the longer text reads 'Because of this a man shall leave his father and mother and cleave to his wife and the two shall be one flesh.' Here the shorter text lacks 'and cleave to his wife'. In support of the shorter text we can suppose that Hort was influenced by the following considerations: (a) one reading is shorter than the other – *lectio breuior potior* – (b) the shorter reading is that of אB and friends, (c) the longer reading is much nearer the Septuagint and so can be regarded as assimilated to it, (d) it can also be explained as harmonization to Matt. 19: 5. The result is a reading which is near to nonsense and translators seem to have felt this; while editors of the Greek text often reproduce Westcott and Hort's shorter reading here, translators who presumably see the difficulty either translate the longer text or mistranslate the shorter text, according to the practice of the English translators that I have seen.

Let us look at the four reasons given above for preferring the shorter reading. As far as we have seen, (a) *lectio breuior potior*, is not true, (b) is now questioned, (c) and (d) have to be taken seriously but with the proviso *ceteris paribus* 'other things being equal'.

What is the position on the other side? First, we have seen that the shorter reading gives a questionable sense and, secondly, there is a paleographical explanation of the shorter text as derived from the longer, the recurrence of a group of some nine letters, the phenomenon that A. C. Clark called ὁμ. It is noteworthy the same variation occurs at Eph. 5: 31 when we have the same quotation with some witnesses giving us the shorter text and some the longer. Reasons (a), (c) and (d) would favour the shorter text, but as far as I can discover no modern editor has printed it. We may conclude that the longer text is right and that the considerations (a)-(d) listed above are inapplicable.

Another passage is Mark 4: 11. Here two readings which differ in word order are in question: (i) has Τὸ μυστήριον δέδοται τῆς βασιλείας, but (ii) has δέδοται τὸ μυστήριον τῆς βασιλείας. (i) differs from the parallel passages in Matt. 13: 11 and Luke 8: 10. In discussing this variation in order we can ignore other variants, interesting as they are.

Here the principle of harmonization seems to apply. (ii) may be regarded as an assimilation to Matthew's and Luke's word-order and so should be secondary. If that were all, we could decide like Hort and other editors that (i) gave us the original text.

As it happens that is not all. There is a linguistic criterion. I know of no other example in Mark of a verb being thrust between a noun and its dependent genitive. Nor is this linguistic phenomenon an accident. Mark's Greek, as is generally recognized, shows the influence of Semitic idiom. We may note, for example, how rarely he will put a genitive before the noun on which it depends. In the same way we may regard (i) as offending against Marcan usage.

Further we know that a more sophisticated word-order was a mark of a more literary style, as we can see from a writer like Philo. We may then regard (i) as a stylistic correction and (ii) as the original reading despite the fact that it brings Mark more nearly into line with Matthew and Luke.

We may then conclude that we cannot follow blindly one or two considerations without considering other possibilities. The nineteenth-century editors often followed the lead of one or two favourite manuscripts, and a criterion like harmonization to the neglect of all else. In particular language criteria fared poorly.

Since Turner's day the use of linguistic criteria has been developed further and other criteria have continued to be employed. Let us, for the moment, assume that they have achieved their end and that we have been able to recover the original text of the New Testament. We shall then have the starting-point for the subsequent developments in the text and, incidentally, be in a position to say how good or bad the text of any one manuscript is. We shall then be in a position to resolve the problem that Griesbach, following on Semler, set us: what is the significance of this classification of the manuscripts for the text of the New Testament?

If I may hazard an opinion, I doubt very much whether any one manuscript or class will show up so much better than others. If this is so, then Griesbach, in his unwillingness to commit himself to any one of his three classes, is justified over against Hort who asserted the superiority of his Neutral witnesses with few exceptions. We can of course so select our material, if we wish, as to give grounds for arguing that any one class of manuscripts is superior to the others. For example, I can maintain that because A and its allies have avoided the substitution of ἔφη for ἀποκριθεὶς εἶπεν (λέγει) five times out of six in Mark, therefore the Syrian witnesses are superior to אB which have the substitution all six times. Hort, partly depending on the argument from conflation, asserted that the Syrian text was secondary and of little value, but he ignored evidence of conflation in B and its friends. In this matter Hort, and Burgon, with his preference for the Syrian witnesses, and A. C. Clark, with his reliance on D and its allies for the text of Acts, are all misleading. If I may repeat my opinion, I suspect that none of our textual types or witnesses will prove to be clearly superior to the rest.

We may take this point further. A general majority of manuscripts is no guide of itself to the truth. Here Hort was right in saying that manuscripts were not to be numbered, and Burgon's attempt to revive the practice of counting manuscripts, however modified, does not convince. Even today when we read in Burgon's pages remarks like, 'overwhelming mass of evidence', 'the great bulk of the witnesses'[20] we may remain convinced that Hort was right.

Nor was Hort afraid to practise what he preached. If he rejected the number of manuscripts in support of a reading as a relevant consideration, this rejection acted both ways. Not only did he refuse to accept a reading just because it was supported by the overwhelming mass of the evidence, but also he chose some readings which occurred in very few witnesses. For example, at Matt. 19: 3 he chose the reading of one cursive 33 against the whole of the rest of the evidence so far reported. Whether Burgon would have thought this a greater offence than Hort's choice of the reading of D at Mark 16: 8 is a nice question, but the important point is that we find New Testament textual critics such as Tischendorf, Hort, Wellhausen, Burkitt and C. H. Turner preferring the reading of one or a few manuscripts against the overwhelming mass of the other evidence.

We may notice a frequent symptom of this procedure. If manuscripts are not to be counted when it comes to deciding between readings, then we may decide on readings on their intrinsic merits, a process usually called eclecticism, of which A. E. Housman was a sturdy protagonist. Unfortunately the word 'eclectic' has now become fashionable, and just as governments which we would hardly describe as 'democratic' glory in the designation, so we may experience a temptation to describe ourselves as eclectic when our hearts are really with the big battalions.

We may then acknowledge that the men who followed in Griesbach's footsteps have made their contributions to the progress of textual studies, even though they may seem not to have found a convincing solution to the problem that Griesbach bequeathed to them. They may, however, have gathered much material for a solution in the body of textual expertise which was built up by the above-named scholars and others even though for the most part they did not see the consequences of what they were doing in this matter.

Consequently we may think that Griesbach was, in his generation, wiser in refusing to commit himself to using his classification as a criterion for establishing the text. It may be tempting to dismiss his non-committal handling of his classification as evidence of the rudimentary and imperfect nature of his hypothesis as he propounded it, but events seem to prove him right in the reserve he displayed towards certain possible developments of his theory exemplified in the work of some later scholars.

III Conclusion

We have then ample grounds in his textual views for doing honour in this bicentenary to Griesbach. This long-suffering scholar made a contribution to the study of the New Testament text that is instructive even today. Scrivener, who adversely and openly criticised him, has borne witness to the character of the man himself:

'It seems needless to dwell longer on speculations which, however attractive and once widely received, will scarcely again find an advocate. Griesbach's text can no longer be regarded as satisfactory, though it is far less objectionable than such a system as his would have made it in rash or unskilful hands. His industry, his moderation, his fairness to opponents, who (like Matthaei) had shown him little forbearance, we may all imitate to our profit. His logical acuteness and keen intellectual perception fall to the lot of the few; and though they may have helped to lead him into error, and have even kept him from retracing his steps, yet on the whole they were worthily exercised in the good cause of promoting a knowledge of God's truth, and of keeping alive, in an evil and unbelieving age, an enlightened interest in Holy Scripture, and the studies which it serves to consecrate.' [21]

8

MODERN TEXT CRITICISM AND THE SYNOPTIC PROBLEM

Gordon D. Fee

That there is an interrelationship between textual criticism and the Synoptic Problem is the presupposition of most Synoptic studies. Nonetheless the specific nature of that relationship, especially as it affects the finding of solutions, is seldom spelled out, and, it would seem, is frequently neglected. This present paper is an attempt, partially at least, to fill up that lacuna.

As far as I know, the last comprehensive study which took both disciplines (textual and Synoptic criticism) seriously as being interrelated in arriving at solutions was B. H. Streeter's monumental *The Four Gospels* (1924). The first two large sections of his book were entitled 'The Manuscript Tradition' and 'The Synoptic Problem'. I may be pardoned for borrowing this *Gattung* for my paper. In part I, some suggestions are offered as to what 'modern textual criticism' means, by overviewing some recent work on method. Since I am part of the debate in this area, I can scarcely be expected to achieve objectivity! But I do hope I have been fair to all, and have touched on the essential issues. In part II, I offer some general observations on the chief area of interrelationship, the problem of harmonization/dis-harmonization. The illustrations in this section are basically concerned with the resolution of textual questions.

I Modern Textual Criticism

The term 'modern textual criticism' can mean precisely what its user intends it to mean. Since it has been suggested (probably rightly so) that I belong to that school of textual criticism which is involved in something like a 'Hort redivivus',[1] that will surely affect my use of this term. Therefore, some comments are in order with regard to four areas of recent discussion in this discipline which will inevitably enter the discussion of the interrelatedness between the two disciplines: (1) the problem of method, (2) the use and evaluation of the manuscript evidence, (3) the use of intrinsic and transcriptional evidence, and (4) the use of Patristic evidence. In the past few years I have offered modified Hortian responses to some current work in each of these areas.

A. *The problem of method (methodology)*

This, of course, is the basic problem in NT textual studies. If as most of us still believe, the quest for the original text is the basic task of our discipline, then how do we go about getting back to that elusive original? The modern answer is eclecticism, which means, as L. Vaganay defined it, that there should be

'no shutting up of the different branches of the science into watertight compartments; verbal criticism, external and internal criticism, all have their parts to play, and they must give each other mutual support. Understood in this way the eclectic method seeks a middle way between the two main systems that at present govern the editing of classical and mediaeval texts [i.e. wholly external; wholly internal]... The most efficacious method... borrows from these two schools the best they have to offer.'[2]

This is the currently reigning method as can be seen by the latest critical edition of a Greek text,[3] the latest handbooks,[4] and the most recent English translations (e.g. RSV, NEB, TEV, NIV).[5]

Discussion on eclecticism has gone in two directions: (1) concern over the method itself and (2) debate over the rigorous application of it, which abandons Vaganay's 'middle way' for wholly internal evidence.

(1) A generation ago there was a period of considerable uneasiness over the method itself. It was viewed as a 'patching up' of the 'failure' of Westcott and Hort (WH),[6] or as a partial method, belonging 'to a day like ours in which we know only that the traditional theory of the text is faulty but cannot yet see clearly to correct the fault'.[7] This unrest, however, was the direct result of a dilemma of our own making. On the one hand, there had been a general disavowal of WH's method and textual theory, but at the same time the critical texts which replaced WH had a distinctively Hortian face.

This phase of unrest seems now to be mostly past. The problem with WH was basically twofold: their use of the genealogical method and their high estimation of Codex Vaticanus (B). Genealogy in New Testament textual criticism was recognized as a failure, and B had come to be considered a recension.[8] However, we have now moved beyond both of the concerns in such a way that the 'Hortian face' of our texts is probably irrelevant. It only means that Hort was essentially on the right path.

For example, although Hort used the name 'genealogy' for his method, as a matter of fact, as several studies have shown,[9] that was something of a misnomer. Properly speaking, genealogy must deal with the descent of manuscripts and must reconstruct stemmata for that descent. This Hort never did; rather, he applied the method to text-types,[10] and he did so *not* to find the original text, but to eliminate the Byzantine manuscripts from further consideration. Even here, his final criterion for judging the Byzantines as late and basically without usefulness was the internal evidence of readings![11] The internal evidence of readings was also the predominant factor in the choice of his 'Neutral' text over the 'Western' and 'Alexandrian' texts as best representing the original text and his choice of B as best representing the 'Neutral' text-type.[12]

The point is that Hort did not come to his conclusions about the Byzantines and B by the genealogical method, at least not in its classical exposition. Rather, he applied his own kind of 'rational eclecticism' to the recovery of the original NT text. First, 'where the two ultimate witnesses agree, the text will be as certain as the extant documents can make it';[13] and secondly, where these disagree, one should generally follow B, for 'the superiority of [B] must be as great in the variations in which Internal Evidence of Readings has furnished no decisive criterion as in those which have enabled us to form a comparative appreciation of the two texts.'[14] Thus the only places where the WH text did not correspond to B were (1) where B had obvious scribal errors, (2) where B had occasionally picked up a corruption also attested in other ancient witnesses, and (3) in those few instances where the other text, D, had the better of it on the basis of the internal evidence of readings, most notably in the so-called Western non-interpolations.

Thus the WH use of genealogy no longer presents formidable methodological problems. The basic difference – and it is considerable – between WH and modern criticism has to do with the point of departure. Hort started with B (and its allies) and followed its text except in cases of obvious clerical errors or where internal principles dictated against it (e.g. the 'Western non-interpolations'; cf. Gal. 2: 12). Rational eclecticism, on the other hand, starts with readings, noting both the various intrinsic and transcriptional possibilities as well as the quality of the manuscripts which contain the various readings.

(2) The second part of the unrest over WH is also phasing out. Recent manuscript discoveries and studies have demonstrated conclusively that B does not represent a third-century revision of the text.[15] In fact P[75] has proven B to be precisely what Hort said it was: 'a very pure line of very ancient text'.[16] This does not mean, of course, that this very ancient text (P[75] B) is the original text. What has been removed is the uneasiness many felt over the facile simultaneous acceptance of *both* the 'recensional' character of B and its 'superiority' as a witness. Not all could live with

Kenyon's avowal that 'even if it is an edited text, it may be a well-edited text; and in the case of all ancient literature a well-edited text is the best we can hope for'.[17] What remained to be demonstrated was that this text is not only not a 'late' recension, but not a recension at all, at least not in any meaningful use of that term.[18] But that is the story of the next section. For now it should be noted that the Hortian appearance of our texts is irrelevant to the validity of our method.

B. *The use and evaluation of the manuscript evidence (external evidence)*

The second area of discussion over the eclectic method has to do with the role of external evidence in making textual choices. On the one hand, there are those who continue to see Hort as essentially on the right path. For example, the editors of the UBS Greek text frequently made their choice on the basis of 'strong external evidence'. As with Hort, this usually meant the combination of early Alexandrian and Western witnesses, or when these divided, the weight of the Alexandrian witnesses.

On the other hand, there are some who disavow the use of the manuscript evidence altogether in making textual choices.[19] Although this method is also called eclecticism – a rigorous application of it – it is not so in Vaganay's sense of the term, but rather is an *eclectic use of internal evidence*. This method reflects two recent trends: (1) the denial that any manuscript or group of manuscripts can be shown to be better than others, and, as a consequence, (2) the placing of all the evidence – Byzantines, Westerns, Egyptians, versions, Fathers – on the same footing.

(1) Because of the apparent weaknesses in Hort's method noted above, especially the conviction of the 'recensional' nature of B, there developed a full reaction to Hort which appears to have thrown out the baby with the bathwater. The logic of the reaction goes something like this: Since no manuscripts have escaped some degree of corruption, therefore all manuscripts must be judged on equal terms. Although no one practising 'rigorous' eclecticism has suggested that all manuscripts are equally corrupt, such a method affirms it in practice.

But recent studies have shown that Hort seems to have been right in this matter. Manuscripts *can* be judged as to their relative quality and such judgements *should* affect textual decisions. Gunther Zuntz, for example, demonstrated the text of P[46] to be 'of outstanding (though not absolute) purity'.[20] My own work on P[66] indicated that its singular and sub-singular readings, for example, are all of secondary character because they reflect the scribe's wildness and editorial tendencies to smooth out the text.[21]

More recently I subjected the manuscript tradition to a rigorous examination to see if one could set up a 'neutral' methodology for discovering

manuscript tendencies.[22] In Luke 10 and 11 all variants were assessed
where any kind of harmonization could have occurred. There were eighty-
five in all, although many of these were less likely to be assimilations than
to reflect other scribal errors or idiosyncrasies. But once all the variables
were taken into account, clear tendencies emerged. D and the Western
tradition had a profusion of such readings, as well as did the Byzantines.
In fact, all but one of the harmonizations judged to be major (large additions, significant wording, etc) belonged to the Westerns or the Byzantines.
Even among those judged to be minor (e.g. add/omit a pronoun in the
Evangelist's narrative) P^{75} and B were seldom guilty.

In the Gospel of John the controls seemed even more certain. Several
features of Johannine style (e.g. asyndeton, anarthrous personal names,
'vernacular possessives') were chosen because they were *both* Johannine
peculiarities in the New Testament *and* generally unidiomatic Greek, thus
on both counts bringing them under the canon of *lectio difficilior*. In each
case the results were the same: P^{75} B scored at the highest level; D fluctu-
ated, scoring high in some (anarthrous personal names) and low in others
(asyndeton); whereas the Byzantine tradition came out very badly at all
points.

Such judgements as these, it seems to me, *must* play a decisive role in
textual decision. And surely Hort was right in arguing further that the
superiority of manuscripts where they can be judged to be so on internal
grounds must carry over to those decisions where the internal evidence
offers us a stalemate.

(2) A corollary to the reaction against the idea of 'superior' manuscripts
has been the total disregard of manuscript relationships. Professor Kilpatrick
has argued that the majority of variants arose in the second century. This
has been partly supported by some of the papyrus finds, which have shown
some Byzantine readings to have existed earlier than was heretofore suspected.[23] But to move from that assertion to the practice of using singular
or sub-singular readings from mediaeval manuscripts seems to be an over-
reaction to Hort's genealogical method.

There is yet a place for genealogy, but under the rubric of manuscript
relationships. The logic here goes back to the early years of this science.
Manuscripts that can be shown to have clear textual affinities thereby bear
a single witness to a variant. In other words, certain kinds of counting do
not count. The obverse of this is that when two early, geographically and
textually diverse, witnesses share a variant, they are thereby independent
at that point and must converge upstream, either at the original or from a
single early copy. All of this has long been practised.

Professor Farmer has recently felt the logic of this procedure by trying to demonstrate the Alexandrian origin of the short ending of Mark.[24] Whereas he has made a strong case with regard to the Armenian evidence, the attempt to show Bobbiensis (k) as also related to B breaks down. Despite C. R. Williams to the contrary,[25] the textual affinities of k and B are extremely distant, and where they do merge, it is not because k has picked up Alexandrian readings, but usually because both independently bear witness to the 'original' text.

It is the fact of manuscript relationships, thus implying some kind of genealogy even if it is not known with precision, that makes textual choices supported by only one or two late manuscripts seem methodologically weak. One should be able to show *how* that manuscript escaped the corruption of all its relatives and *why* it should inspire confidence when it has singular readings before choosing its variant simply because the variant exists.

Thus again, Hort has led the way. We hesitate to follow him totally, because later discoveries and the refining of method have made us put more emphasis on 'comparative' than he did when speaking of the 'comparative purity' of ancient texts.

C. The use of intrinsic and transcriptional evidence (internal evidence)

Because the rigorous eclectics have had to rely solely on internal evidence, their attention has often been given to a greater refinement of author's stylistic traits and new assessments of possible scribal habits. For this we are greatly in their debt. The studies by C. H. Turner on Mark served as models in this regard,[26] and G. D. Kilpatrick has followed his lead with several significant studies.[27] Such studies have also appeared in the 'sources' debate in John[28] and in the Synoptic Problem.[29] My point here is simply to register a caution as to the use of this evidence.

One should not – indeed must not – assume authors to be consistent.[30] For in many cases there are just enough instances of variation in an author to render judgements uncertain at points where there is textual variation. Ordinarily a reading more in keeping with an author's style is judged to be original. But this can become a Procrustean bed which logically should lead to fullscale emendation. The fact is that a variant may be regarded as original *because it conforms* to the author's style, or it may be regarded as secondary *because a scribe may have made it conform* to the author's prevailing style.

Moreover, there are objections to be raised to the exclusive use of internal evidence. Hort cautioned long ago that 'in dealing with this kind of evidence equally competent critics often arrive at contradictory conclusions as to the same variations'.[31] This is recently illustrated in the differences between M.-E. Boismard and G. D. Kilpatrick on the canon of 'shorter reading'.[32] The problem here is that, having abandoned the outside corrective of the manuscript evidence, one is tempted to use one canon of internal criticism to the exclusion of others as 'more objective'.

For example, Professor Kilpatrick has greatly put us in his debt through his analysis of Atticism and its possible influence on the New Testament text.[33] But one must be cautious of turning possibility into probability, and probability into necessity. Atticism may indeed have been a factor in textual variation, but it can be shown that scribes were also influenced by the LXX.[34]

At every variant the full range of possibilities must be kept in view. Most of us still consider the manuscripts themselves to be a part of this 'full range'.

D. The use of Patristic evidence

The evidence of the early Fathers has long played a decisive role in textual criticism. It served as one of Hort's three criteria for dispensing with the Byzantines.[35] More recently, it has emerged on equal footing with the manuscript evidence in making textual decisions. In fact, M.-E. Boismard, with great erudition, has used it with the versional evidence to establish a whole new theory of textual origins and transmission in the Gospel of John.[36] But here especially cautions must be raised. From my close work with the Greek Fathers in the Gospels over several years, I make the following observations.[37]

(1) There is still need for good critical editions of all the Fathers, especially Chrysostom, Athanasius, and Didymus. My experience is that in every instance a critical edition of the Father moves his New Testament text in some degree *away from* the Byzantine tradition.[38] This suggests that the Father's texts have tended to be made to conform to the ecclesiastical text in much the same way as the manuscripts themselves. Furthermore, the more a Father was used and his text reproduced, the greater the degree of corruption toward the Byzantine text.

(2) Fathers may, and *must*, be evaluated in the same way as the manuscript evidence. Some cite with precision; others do not. Some show care for the wording *per se*; others adapt and paraphrase at will. How a Father cites is often as important as what.

(3) A 'shorter text' in the Fathers must always be used with caution;[39] and it can *never* be used with certainty when the 'omission' stands at the beginning or end of his citation. Our textual apparatuses are filled with such evidence and should be cleaned out as soon as possible.[40]

(4) It is possible to distinguish degrees of certainty as to whether a Father knew or used a given variant. There are some that are absolutely

certain: for example, where he comments on the very word(s) in dispute; or when he calls attention to other variations; or where further allusions or uses of the word(s) in question verify the citation itself. These should be distinguished from others, especially those which are extremely tenuous.

Finally, it should be noted that the listing of the Fathers in our modern editions of the Greek text cannot be trusted in the same way as the manuscript evidence. At any single point of variation one should check the Father's text for himself before citing his evidence. It will save grief and embarrassment.

The point is, the Fathers are still extremely important. At times they offer datable evidence every bit as good as any manuscript. But they present a 'mixed bag'; and therefore must be used with great care.

From this overview of 'where we are' in modern textual criticism we must turn to see how all of this is related to the Synoptic Problem.

II Textual criticism and the Synoptic Problem

The fact that J. J. Griesbach's work is foundational *both* for NT textual criticism *and* for Synoptic studies highlights the significant interrelatedness that exists between the two disciplines. This relationship goes both ways. On the one hand, Synoptic parallels and one's view of the Synoptic Problem will often be a factor in making textual choices; on the other hand, the establishment of the 'original' text of each Gospel is a mandatory prerequisite to the discussion of Synoptic relationships at its basic level, namely the comparison of the Gospels pericope by pericope.[41]

A. *Harmonization*

The first, and most obvious, area where the two disciplines overlap is that of harmonization. The problem here is especially complex, for we are dealing both with *authors* who used the text of one (or two) of the others in varying degrees of exactness and with *scribes* who in a variety of ways made parallel passages conform, but who also, by intent or otherwise, could disharmonize passages.

My more immediate concern in this section is with textual criticism. How does one make textual choices where Synoptic parallels are involved? Before looking at a few examples, several preliminary considerations should be noted.

(1) Harmonizations can be of four kinds: (a) between, or among, the Gospels, (b) within a single Gospel, (c) to the LXX, or (d) to a well-known phrase or idea quite apart from any immediate parallel. The addition of ἄρτον μὴ λίθον ἐπιδώσει αὐτῷ; ἢ καί at Luke 11: 11 by the majority of manuscripts is an example of the first kind (despite the split decision of

the UBS committee); the addition of ὅπου ὁ σκώληξ αὐτῶν οὐ τελευτᾷ καὶ τὸ πῦρ οὐ σβέννυται at Mark 9: 44 and 46 under the influence of 9: 48 is an example of the second; the addition of θρῆνος καί at Matt. 2: 18 by the majority illustrates the third; and the addition (probably) of τοῦ θεοῦ in Matt. 6: 33 is an example of the fourth. This problem is especially complex when two or three of these kinds can be active at any variation unit. However, the second and fourth of these types, because they are more immediate to the scribe, are more likely to have occurred in 'minor harmonizations' (see below) than the first type.

(2) One must be careful not to presuppose automatically what an author or scribe would have done. The problem with the authors here is probably greater than with the scribes. As is well known, Synoptic relationships are sometimes extremely close. For example, in the standard text of the Matthew/Luke account of John's preaching of repentance, Luke has sixty-four words and Matthew sixty-three; they have sixty-two words in common, without a single change of word-order and only one difference between a singular and a plural. Although this level of agreement occurs infrequently and is almost exclusively limited to the double tradition between Matthew and Luke, it is evidence that it can occur. For the most part, however, the writers tend to rewrite in varying degrees of exactness.

Copyists, on the other hand, show extremely strong tendencies to make passages conform to one another. Yet not every possible harmonization must be adjudged to be so. Harmonization is far more likely to have occurred in the sayings of Jesus than in the Evangelist's narratives; similarly it is far more likely to have occurred in major additions/omissions or with significant words (= 'major harmonizations') than with add/omit pronouns, conjunctions, articles, etc, or with word-order (= 'minor harmonizations'). These latter especially may be due to all kinds of other factors. Those of us who are aware of 'harmonization' *only* because we have a Gospel synopsis before us cannot presume that early copyists worked from synopses (!) or that their memories of parallels were so keen as to recall the jots and tittles.

(3) By the very historical fact of the greater use of Matthew in the early Church as compared with Mark or Luke, the manuscript traditions of the latter two have far more variants that could be attributed to harmonization than does Matthew, and between them, Mark far more so than Luke. It is almost inevitable that this factor will weigh heavily in making textual choices in Matthew and Mark.

(4) Similarly, although no manuscript or manuscript tradition has escaped some degree of harmonizing corruption to its text, this phenomenon is a hallmark of the Western and Byzantine traditions, whereas the

earlier Alexandrians are relatively pure at this point. Again, this factor simply cannot be lightly put aside when making textual choices. How great a role it plays will undoubtedly vary from scholar to scholar. Its influence on the editors of the UBS Greek text can be seen in two 'D' readings in Luke 11: 33 and 12: 27. In 12: 27 they retained a harmonization where only D and the Old Syriac have a disharmonized reading; in 11: 33 they retained the harmonized reading in brackets, probably because the early Alexandrians were split.

(5) It should candidly be admitted that our predilections toward a given solution of the Synoptic Problem will sometimes affect textual decisions. Integrity should cause us also to admit to a certain amount of inevitable circular reasoning at times. A classic example of this point is the well-known 'minor agreement' between Matt. 26: 67–8 and Luke 22: 64 (// Mark 14: 65) of the 'addition' τίς ἐστιν ὁ παίσας σε. B. H. Streeter,[42] G. D. Kilpatrick,[43] and W. R. Farmer[44] each resolve the textual problem of Mark in a different way. In each case, a given solution of the Synoptic Problem has affected the textual decision.

At this point one could offer copious illustrations. The four given here were chosen partly because in each case they illustrate in a different way the complexity of the textual problems involved and partly because in some instances I disagree with the conclusions of some of my colleagues.

(a) The choice between ὑποκάτω and ὑποπόδιον at Matt. 22: 44 // Mark 12: 36 // Luke 20: 43 especially illustrates the complexities involved. First, there is similar textual variation in all three Gospels; secondly, all known Greek manuscripts of the LXX read ὑποπόδιον, as do all manuscripts of Heb. 1: 13; thirdly, although the critical editions disagree among themselves, they all agree that the Synoptists do not all have the same reading. The variations in the Synoptic accounts have the following support:

Matt. 22: 44	ὑποκάτω	ℵ B D G L U Z Γ Θ 047 λ 22 472 2145
	ὑποπόδιον	E F H K M S U V W Δ 33 1241 pler
Mark 12: 36	ὑποκάτω	B D W 28
	ὑποπόδιον	ℵ L rell
Luke 20: 43	ὑποκάτω	D
	ὑποπόδιον	ℵ B L W rell

In Matthew and Luke the text is certain. The widespread disharmonized form ὑποκάτω must be the original in Matthew; on the other hand, the fact that D's singular readings are generally suspect, plus its proclivities toward harmonization (in this case to Matthew), indicates that ὑποπόδιον is original in Luke. The text of Mark is less certain. Here one's judgement of the manuscripts as well as his disposition toward a Synoptic solution play a role. For those, as myself, inclined toward Marcan priority, then the ὑποκάτω is original with Mark, which Matthew copied, but Luke 'corrected'. For those inclined toward Matthean priority, the textual choice in Mark is less certain. Did Mark copy Matthew or Luke (more likely) in this case? If Luke, then B D W 28 represent conformity to Matthew by early scribes.[45]

(b) The next illustration is taken from the parallel passages: Matt. 4: 17 and Mark 1: 14b-15. The texts read as follows:

Matt. 4: 17	Mark 1: 14b-15
' Απὸ τότε ἤρξατο ὁ Ιησοῦς	
κηρύσσειν	κηρύσσων τὸ εὐαγγέλιον τοῦ
καὶ λέγειν·	θεοῦ καὶ λέγων, ὅτι πεπλήρωται
μετανοεῖτε· ἤγγικεν γὰρ	ὁ καιρὸς καὶ ἤγγικεν
ἡ βασιλεία τῶν οὐρανῶν.	ἡ βασιλεία τοῦ θεοῦ· μετανοεῖτε
	καὶ πιστεύετε ἐν τῷ εὐαγγελίῳ

The variant add/omit μετανοεῖτε...γάρ in Matt. 4: 17 illustrates both the complexity of the possibilities of harmonization (internal and external) as well as the need for greater care in using Patristic evidence. This omission here made the margin of WH and has been opted for by Kilpatrick[46] and J. N. Birdsall,[47] where apart from any Greek evidence Codex Bobbiensis and the Old Syriac, supported by early Fathers, are said to preserve the original dissimilated reading. Kilpatrick further argues that this is supported by Matthew's tendency to dissimilate John the Baptist and Jesus.

The alleged Patristic support of this omission is totally deceiving. Justin's 'citation' is a loose adaptation (καὶ αὐτὸς λέγων ὅτι ἐγγύς ἐστιν ἡ βασιλεία τῶν οὐρανῶν Dial. 51). This is an *argumentum e silentio* of the worst kind. So with Clement (*Protr.* IX. 87 3): βοᾷ γοῦν ἐπείγων εἰς σωτηρίαν αὐτός· ἤγγικεν ἡ βασιλεία τῶν οὐρανῶν. Furthermore, both of these could just as easily be citations of Mark, conforming to Matthew's use of τῶν οὐρανῶν (cf. W). The partial support by Origen, of which Kilpatrick says 'the reading seems at least to have been known to Origen' is completely in error. In his commentary on John at the beginning of book X, Origen cites Matt. 4: 17 in full, and includes the disputed words. Likewise a little later (X. 11), in a comment on Heracleon's exegesis of John 2: 12, he cites from μετανοεῖτε on. In two closely following citations, where his interest is only in this clause, he then cites ἤγγικεν κ.τ.λ. without μετανοεῖτε. Origen, therefore, knew nothing of a text of Matthew which omitted these words, a conclusion further attested in the catenae fragments of his commentary on Matthew. Eusebius' evidence is scarcely more certain. In Ps. 84: 13 he has a citation similar to Clement's. In the *Demonstratio* (IX. 8) he has a long citation of Matt. 4: 12-25. Most of the citation seems

to follow the text with care. However at v. 17 he writes: ἀπὸ τότε γοῦν
ἤρξατο ὠ Ἰησοῦς κηρύσσεω καὶ λέγεω, ὅτι ἤγγικεν ἡ βασιλεία τῶν
οὐρανῶν. This is adapted just enough to give doubts as to the Greek text
Eusebius actually knew. Among the Fathers, that leaves only the evidence
of Victor of Antioch in his commentary on Mark.[48] But his reference is
completely puzzling in that he cites the full text in one paragraph, while
in the next paragraph he seems to deny the preaching of repentance to
Jesus.[49] The explanation of this, however, lies *not* in his text of Matthew,
but in his attempt to reconcile Matthew with Mark as to what Jesus
preached *after* he went to Capernaum. In any case this is the *only*
Patristic evidence for the 'omission', and it is flimsy indeed.

The point, then, is that we have here not a widespread early witness to
Matthew's original, but the coincidence of omission in two versional texts,
the omissions of which at other points do not inspire confidence in their
originality here. It is these traditions, either dependent on an earlier source
or more likely independently but typically, which dissimilate John the
Baptist and Jesus. Here, then, is an example of an author's redaction
effecting an internal assimilation, which probably for theological reasons
was disharmonized by scribes.

(c) The next example is taken from the parallel texts of Matt. 3: 1-2
and Mark 1: 4 (cf. also Luke 3: 2-3). These verses read as follows:

Matt. 3: 1-2	Mark 1: 4
παραγίνεται	ἐγένετο
Ἰωάννης ὁ βαπτιστὴς κηρύσσων	Ἰωάννης ὁ βαπτίζων
ἐν τῇ ἐρήμῳ τῆς Ἰουδαίας,	ἐν τῇ ἐρήμῳ
λέγων· μετανοεῖτε·	κηρύσσων βάπτισμα μετανοίας
ἤγγικεν γὰρ ἡ βασιλεία τῶν	εἰς ἄφεσιν ἀμαρτιῶν.
οὐρανῶν.	

The use of ὁ βαπτίζων or βαπτίζων in Mark 1: 4 is related to a whole
set of variants in Mark where either internal, cross-Synoptic, or common-
idiom harmonization has taken place. The evidence:

Mark 1: 4   ὁ βαπτίζων ℵ B L Δ 33 892 bo
              βαπτίζων rell
   (// Matt. 3: 1 ὁ βαπτιστής – no variation)

Mark 6: 14   ὁ βαπτίζων ℵ A B pler
              ὁ βαπτιστής D
   (// Matt. 14: 2 ὁ βαπτιστής – no variation)

Mark 6: 24   τοῦ βαπτίζοντος ℵ B L Δ Θ 28 pc
              τοῦ βαπτιστοῦ A C D W Byz pler
   (no Syn. parallel)

Mark 6: 25 τοῦ βαπτίζοντος L 700 892
τοῦ βαπτιστοῦ ℵ A B C D Byz rell
(// Matt. 14: 8 – τοῦ βαπτιστοῦ – no variation)

Mark 8: 28 τὸν βαπτίζοντα 28 565
τὸν βαπτιστήν ℵ A B D Byz rell
(// Matt. 16: 14; Luke 9: 19 – τὸν βαπτιστήν – no variation)

Besides these Matthew has three other instances and Luke two with ὁ βαπτιστής without variation. J. K. Elliott, arguing from internal evidence alone, has opted for ὁ βαπτίζων as Mark's style and therefore to be read in each instance.[50] But that is probably too easy. That is surely true at 6: 14 and 24, and probably to be preferred at 1: 4 (this was never made to conform to ὁ βαπτιστής because the other 'correction' of dropping the article came to predominate). Furthermore, the normal direction of harmonization is to the more common ὁ βαπτιστής . But in 6: 25 another kind of harmonization was carried out by two scribes (700 and an earlier exemplar of L and 892) – to the more immediate context of 6: 24 (they are among the first to believe that an author must be consistent!). That factor should also decide in favour of βαπτιστής at 8: 28, but here because it is otherwise difficult to explain how 28 and 565 alone among their immediate and more distant relatives both escaped corruption. Thus we have examples of what is often found in the textual tradition – a scribe making an author's text conform to his own, albeit more unusual, style.

(d) In his article on Atticism, Professor Kilpatrick has argued that wherever there is a variant between the ἀποκριθεὶς εἶπεν idiom and ἔφη, the former is to be preferred as original because the latter is an Atticistic 'improvement'. Professor Kilpatrick maintains: 'No Greek at any period, left to himself, would say or write ἀποκριθεὶς εἶπεν.'[51]

I have already responded to this argument at some length and have shown that Biblical scribes were not 'left to themselves'. Especially in the Gospel of John the manuscript evidence demonstrates the exact opposite, that scribes tended more often toward the full Semitic idiom than away from it. Even John Chrysostom does it in two places where there is no manuscript support![52]

The textual variation at Mark 9: 38 // Luke 9: 49 presents another interesting case of this variation in terms of Synoptic relationships:

Mark 9: 38   Luke 9: 49

ἔφη αὐτῷ ὁ Ἰωάννης   ἀποκριθεὶς δὲ ὁ Ἰωάννης εἶπεν

In Luke's Gospel the *only* known variation is in codex 16, which reads καὶ ἀποκριθείς for ἀποκριθεὶς δέ. However, in Mark there are the following variations:

ἔφη . . .	א Β Δ Θ Ψ 33 579 892 1071
ἔφη . . . λέγων	L
ἀποκριθεὶς δὲ ἔφη . . .	C 1573 a
ἀπεκρίθη δὲ . . . λέγων	Α Γ Π Byz pler
ἀπεκρίθη . λέγων	D 21 517 954 1012 1574 1675 pc
ἀπεκρίθη δὲ . . . καὶ λέγει	fam 1 544 b r i
ἀπεκρίθη δὲ . . . καὶ εἶπεν	28
καὶ ἀποκριθεὶς . . . λέγει	565 700
καὶ ἀποκριθεὶς . . . εἶπεν	W fam 13ᵖˡ

Several other data are significant here: (1) Matthew and Luke fluctuate regularly between these two idioms, but with much less textual variation than one finds in Mark. This is clear evidence that both can be used by first-century Greek writers. (2) Wherever ἔφη appears in Mark in Nestle–Aland, there is always this multiple variation. (3) In Mark such variation occurs irregularly either with ἀποκριθεὶς εἶπεν or with εἶπεν by itself. But when variation does occur it can go either way. (4) The other occurrences of ἔφη in Mark are all in Synoptic parallels, but in no case does the parallel read ἔφη. On the other hand, as in this case the parallel sometimes reads the ἀποκριθεὶς εἶπεν idiom.

The best explanation of all these data, and of the multiple variation in this passage, is *not* the Atticizing of Mark's text, but rather its harmonization either to Mark's more common idiom or to its Synoptic parallel (less likely). If this is so, then either Luke Semitizes Mark or Mark Atticizes Luke!

B. *Textual principles and the Synoptic Problem*

It was Griesbach who first spelled out clearly the first principle of textual criticism: that reading is to be preferred as the original which best explains the existence of all the others. It is always under this rubric that the further questions of scribal tendencies and author's style must be asked. Consciously or unconsciously, this is also the *sine qua non* in resolving the Synoptic Problem: given that there is direct literary dependence among our Gospels, that Gospel is to be preferred as having priority which best explains how the others came into existence. It seems to this textual critic that this must include *both* the arrangement of the materials (order, form, etc) *and* the close study of the parallels.[53]

In this instance, of course, there are crucial differences: (1) We are dealing with more complex issues, since we have three known documents plus unknown hidden factors, such as the possibility of written fragments and the tenacity of oral tradition. (2) Whereas copyists (apart from some early expressions in the Western tradition) are trying basically to reproduce an exemplar, Gospel writers are doing the precise opposite. The Gospels they are using are not adequate for them (or their community), and they are *rewriting* the story of Jesus, not merely copying it. For this reason, as E. P. Sanders has demonstrated,[54] one cannot speak of tendencies in the Synoptic tradition with the same sense of confidence one has about scribal tendencies. One who is rewriting, and who also has access to many other sources (either written or oral) unknown to us may do things which from our perspective are inexplicable. It is for these reasons that J. A. Fitzmyer said at the Pittsburgh Festival: 'The history of Synoptic research reveals that the problem is *practically insoluble.*'[55]

With Fitzmyer's judgement I tend to agree. Nonetheless there must be some kind of solution – either one of the existing ones or one yet to come. Our problem is that we have not yet reached agreement on the known; whereas the real problems most likely lie with the unknown. The consensus of even fifteen years ago is less certain today. The Griesbach Hypothesis is receiving a new and full hearing, and gaining converts. Although some have felt it could be 'falsified',[56] others have doubted whether it has been so in fact.[57] But the real question is not whether it can be falsified, any more than whether the two-source theory can (if indeed either could be; then of course we must look elsewhere). *The real question is, which theory best explains the phenomena.* Here we have competing theories, the two most common of which can give reasonable explanations, but which are likewise mutually exclusive. And here it must be insisted upon that *although all things are theoretically possible, not all possible things are equally probable.* The question is not, But is it not possible that. . . ? To which the answer usually must be, Yes. The question is, Is that more probable? In the final analysis, text critics and Synoptic critics are historians and must ultimately come down on the side of what they think is most probable, given all the data now in possession.

At this point textual criticism may yet have a contribution to make to the historical task. If we allow, as the majority of scholars on both sides do, that there is a *direct* literary relationship between any two of the Synoptists, then the kinds of questions textual criticism brings to such literary relationships are a pertinent part of the analytical task.

Indeed, Farmer assumes this to be true in Step XII in his 'new introduction'. He states: 'Assuming that there is direct literary dependence between Matthew and Luke, internal evidence indicates that the direction of dependence is that of Luke upon Matthew.'[58] What Farmer means by 'internal evidence' is precisely the kind of textual/literary arguments Streeter used to show Matthew dependent upon Luke.[59] And it is this argument of Streeter's which Butler, though in disagreement, candidly recognized as tending 'to support the theory of Marcan priority to the exclusion of all other solutions.'[60]

My point, in conclusion, is a simple one. Since both Marcan and Matthean priorists allow (1) that Luke is secondary, and (2) that Mark and Matthew have a *direct* literary relationship, then a crucial part of a Synoptic solution must be the careful pericope-by-pericope, word-by-word analysis of Matthew and Mark (preferably where Luke is absent) to determine the most likely direction of literary dependence. It has recently been argued that such a procedure is irrelevant.[61] I demur. It is a matter of doing redaction criticism at its primary level. If Matthew used Mark, then explanations of his redactional work must be given; but so also is this true if Mark used Matthew. My point is that such questions must be a part of the process in arriving at a solution of the Synoptic Problem, not simply an exercise engaged in after the solution is found; and it is here that textual criticism, by its way of asking questions, has a direct tie to the Synoptic Problem.

9

AT THE COLLOQUIUM'S CONCLUSION

Thomas R. W. Longstaff

It is, of course, impossible to provide in this brief essay a complete or comprehensive account of the Griesbach Bicentenary Colloquium. The papers prepared for circulation among the participants were all of very high quality and the discussion which they stimulated, while often intense and vigorous, was always considerate and productive. In this essay I can do no more than indicate a few of the more important topics raised for discussion together with some of the conclusions reached and suggestions made for further research.

In the first place, although the three areas of specialization chosen for emphasis[1] were approached separately, the participants soon came to see that both in the work of Griesbach and in contemporary research the three areas are in fact very closely interrelated. In the second place, although the papers included in this volume (as has been explained in the editors' preface) deal primarily with Griesbach's own work and the influence which it has had on continuing New Testament studies, the discussion itself knew no such limitation. Indeed, many exciting hours were spent by the participants (both in formal meetings and in casual conversations) considering the present state of research on the important questions involved in the three areas chosen for emphasis. An attempt was made to define the important questions which must henceforth be considered if further progress is to be made in those areas where Griesbach's interest and contribution were greatest. I will return to this point toward the end of this essay.

A. Gospel synopses

In the discussion of Gospel synopses (stimulated by Greeven's 'The Gospel synopsis from 1776 to the present day' and Léon-Dufour's 'The Gospel synopsis of the future') considerable attention was given to the following questions:

1 The arrangement of Gospel synopses

Here attention was given to such matters as the criteria useful for defining 'parallel' material and the manner in which the material from the several Gospels can best be presented so that the user can quickly and accurately see the similarities and differences among the Gospels. In connection with this latter point the merits of printing the texts of the Gospels in parallel columns or on horizontal lines, the use of different type styles (or colours), etc were carefully considered.

2 Complicating factors

Considerable discussion centered around the question of how problematic sections of the Gospels have been and should be treated. Among the texts considered were the Sermon on the Mount/Sermon on the Plain, and the so called 'Parables Chapter' (Matt. 13 // Mark 4). The manner in which 'doublets' should be printed to illustrate both the repetition and the parallels was also considered.

3 The material to be included in Gospel synopses

Here particular attention was given to the questions of whether the Gospel of John and non-canonical material (i.e. apocryphal Gospels, citations in the Apostolic Fathers, etc) should be included. Considerable attention was also given to the question of the nature of the text-critical apparatus (if any) appropriate for inclusion in a synopsis.

4 The neutrality of synopses

The question of whether the arrangement of a Gospel synopsis (i.e. which Gospel is placed in the left-hand, the centre, and the right-hand columns; the way in which pericopae are divided and titled; etc) *necessarily* presupposes some judgements about the Synoptic Problem was debated. Among the participants Farmer and Orchard represented those who argued that a neutral synopsis is not possible whereas Greeven and Neirynck represented the position that the arrangement of a neutral synopsis is indeed possible.

Even in these brief remarks the reader will see clearly that in the discussion of the papers the close interrelationship of the three topics chosen for emphasis was recognized.

B. The Synoptic Problem

The discussion of the Synoptic Problem (introduced by Reicke's 'Griesbach's answer to the Synoptic Question' and Farmer's 'Modern developments of Griesbach's hypothesis') was, understandably, some of the most vigorous and forceful. Some key points among many considered fell into the following general areas:

1 The two-document hypothesis

The continuing strength of the two-document hypothesis as a widely accepted solution to the Synoptic Problem was recognized and affirmed.

2 The Griesbach Hypothesis

Griesbach's solution to the problem (as reformulated in recent years by Farmer and others) was, however, generally acknowledged to provide a strongly viable alternative to the two-document hypothesis.

3 New methods of investigation

The importance of text criticism, form criticism, redaction criticism, etc for the continuing discussion of the Synoptic Problem was also emphasized. There was general agreement that new lines of inquiry need exploration – that the discussion has too often 'gone over old ground'. In the course of the discussion frequent reference to recent work was made and several important passages were subjected to preliminary analysis as 'test cases'.

C. Text criticism of the New Testament

Some of the salient points considered in the discussion of text-critical questions (introduced by Kilpatrick's 'Griesbach and the development of text criticism' and Fee's 'Modern text criticism and the Synoptic Problem') were the following:

1 Methodological considerations

The methods by which the text most closely approximating the original can be established was the most important topic. Here considerable discussion was centered around the question of establishing genealogies for families of manuscripts. Also important was the discussion of the use of 'internal' (e.g. stylistic) and 'external' (e.g. citations) evidence as defined by Fee for establishing the text. The recent emphasis on an 'eclectic' method was extensively considered.

2 The Synoptic Problem

The question of the importance of text criticism in the continuing search for a solution to the Synoptic Problem (its role in this task being generally recognized) and the question of whether presuppositions about the relationships among the Gospels are important in making text-critical decisions were discussed. The possible danger of circular reasoning was also considered.

3 Illustrative passages

In these discussions frequent reference was made to important (and problematic cases (e.g. Matt. 4: 17 // Mark 1: 14b–15; Matt. 3: 1–2 // Mark 1: 4; Matt. 22: 44 // Mark 12: 36 // Luke 20: 43; and Mark 9: 38 // Luke 9: 49) and clear illustration of methodological suggestions given.

D. Areas of general agreement

Although the participants in the Colloquium often held quite different views with regard to important issues, there were significant points of agreement reached in the discussions. While these cannot all be reported in detail here it seems to me that some of the most noteworthy were the following:

1 Gospel synopses

During the discussion of the progress made during the past 200 years in the arrangement and printing of synopses it became evident that all of the participants were agreed that a modern synopsis should enable the user to see each passage in its own context in the Gospel to which it belongs as well as to see it 'synoptically' (i.e. in comparison with the parallel passages in the other Gospels). Most of the participants also seemed to concur in the opinion that the arrangement of parallel passages in vertical columns (as is generally done) rather than on horizontal lines (as in the synopses of Veit and Swanson[2] provides a more useful format. Nevertheless, there was general agreement that further refinements in the means of presenting parallel passages synoptically should be sought.

It was further agreed, however, that a synopsis ought not to be employed as the primary text for study of individual pericopae or of a particular Gospel. Therefore, the participants concluded that a synopsis need not include a complete or an exhaustive text-critical apparatus but rather could include only those variant readings important for comparing the agreements and disagreements in wording among the Gospels.

2 The Synoptic Problem

Perhaps one of the most important results of the Colloquium was the clear articulation (voiced, for example, by Professors Reginald Fuller and Harald Riesenfeld) of the view that New Testament scholarship has entered upon a new period of pluralism with regard to proposed solutions to the Synoptic Problem. Although the strength of the two-document hypothesis was frequently stressed, nearly everyone present agreed that this solution was not without its difficulties and that it could no longer be considered to be established beyond reasonable doubt. In fact, most participants acknowledged that New Testament research would profit from a climate in which a plurality of hypotheses could be accepted as legitimate starting-points for exegetical studies. In this manner it is hoped that our understanding of individual pericopae, of the growth of the Gospel tradition, and of the interrelationships among the Gospels will be further advanced.

3 Text criticism and the New Testament

In recent New Testament scholarship text-critical studies have become extremely complicated and complex. The technical expertise required for this work is great. Therefore many of us (and I particularly include myself in this regard) were often helpfully instructed (both in the formal sessions and in informal discussions) by the scholars who have specialized in this area. In the discussions, which were often related to specific problem texts, there were a number of occasions where general agreement was reached with regard to the best reading of a particular passage. In addition, there was clear agreement that text criticism had played an important role in the earlier discussion of the Synoptic Problem (especially in the work of B. H. Streeter) and that it will continue to do so in the future. Finally, all of the participants acknowledged that both internal and external evidence must be employed in the continuing search for the best text of the New Testament.

E. Suggestions for further study

The last formal meeting of the Colloquium was devoted to a review of the results of our deliberations (comments made during this portion of the discussion have been taken into account in my remarks above) and to suggestions for further research in the several areas considered. Many such suggestions were made and taking account of the response which I perceived among the participants I have selected two general suggestions and four specific ones for mention here as the most important to emerge from the discussion. In several of these areas the work envisioned has already begun, and in these cases it was the judgement of those present that it should be pursued vigorously.

(1) It was strongly argued that in the discussion of the Synoptic Problem due consideration must be given to the unity of each Gospel. It was stressed that each Gospel must be considered as a whole with a view to identifying the traditions which it preserves. In the discussion it was recognized that whatever solution to the Synoptic Problem one adopts it will be necessary to recognize that no Gospel invariably preserves the earliest form of tradition; the earliest form of a tradition will at times be found in a Gospel which one considers to be secondary (or tertiary!). Therefore it is necessary that criteria should be developed for distinguishing relatively earlier from relatively later forms of tradition, criteria independent of any presupposi-

tions about the way in which the Gospels are related to one another.

(2) A number of participants emphasized the need for particular attention to the words of Jesus as they are preserved in the several Gospels. It would be important to know whether these words (as many suspect) are treated differently from other material and if so whether this can help us to understand better the manner in which the Gospels were produced.

(3) Several people indicated that our understanding of the stylistic characteristics which are representative of each Evangelist's writing needs to be increased and refined.

(4) A number of participants also called for a more careful and thorough study of the so called 'minor agreements' (and major agreements). It was stressed that this study must give due consideration to agreements of omission and to text-critical questions.

(5) As I have suggested above, the participants in the Colloquium did not resolve the question of whether it is possible to produce a Gospel synopsis which is neutral with regard to the Synoptic Problem. In the closing session it was recognized that this constitutes an important question which must be further considered.

(6) Finally, the participants suggested that the question of the manner in which internal and external evidence is to be used in text-critical studies, and especially the way in which the two kinds of evidence are to be weighed against one another, needs further consideration and clarification.

The Griesbach Bicentenary Colloquium held in Münster in 1976 was clearly an important gathering of New Testament scholars with diverse interests and opinions. Although unanimity with regard to all points was neither expected nor achieved, the Colloquium was one in which some of the most vexing problems in New Testament research were faced squarely and with an unusual regard for divergent opinion. The effects of this Colloquium will be reflected, not only in this volume, but in the contributions and influence of the participants in the months and years to come.

In his opening remarks Professor Farmer described the context in which the assembled scholars would begin their tasks. Although somewhat dramatic, it would nevertheless be accurate to remark that as the participants dispersed it was with the rewarding feeling 'we have begun', and with the expressed wish that a second Colloquium could be convened in the near future to deal further with some of the problems which still await resolution.

10

THE GRIESBACH HYPOTHESIS: A BIBLIOGRAPHY

*Compiled by Frans Neirynck and
F. Van Segbroeck*

This bibliography is not intended to be a complete list of works cited or referred to in this book. Rather, Professor Neirynck and his colleague have presented a bibliography of works dealing with Griesbach's solution to the Synoptic Problem, chronologically arranged, for the use of scholars interested in the history of this theory and its current revival. (Eds.)

1   OWEN, Henry. *Observations on the Four Gospels.* London, 1764.
    Cf. pp. 53-75.

2   BÜSCHING, Anton Friedrich. *Die vier Evangelisten mit ihren eigenen Worten zusammengesetzt und mit Erklärungen versehen.* Hamburg, 1766.
    Cf. pp. 109-19 (Luke - Matthew - Mark).

3   Anon. [Friedrich Andreas STROTH]. 'Von Interpolationen im Evangelium Matthaei', *Repertorium für biblische und morgenländische Litteratur* (ed. J. G. EICHHORN) 9 (1781), 99-156.
    Cf. p. 144.

4a GRIESBACH, Johann Jakob. *Inquiritur in fontes, unde Evangelistae suas de resurrectione Domini narrationes hauserint.* Jena, 1783.
    Reprinted in *Opuscula academica* (ed. J. P. GABLER), vol. II, Jena, 1825. Pp. 241-56.
    Cf. pp. 255-6.

4b *(Commentatio qua) Marci Evangelium totum e Matthaei et Lucae commentariis decerptum esse monstratur.* Jena, 1789, 1790.
    Enlarged edition in *Commentationes Theologicae* (ed. J. C. VELTHUSEN, C. T. KUINOEL and G. A. RUPERTI), vol. 1, Leipzig, 1794. Pp. 360-434; 'Commentatio qua..., scripta nomine Academiae Jenensis, (1789. 1790) jam recognita multisque augmentis locupletata'.
    Reprinted in *Opuscula academica* (ed. J. P. GABLER), vol. II, Jena, 1825. Pp. 358-425.

5   EVANSON, Edward. *The Dissonance of the Four Generally*

*Received Evangelists and the Evidence of Their Respective
Authenticity.* Ipswich, 1792.

(Luke - Matthew - Mark)

6a PAULUS, Heinrich Eberhard Gottlob. *Philologisch-kritischer und
historischer Kommentar über die drey ersten Evangelien.* Philologisch-kritischer und historischer Kommentar über das neue
Testament, 1. 3 vols., Lübeck, 1800–4. 2nd ed., 1804–5 =
Leipzig, 1812.

6b *Theologisch-exegetisches Conservatorium, oder Auswahl auf-
bewahrungswerther Aufsätze und zerstreuter Bemerkungen über die
alt- und neutestamentlichen Religionsurkunden... 1ste Lieferung:
Eine Reihe von Erörterungen über den Ursprung der drey ersten
Evangelien.* Heidelberg, 1822.

6c *Exegetisches Handbuch über die drei ersten Evangelien.* 3 vols.,
Heidelberg, 1831–3. 2nd ed., 1842.

Cf. I/1, p. 37.

7 AMMON, Christoph Friedrich von. *Dissertatio de Luca emendatore
Matthaei.* Erlangen, 1805.

8a SCHLEIERMACHER, Friedrich Daniel Ernst. *Ueber die Schriften
des Lukas, ein kritischer Versuch,* vol. I. Berlin, 1817.
Reprinted in *Sämtliche Werke. Erste Abteilung: Zur Theologie,*
vol. II. Berlin, 1836. Pp. 1–220.

8b *Einleitung ins Neue Testament. Aus Schleiermacher's handschrift-
lichem Nachlasse und nachgeschriebenen Vorlesungen mit einer
Vorrede von Dr Friedrich Lücke* (ed. G. WOLDE). Berlin, 1845.

Cf. p. 313. (Comp. de Wette's *Lukas und Markus,* p. 3.)

9a THEILE, Karl Gottfried Wilhelm. *De trium priorum evangeliorum
necessitudine.* Leipzig, 1825.

9b 'Kritik der verschiedenen Berichten über das Wechselverhältniss
der synoptischen Evangelien', *Neues kritisches Journal der theologischen Literatur* 5. 4, 385ff.

Cf. pp. 400–1.

9c *Zur Biographie Jesu.* 3 vols, Leipzig, 1837.

10 SAUNIER, Heinrich. *Ueber die Quellen des Evangeliums des Marcus.
Ein Beitrag zu den Untersuchungen über die Entstehung unserer
kanonischen Evangelien.* Berlin, 1825.

11a DE WETTE, Wilhelm Martin Leberecht. *Lehrbuch der historisch
kritischen Einleitung in die kanonischen Bücher des Neuen Testaments.* Berlin, 1826. 2nd ed., 1830. 3rd ed., 1834. 4th ed., 1842.
5th ed., 1848. Pp. 131–79 (E. T., F. Frothingham, Boston, 1858).
6th ed., 1860 (ed. H. MESSNER and G. LÜNEMANN), §§ 79–95,

pp. 144–195: 'Verwandtschaft der drei ersten Evangelien'.

11b *Kurze Erklärung der Evangelien des Lukas und Markus.* Kurz-gefasstes exegetisches Handbuch zum Neuen Testament, I. 2. Leipzig, 1836. 2nd ed., 1839. 3rd ed., 1846. 4th ed., 1857 (ed. H. MESSNER).

12a BLOOMFIELD, Samuel Thomas. *Recensio synoptica annotationis sacrae, Being a Critical Digest and Synoptical Arrangement of the Most Important Annotations on the New Testament, Exegetical, Philological and Doctrinal*, vol. II. London, 1826.

12b *The Greek Testament with English Notes.* 2 vols, London, 1832. 3rd ed., 1839. 6th ed., 1845.
    Cf. vol. I, pp. 182–3 (Hales).

13 CLAUSEN, Henrik Nicolai. *Quatuor Evangeliorum tabulae synopticae.* Copenhagen, 1829.
    Cf. p. xx.

14 FRITZSCHE, Karl Friedrich August. *Evangelium Marci.* Quatuor Evangelia recensuit et cum commentariis perpetuis edidit, 2, Leipzig, 1830.

15 SCHOTT, Heinrich August. *Isagoge historico-critica in libros Novi Foederis sacros.* Jena, 1830.

16 MEYER, Heinrich August Wilhelm. *Kritisch exegetisches Handbuch über den Evangelien des Matthäus, Markus und Lukas.* KEK, I; Das Neue Testament griechisch nach den besten Hülfsmitteln kritisch revidirt... Zweiter Theil, den Kommentar enthaltend, I, Göttingen, 1832.
    Kritisch exegetisches Handbuch über das Evangelium des Matthäus. KEK, I. 1. 2nd ed., 1844.
    Cf. *Einleitung* § 6.
    Kritisch exegetisches Handbuch über die Evangelien des Markus und Lukas. KEK, I. 2. 2nd ed., 1846.

17 SIEFFERT, Friedrich Ludwig. *Ueber den Ursprung des ersten kanon-ischen Evangeliums. Eine kritische Abhandlung.* Königsberg, 1832.
    Cf. pp. 55 and 109.

18 KERN, Friedrich Heinrich. 'Ueber den Ursprung des Evangeliums Matthaei', *Tübinger Zeitschrift für Theologie* 7 (1834), fasc. 2, 3-132.

19a STRAUSS, David Friedrich. *Das Leben Jesu kritisch bearbeitet*, vol. I, Tübingen, 1835. Vol. II, Tübingen, 1836. Reprinted Darmstadt, 1969 (cf. vol. I, § 12, p. 65 and § 139, p. 682). 2nd ed., 1837 (§ 13, p. 69). 3rd ed., 1838-9. 4th ed., 1840. (E. T., G. Eliot, 1846; 2nd ed., 1892; reprinted 1972, p. 71.)

19b *Das Leben Jesu für das deutsche Volk bearbeitet.* Leipzig, 1864.

Cf. pp. 127ff.

20   GFRÖRER, August Friedrich. *Die heilige Sage.* Geschichte des Urchristentums, 2. Stuttgart, 1838.

21   KUHN, Johann. *Das Leben Jesu wissenschaftlich bearbeitet,* vol. I, Mainz, 1838. (F. T., Paris, 1842.)
     Cf. pp. 33ff.; F.T. pp. 30–5.

22   NEUDECKER, Christian Gottholl. *Lehrbuch der historisch-kritischen Einleitung in das Neue Testament.* Leipzig, 1840.
     Cf. pp. 145ff.

23a SCHWEGLER, Albert. 'Die Hypothese vom schöpferischen Urevangelisten in ihrem Verhältnis zur Traditionshypothese', *Theologische Jahrbücher* 2 (1843), 203–78.

23b *Das nachapostolische Zeitalter in den Hauptmomenten seiner Entwicklung.* Tübingen, 1846.

24a SCHWARZ, Franz Josef. *Neue Untersuchungen über das Verwandtschafts-Verhältniss der synoptischen Evangelien mit besonderer Berücksichtigung der Hypothese vom schöpferischen Urevangelisten.* Tübingen, 1844. (Preisschrift Kath.-Theol. Fakultät.)

24b 'Evangelien (und Apostelgeschichte)', in *Kirchen-Lexikon* (ed. H. J. J. WETZER and B. WELTE), vol. III. Freiburg, 1849. Pp. 779–801. (F. T., Paris, 1860, vol. VIII, pp. 183–207.)
     Cf. pp. 794–5.

25   Anon. = 'sächsischer Anonymus' [Christian Adolf HASERT]. *Die Evangelien, ihr Geist, ihre Verfasser und ihr Verhältniss zu einander. Ein Beitrag zur Lösung der kritischen Fragen über die Entstehung derselben.* Leipzig, 1845. 2nd ed., 1852.
     Cf. Holtzmann's *Einleitung,* p. 361.

26a BLEEK, Friedrich. *Beiträge zur Evangelien-Kritik.* Berlin, 1846.
     Cf. pp. 72–5.

26b *Einleitung in das Neue Testament* (ed. J. F. BLEEK). Berlin, 1862. Pp. 242–57. 2nd ed., 1866 (E. T. 1869). 3rd ed., 1875 (ed. W. MANGOLD). 4th ed., 1886.
     Cf. § § 67–71, pp. 184–200; p. 186: 'stets in meinen Vorlesungen (zuerst 1822/23)'.

26c *Synoptische Erklärung der drei ersten Evangelien* (ed. H. HOLTZMANN). Leipzig, 1862.
     Cf. vol. I, pp. 4–5.

27a BAUR, Ferdinand Christian. *Kritische Untersuchungen über die kanonischen Evangelien, ihr Verhältniss zu einander, ihren Charakter und Ursprung.* Tübingen, 1847.
     Cf. pp. 533–67: 'Das Evangelium des Markus'.

27b Das Markusevangelium nach seinem Ursprung und Charakter.
Tübingen, 1851.

27c 'Rückblick auf die neuesten Untersuchungen über das Markus-evangelium', *Theologische Jahrbücher* 12 (1853), 54–93.

28a MAIER, Adalbert. 'Beiträge zur Einleitung in das Neue Testament. Die drei ersten Evangelien im Allgemeinen', *Zeitschrift für Theologie* 20 (1848), 3–76.
Cf. § 5, pp. 27–38.

28b Einleitung in die Schriften des Neuen Testaments. Freiburg, 1852.
Cf. pp. 32–7.

29 KÖSTLIN, Karl Reinhold. Der Ursprung und die Komposition der synoptischen Evangelien, Stuttgart, 1853.
Cf. pp. 351–7.

30 DELITZSCH, Franz. Neue Untersuchungen über Entstehung und Anlage der kanonischen Evangelien. Erster Theil: Das Matthäus-evangelium. Leipzig, 1853.
Cf. pp. 110–12.

31 LUTTEROTH, Henri. Essai d'interprétation de quelques parties de l'évangile selon saint Matthieu, vol. I (chs. 1–2), Paris, 1860. Vol. II (chs. 3–7), Paris, 1864. Vol. III (chs. 8–13), Paris, 1867. Vol. IV (chs. 14–28), Paris, 1876.

32 DÖLLINGER, Johannes Josef Ignaz von. Christentum und Kirche in der Zeit der Grundlegung. Regensburg, 1860. 2nd ed., 1868.
Cf. pp. 133–4.

33 KAHNIS, Karl Friedrich August. Die Lutherische Dogmatik historisch-genetisch dargestellt, vol. I. Leipzig, 1861.
Cf. p. 409.

34 ANGER, Rudolf. Ratio, qua loci Veteris Testamenti in Evangelio Matthaei laudantur, quid valeat ad illustrandam huius evangelii originem, vol. I, Leipzig, 1861. Vols II–III, Leipzig, 1862.
Cf. Holtzmann's Einleitung, 1886, p. 361.

35a ZELLER, Eduard. 'Strauss und Renan', Historische Zeitschrift 12 (1864), 70–133.
Cf. p. 92.

35b 'Zum Marcus-Evangelium', Zeitschrift für wissenschaftliche Theologie 8 (1865), 308–28, 385–408.

36 MEIJBOOM, Hajo Uden. Geschiedenis en critiek der Marcushypo-these. Amsterdam, 1866. (Doctoral Dissertation Groningen.)

37 KEIM, Theodor. Geschichte Jesu von Nazara. 3 vols., Zürich, 1867, 1871, 1872.
Cf. vol. I, p. 86.

38 DAVIDSON, Samuel. *An Introduction to the Study of the New Testament, Critical, Exegetical, and Theological.* London, (1848). Revised edition 1868. 2nd ed., 1882. 3rd ed., 1894.
      Cf. pp. 352-584; see Farmer's *The Synoptic Problem*, p. 71.
39 LANGEN, Josef. *Grundriss der Einleitung in das Neue Testament.* Freiburg, 1868. 2nd ed., Bonn, 1873.
      Cf. pp. 55-6, 60-1.
40 GRIMM, Josef. *Die Einheit der vier Evangelien.* Regensburg, 1868.
41 NIPPEL, Karl. 'Das Verhältniss der Evangelien des Marcus und Lucas', *Theologische Quartalschrift* 58 (1876), 551-79.
42 NÖSGEN, Karl Friedrich. 'Der Ursprung und die Entstehung des dritten Evangeliums', *Theologische Studien und Kritiken* 53 (1880), 49-137.
      Cf. pp. 116-18.
43 PASQUIER, Henri. *La solution du problème synoptique.* Tours, 1911.
      Cf. review M.-J. Lagrange in *RB* n. s. 9 (1912), 280-4.
44 FARMER, William R. *The Synoptic Problem. A Critical Analysis.* New York-London, 1964. Reprinted 1976.
      For reviews cf. 'The Synoptic Problem: After Ten Years', *The Perkins School of Theology Journal* 28 (1975), 63-74, esp. p. 68.
45a DUNGAN, David L. 'Mark – The Abridgement of Matthew and Luke', *Perspective* 11 (1970), 51-97.
45b 'Reactionary Trends in the Gospel Producing Activity of the Early Church: Marcion, Tatian, Mark', in M. SABBE (ed.), *L'évangile selon Marc. Tradition et rédaction*, BETL, 34. Gembloux-Louvain, 1974. Pp. 179-202.

See additional entries on p. 219

NOTES

2 Gerhard Delling: Johann Jakob Griesbach: his life, work and times

1   Martin-Luther-Universität Halle – Wittenberg, Department of Theology DDR 402 Halle/S. This essay was published in its original German form in *Theologische Zeitschrift* 33 (1977), 81–99.

2   The literature listed in the attached bibliography (pp. 16–21) is referred to by the numbers of that list. These are printed in italics. The bibliography number is followed sometimes by the volume-number and then, after a colon, by the page-number. As far as possible these follow Gabler's edition – as, for example, for Griesbach's programmes (*37*). I have specially to thank the staff at the university libraries of Halle and Jena for having put the material at my disposal.

3   *Aus meinem Leben. Wahrheit und Dichtung*, near the end of book 4.

4   Hieronymus Peter (1735–97) and Johann Georg (1739–99). On them see R. Jung in: *Allgemeine deutsche Bibliothek*, vol. XXXI (Leipzig, 1890), pp. 543–7.

5   In his letters to Gabler Griesbach often signed himself 'Jh. Griesbach'; see C. Ranft, 'Briefe von Johann Griesbach in Jena an Johann Philipp Gabler in Altdorf', *Zeitschrift des Vereins für Thüringische Geschichte und Altertumskunde* 45 (n.s. 37) (1943), 316–25.

6   H. Meinert, 'Frankfurt am Main', *Handwörterbuch zur deutschen Rechtsgeschichte*, vol. I (Berlin, 1971), columns 1203–8, esp. 1205.

7   Not only those of the Rothschilds. On the whole subject see Friedrich Bothe, *Geschichte der Stadt Frankfurt am Main* (Frankfurt, 1913); on the banking houses in the period before 1800 see pp. 586f.

8   *Aus meinem Leben*, book 5 (to the end).

9   In the baptismal register of St George's, Halle (28 June 1725) the first godparent of Dorothea Rambach is named as Anna Magdalena, 'beloved spouse' of A. H. Francke; the second is the wife of Prof. Joachim Lange (Pietist; grandparents of Dorothea, *34*: xi); the third is master-joiner Johann Jacob Rambach.

10 Friedrich Wilhelm Strieder, *Grundlage zu einer Hessischen Gelehrten und Schriftsteller Geschichte*, vol. V (Kassel, 1785), pp. 101–8, esp. pp. 104–6.

11 Entry in baptismal register of Butzbach/Hessen: 'The godfather was Jacob Theodor Frantz Rambach – son of the late Johann Jacob Rambach... – who named the child Joh. Jacob after his father of blessed memory.'

12 *Aus meinem Leben*, book 8. Goethe made his acquaintance through Susanne von Klettenberg.

13   According to a letter of Friederike Griesbach's, dated 17 March 1829 (*40*:
      21), in Frankfurt she had learned 'Latin, English and French'. *40*: 46.
14   Cf. what was said above about Rambach's Moral Theology. For Griesbach
      'conversion' (used by Griesbach in the footnote to para. 152) is a figurative
      ('non-factual') Biblical expression (para. 153).
15   On him, see Albrecht Ritschl, *Geschichte des Pietismus*, vol. III 2 (Bonn,
      1886), pp. 120-6.
16   Supported by J. A. Ernesti whom he also heard - and others. (*35*: 538; *34*:
      xii); cf. below n. 59.
17   1734-1815. The 'well curled cloud' ('a machine of that sort...'), the wig
      that Griesbach is wearing here, he had discarded by 1792. See a letter dated
      9 April 1804 in Ranft, 'Briefe' (see above n. 5), p. 322.
18   *34*: xv. After the beginning of the preface to the *Symbolae*, a considerable
      part of vol. I had already been printed ten years earlier (1775). See *22* I:
      1-242 etc.
19   In his time the 'capital city of the Saale region' numbered 'over 20,000
      inhabitants, besides the military and students'. These latter numbered 2000
      and 1000-1100 respectively. Jena was a city of 'medium size, with about
      800 houses and 5000-6000 inhabitants' (*Akademisches Taschenbuch*
      (Halle, 1792), pp. 133 and 177).
20   R. Hoche, *AdBiog*, vol. XXXIII (1891), pp. 111-15.
21   Below the signature to the preface of *23*.
22   The way in which Griesbach, in his early years at Jena, interpreted his
      career so far is indicated by a section well on in the *Vita*, that was written
      on the occasion of his promotion to Doctor of Theology (*34*). It is written
      with the gusto of the young professor who, having arrived, is proud of his
      educational position and of belonging to a many-sided educated world. As
      a mature man in his prime (1790), who has accomplished much and played
      a versatile part in public life, Griesbach writes in a different manner (*35*).
      The change is due not simply to a difference in language and style (the
      contrast between the Latin of an academic discourse and the German of
      a newspaper article), but to the sheer practical sobriety of the content.
      That the latter are from Griesbach's pen (Heinrich Carl Eichstädt, *Opuscula
      oratoria*, 2nd ed. (Jena, 1850), p. 566, n. 4; his *Vita Griesbachs* - to 1770 -
      pp. 565-71, 577-82), seems most probable, to judge by the style.
23   Among Griesbach's audience at Jena we find, for example, Wilhelm Martin
      Leberecht de Wette (1800-3), Georg Carl Benjamin Ritschl (1801-2), the
      father of Albrecht Ritschl, Ernst Moritz Arndt (1793-4; see E. M. Arndt,
      Erinnerungen aus dem äusseren Leben (Leipzig, 1840), p. 73).
24   Also in winter 1783/4 and 1784/5.
25   *Historia religionis et ecclesiae christianae adumbrata in usus lectionum*
      (Berlin, 1777; 5th ed., 1805).
26   Griesbach was a keen autograph collector, - a pastime common in his time.
      His catalogue numbers 745 autographs of Luther alone (Nos 9636-69, filed
      according to years, 797 of Luther's contemporaries). It is doubtful, admit-
      tedly, in what sense the word 'autograph' is used here: it could extend to
      include first editions.
27   And quite clearly on the interleaves he entered exclusively the variants
      found in the Alexandrian. Griesbach used a copy of the New Testament

printed in 1750 in Glasgow. Friedrich Andreas Stroth, who congratulated Griesbach at the beginning of his lectures with a short treatise *De codice Alexandrino* (Halle, 28 Sept. 1771) says there: 'adamantina diligentia opera... *Adamantii Origenis* perlegisti' (p. 12).

28 Ranft, 'Briefe' (see above n. 5), p. 321.

29 Possibly once more in 1792, 1792/3 or 1793.

30 As in the lecture-index for winter 1779/80. Summer 1780: 'locos dogmaticos de salutis consequendae ordine et mediis...' Otherwise Griesbach delivered this course at intervals of three or four semesters.

31 Cf. further the title of the first edition of 1779; see the appendix.

32 *35*: 538. A contrast is made here with 'what is genuinely useful and practical in the theological disciplines'; in his Tübingen period Griesbach had already been pointed in this direction by the Pietist J. Fr. Reuss (*ibid.*; see above p. 6).

33 On the redemptive action of God in the death of Jesus on the cross, Griesbach says (para. 145): 'The *simple concept* in the Bible of this marvellous economy for the restoration of the human race can and must be separated from the well-intentioned *hypotheses* about this doctrine', hypotheses in which, for example, the sufferings of Christ are set in the balance against the punishment due to men.

34 On the 'differentiation of Biblical, from dogmatic, theology' cf. the inaugural address of J. Ph. Gabler at Altdorf on 30 March 1787; see Otto Merk, *Biblische Theologie des Neuen Testaments in ihrer Anfangszeit* (Marburg, 1972), esp. pp. 31–45; translation of the address in pp. 273–84.

35 J. S. Semler contests this religious value in his *Abhandlung von freier Untersuchung des Canon* (Halle, 1771–5; 2nd ed., 1776), para. 24, ed. Heinz Scheible (Gutersloh, 1967), pp. 91–4. Griesbach, in a letter to Paulus dated 16 February 1807, speaks most critically of the Apocalypse. See Karl Alexander Frh. von Reichlin-Meldegg, *Heinrich Eberhard Gottlob Paulus und seine Zeit*, vol. I (Stuttgart, 1853), pp. 370f.

36 Griesbach to Gabler 4 April 1804; Ranft, 'Briefe' (see above n. 5), p. 320.

37 Unless I have overlooked something.

38 Six times these are the accounts of the Passion and the Resurrection.

39 Griesbach was already lecturing in hermeneutics in Halle (*35*: 540).

40 Cf. J. S. Semler, *Vorbereitung zur theologischen Hermeneutik*, vol. I (Halle, 1760), pp. 16f.

41 Cf. Semler, *Vorbereitung* (see above n. 40), vol. I, p. 160: 'In short, *hermeneutic* skill depends most of all upon the certain and exact knowledge of the *linguistic usage* of the Bible, and also the capacity to discern the *historical* circumstances of a Biblical discourse.'

42 The Academia Ienensis always announced to their *cives* the celebration of the current feast on the title-page of the programme (the university was regarded as a *respublica*); on the next page the *cives* were greeted by the Duke Carl August in his role as *rector magnificentissimus*. The anonymous author of the programme uses the 'I' form notwithstanding.

43 That is the theme especially of paras. 21–3 of the treatise on the canon by his teacher Semler (see above n. 35; Scheible, pp. 84–7, 90). Cf. Gottfried Hornig, *Die Anfänge der historisch-kritischen Theologie* (Göttingen, 1961) (Diss. theol. Lund, 1961), chapter 3, 'Das historisch-kritische Schrift-

verständnis Semlers'.

44 Cf. Hornig, *Anfänge* (see above n. 43), pp. 72–4.
45 *37* II: 167f., (*13*); cf. pp. 185 (*14*), 485f.; further, *24*: conclusion of I; *31*: conclusion of II, III.
46 *37* I: 391, 404 (*8*); cf. II: 469f., (*26*); further, pp. 428, 431f., (*25*), 136 (*12*).
47 This applies also to the treatise on Hebrews 1: 2 (*16*); here Griesbach prefers 'for he has also...' to 'through which he also...' (ΔΙΟΤΙΚΑΙ in place of ΔΙΟΤΚΑΙ; *37* II: 202f.). Gabler subjects this to severe criticism (*37* II: l–lvi); he says that here Griesbach has 'definitely not accomplished anything; he has only wasted much time and trouble' (p. li). Gabler's verdict on the interpretation of 1 Pet. 1: 19–21 (*17*), which likewise he rejects, is much milder. This text, according to Griesbach, concerns the primitive Christian prophets and Christ's second coming (*37* II: lvi–lxi).
48 According to Semler, the priority of St Matthew's Gospel is 'incontrovertible': *Abhandlung* (see above n. 35) para. 21 (Scheible, p. 83).
49 To these belong, at all events, the Gospels of Matthew and John, the thirteen Pauline letters, 1–3 John. On Hebrews see below n. 51.
50 Griesbach is a zealous apologist of, for example, the account of Luke in Acts 2: 9–11 (see *37* II: 153f.; *13*), and likewise – in *18* – of the Resurrection Narratives of the Evangelists (on Luke see *37* II: 252–5).
51 Thus Ephesians is by Paul; and so 'the first rule' for the exposition of the letter is this: no contradiction can be allowed to arise between the parallel passages in Ephesians and Colossians (*37* II: 137; *12*). In his treatise on Heb. 1: 2, Griesbach starts from the assumption that Hebrews was written by Paul (*16*); in 1791 and 1792 (*25*; *26*) he speaks simply of the 'author' of the letter.
52 Griesbach had been very active in getting Gabler to move from Altdorf to Jena. See the texts in Ranft, 'Briefe' (see above n. 5).
53 The scientific possibilities which Griesbach had left unutilized on account of his administrative duties, were already mentioned by H. E. G. Paulus, 'Nekrolog', *Heidelb. Jahrbb. der Litteratur*, 5 (1812), Intelligenzbl. no. 7 40–7, esp. 43f.
54 The preface to *32b* I (1805) speaks of a 'failing in health, especially in the sight' (p. iv). On 18 August 1803 Schiller wrote: 'Griesbach will not last out the winter'; and on 12 September 1803 that 'Griesbach is hopelessly ill'. (Fritz Jonas, *Schillers Briefe*, complete critical edition (7 vols., Stuttgart, 1892–6), vol. VII, pp. 66, 67.) Cf. Goethe on Griesbach on 1 September 1803: 'I saw the venerable, very sick man, driving daily, very early, through the castle yard, in order to carry on teaching without interruption' ('Griesbach comes from the garden-house'); Hans Wahl (ed.), *Briefwechsel des Herzogs-Grossherzogs Carl August mit Goethe*, vol. I (Berlin, 1915), pp. 318f. See Paulus to Schnurrer on 9 January 1803, von Reichlin-Meldegg (see above n. 35), vol. I, p. 333. And yet in 1804 Griesbach was able to report that 'now he felt better and stronger than he had in five years', Letter, *40*: p. 60.
55 Several things make it evident that Griesbach had a gift for, and an interest in, financial administration. Cf. Abeken's description *40*: 25–7 and the remark of Friederike's cited in pp. 25f. Cf. also Paulus, 'Nekrolog' (see

above n. 53), pp. 43f.; 'componendis novis calculis', Gabler *37* I: viii; Griesbach himself, *35*: 542.

56 Cf., say, Fritz Hartung, *Das Grossherzogtum Sachsen unter der Regierung Carl Augusts 1775-1828* (Weimar, 1923), pp. 143f., 215, 218.

57 On 2 July 1800, Schiller wrote to Friederike Griesbach from Weimar: 'How I wish he could have had some rest after these arduous four weeks that he spent here! But he has so pampered the people, and they have found his counsel to be so good, that they just cannot do without him.' Jonas, *Briefe* (see above n. 54), vol. VI, p. 166.

58 It is clearly Griesbach whom Herder describes on 1 February 1783, in contrast to Eichhorn, as 'the most illustrious despot and university visitator'. See *Von und an Herder. Ungedruckte Briefe aus Herders Nachlass*, vol. II (Leipzig, 1801), p. 277, ed. Heinrich Düntzer and Ferdinand Gottfried Herder. Cf. the previous letter from Eichhorn to Herder.

59 Concerning the theological faculty, see Herder to Eichhorn, 12 July 1782 (Düntzer–Herder, *Briefe* (see above n. 58), vol. II, p. 274): 'Are you happy with Döderlein's election? Nothing could be done about it, for Griesbach had taken charge of everything, and Matthaei didn't stand a chance against him.' According to letters of Herder's of May 1782 (*ibid.* pp. 273, 193f.), this concerned Christian Friedrich Matthaei (1744–1811), pupil of J. A. Ernesti, who was at that time making the effort to get back to Germany (O. von Gebhardt, 'Christian Friedrich Matthaei und seine Sammlung griechischer Handschriften', *Centralblatt für Bibliothekswesen* 15 (1898), 345–57, 393–420, 441–82, 537–66, esp. 350f.). His edition of the New Testament first began to appear in 1782 in Riga. His satirical and sarcastic type of critique of the methods and findings of those named in the title was published in German in: *Über die sogenannten Recensionen welche der Herr Abt Bengel, der Herr Doctor Semler und der Herr Geheime Kirchenrat Griesbach in dem griechischen Texte des N. Testaments wollen entdeckt haben* (Ronneburg und Leipzig, 1804). According to Matthaei, p. 92, the discussion of Matthaei's *SS. Apostolorum septem epistolae catholicae* and *S. Lucae Actus Apostolorum Graece et Latine* (Riga, 1782), originated in: *Jenaische gelehrte Zeitungen auf das Jahr 1782*, 328–36, by Griesbach. The reviewer is obviously trying to write an objective criticism of Matthaei's edition; his style, judged by the review-style of the period, can be described as moderate. Matthaei only occasionally mentions the edition by Griesbach in the second volume (pp. xix, 212, 237, 327), whereas he mentions Mill and Wettstein frequently. Matthaei, *D. Pauli epistolae ad Romanos, Titum et Philemonem Graece et Latine* (Riga, 1782), was reviewed in the same journal, pp. 721–4, 729–31 (in this volume Matthaei refers to Griesbach on pp. 54, 68, 126, 138). The bibliography of Matthaei (consisting chiefly of editions) is in Heinrich Doering, *Die gelehrten Theologen Deutschlands im achtzehnten und neunzehnten Jahrhundert*, vol. II (Neustadt/Orla, 1832), pp. 427–30.

60 The 'protectors' of Jena (cf. below n. 61) were 'the Dukes of Saxony, of the Ernestine line', i.e. those of Sachsen-Weimar, Sachsen-Gotha, Sachsen-Coburg and Sachsen-Meiningen (see *Akademisches Taschenbuch*, p. 167). But Carl August had been *Rector magnificentissimus* since the government took over in 1775. The acting Rector at Jena held the title of *Prorector*.

Griesbach held this office at all events in the winters of 1780/1, 83/4, 87/8 and 96/7.

61 The regard of this man for Griesbach is shown, for example, by his having sent him greetings through Goethe, for no apparent reason. Wahl, *Briefwechsel* (see above n. 54), vol. I, p. 296 (29 June 1801). Only thirty-nine years of age, Griesbach already held the title *geheimer Kirchenrat*, 'privy Church councillor' (1784). That Griesbach was completely at ease with the whole protocol of dealing with the government is shown in his manner of speaking to Gabler on 4 April 1804: 'I expect to receive from them a... declaration of their devout gratitude to the illustrious protectors' (Ranft, 'Briefe' (see above n. 5), p. 321).

62 On Griesbach's humour cf. nn. 17, 61.

63 29 August 1787 (Jonas, *Briefe* (see above n. 54), vol. I, pp. 402f.).

64 Cf. what Griesbach says in his correspondence in Abeken, *40*: 26: 'Your W. is one of those men of whom it is said that they have a good heart and a good will. I hate these kind of men. They have no energy.'

65 Paulus, 'Dankbare Erinnerungen an die durch... Carl August... zu Jena geschützte Lehrfreiheit', in: *Sophronizon* 11, part 2 (Heidelberg, 1829), 1–115, esp. p. 75, which corresponds to 'Nekrolog' (see above n. 53), p. 45.

66 However, after his Italian tour (1786–8) Goethe withdrew from important state functions, although not perhaps from those concerning the arts and science. See Hartung, *Grossherzogtum* (see above n. 56), p. 26.

67 Cf. Hartung, *Grossherzogtum* (see above n. 56), pp. 22f.

68 Goethe distinguishes between official and friendly meetings with Griesbach. Letter dated 1 September 1803 (Wahl, *Briefwechsel* (see above n. 54), vol. I, p. 319).

69 Bernhard Rudolf Abeken, *Goethe in meinem Leben*, ed. Adolf Heuermann (Weimar, 1904), p. 57.

70 Goethe mentions such visits ('as I usually do') 1 September 1803, (Wahl, *Briefwechsel* (see above n. 54), vol. I, p. 319). 'Griesbach's Garden' still is – or has again become – the name of that plot of land.

71 Schiller, Weimar 29 August 1787: Griesbach 'stays during the summer in a large recently built garden-house on the outskirts of the city; the house commands a magnificent view of the countryside' (Jonas, *Briefe* (see above n. 54), vol. I, p. 402). On the ground floor cattle were kept. See Schiller's poem *40*: 52f.

72 Cf. Wieland's almost rapturous letter to Frau Griesbach on 29 July 1809, *40*: 54f.

73 Abeken, *Goethe* (see above n. 69), p. 119.

74 A letter of Griesbach's dated 3 December 1802 (*40*: 50): 'We are so happy at the Vosses. They are splendid people, and we have gained much through their settling in Jena.' Voss lived in Jena from 1802–5; according to von Reichlin-Meldegg, *Paulus* (see above n. 35), vol. II, p. 242, he lived with Griesbach.

75 Abeken, *Goethe* (see above n. 69), p. 127.

76 Schiller, 23 February 1795. Jonas, *Briefe* (see above n. 54), vol. IV, p. 134.

77 Architect of – among others – the castles of Gotha (Friedenstein), Jena, Zeitz (*Allgemeines Lexikon der bildenden Künstler*, ed. Hans Vollmer, vol. XXVIII (Leipzig, 1934), pp. 295f.).

78 Jonas, *Briefe* (see above n. 54), vol. II, p. 296.
79 29 August 1787 (Jonas, *Briefe* (see above n. 54), vol. I, p. 402). In the
    letters to the sisters von Lengefeld, dated 1789-90, Schiller admittedly
    makes ironic and sarcastic remarks about the 'Laurel wreath' (Friederike).
    See, for example, Jonas, *Briefe* (see above n. 54), vol. II, p. 348 (26 Oct-
    ober 1789), p. 382 (24 November); vol. III, pp. 3f. (5 January 1790), p.
    29 (25 January), p. 52 (14 February). The good relationship was, however,
    unsettled on Schiller's side, but only temporarily. K. Th. Gaedertz, 'Schiller
    und die Griesbachs in Jena', *Zeitung für Literatur, Kunst und Wissenschaft,
    Beilage des Hamburgischen Korrespondenten*, 28, No 10 (1905), 39f. On
    17 December 1801 Schiller signed a letter to Friederike: 'Wholly and always
    yours' (in Gaedertz, p. 40). According to Gaedertz, Schiller's youngest
    daughter was born in 1804 in Griesbach's garden-house (*ibid.*).
80 Letters of 4 November and 8 December 1799 (Jonas, *Briefe* (see above n.
    54), vol. VI, pp. 107, 121).
81 I know nothing about Griesbach's relationship with, say, Fichte (Jena
    1793-9) or August Wilhelm Schlegel (Jena 1796-1801). To judge, how-
    ever, from one or two ironic remarks made by Herder (Weimar 1776-1803)
    in letters (Düntzer-Herder, *Briefe* (see above n. 58), vol. II, pp. 274, 277)
    no friendly relationship can be presumed, even though Herder makes
    equally sarcastic remarks about other people as well (*loc. cit.* p. 276,
    summer 1782, about Doederlein: 'This snub-nose will get on with what he
    is doing.' A portrait of Doederlein owned by the University of Jena cor-
    roborates the nickname.). Eichhorn makes like comments on Griesbach
    (*loc. cit.* pp. 277, 278).
82 Heyd, *AdBiog*, vol. XXXII (1891), pp. 196-8. On visits to Schnurrer and
    Paulus, see Griesbach in von Reichlin-Meldegg, *Paulus* (see above n. 35),
    vol. II, pp. 60f.
83 'In his [Griesbach's] view diversity of exegetical views should always be
    pardoned in the *enfant perdu*', wrote Paulus on 21 February 1802 to
    Schnurrer, with reference to Part III of his (Paulus') *Commentary on the
    Synoptics* (von Reichlin-Meldegg, *Paulus* p. 219 (see above n. 54)).
84 Hartung, *Grossherzogtum* (see above n. 56), p. 151. Griesbach had objec-
    tions, too, to the nomination of Johann Gottfried Eichhorn (professor of
    oriental languages at Jena from 1775 to 1788) as Doederlein's successor.
    See Paulus to Schnurrer, 13 January 1793: 'Griesbach very much wants an
    irreproachable theologian – certainly not friend Eichhorn.' Von Reichlin-
    Meldegg, *Paulus* (see above n. 35), vol. I, p. 197. From 1777 to 1786
    Eichhorn was editor of the *Repertorium* (see *10, 11, 15*).
85 Paulus, 'Erinnerungen' (see above n. 65), p. 71; quotation from p. 75.
86 Griesbach emphasizes this repeatedly. Thus with regard to 1 Cor. 12 he
    stresses that the miracles of the apostolic age confirmed 'the divine origin
    of Christian doctrine' and corroborated 'the divine authority of its heralds'
    (*37* II: 179).
87 In the Introduction to the programme for Easter 1783 (*37* II: 241f.)
    Griesbach expounds in detail that the resurrection of Jesus is excellently
    and variously evidenced. For a development see above p. 12. (Sequel to
    37 II: 241.)
88 See above p. 11 (*23*, paras. 147f.; cf. *37* II: 177f.; *14*).

89   On the textual critic as critic of the ancient traditional texts see above
     pp. 10ff.

90   'Abriss einer Geschichte der Umwälzung, welche seit 1750 auf den Gebiet
     der Theologie in Deutschland statt gefunden', *Vermischte Schriften
     grösstenteils apologetischen Inhalts*, vol. II (Hamburg, 1839), pp. 1–147,
     esp. 134f.

3 Heinrich Greeven: The Gospel synopsis from 1776 to the present day

1   The literature from the German-speaking area was naturally more accessible
    to me. Therefore I am sure that I will be excused if I should have missed
    synopses published abroad – especially older ones.

2   Some friends and I hope to be able to show elsewhere that Tatian was not
    necessarily the ancestor, i.e. the source, of the tradition of all later harmo-
    nies, as has been widely assumed.

3   So F. C. Burkitt, *The Old Latin and the Itala*, Texts and Studies 4, 3
    (Cambridge, 1894), pp. 59, 72–8; cf. Th. Zahn, *Einleitung in das NT*, 3rd
    ed. (Leipzig, 1924), vol. II, p. 200 (§ 50 n. 3); P. Feine, RE[3], vol. XIX
    (1907), p. 278, 9ff.

4   *De Consensu* I. 2. 4; I. 3. 5; I. 4. 7; IV. 10. 11.

5   Jh. Alb. Fabricius, *Bibliotheca Graeca* (Hamburg, 1790/1809), vol. IV,
    pp. 882–9; reference in Clausen (n. 37), p. vii.

6   Jo. Jac. Griesbach, *Synopsis evangeliorum Matthaei, Marci et Lucae una
    cum iis Joannis pericopis quae historiam passionis et resurrectionis Jesu
    Christi complectuntur...*, 2nd ed. (Halle, 1797), preface, p. v. The two
    other synopses mentioned there appeared at almost the same time as
    Griesbach's first edition: Jos. Priestley, *A Harmony of the Evangelists, in
    Greek; to which are prefixed critical dissertations in English* (London,
    1777); William Newcome, *An Harmony of the Gospels; in which the text
    is disposed after Le Clerc's general manner...* (Dublin, 1778).
       Subsequently the latter is joined by: E. Robinson, *A Harmony of the
    Gospels in Greek, in the general order of Le Clerc and Newcome, with
    Newcome's Notes...* (Andover (Mass.), 1834). A later edition by the same
    author, but with a different textual basis, follows in 1845 (Boston). Be-
    longing to the era before the period of our narrative there should perhaps
    be mentioned the work of Nic. Toinard, *Evangeliorum harmonia graeco-
    latina* (Paris, 1707), which followed quickly on that of Le Clerc and is at
    least of the same quality. In this folio volume the various chronological
    and archaeological excursuses, also pictures of coins, charts for chrono-
    logical comparisons and to determine the time of the new moon, all bear
    witness to his quite predominant interest in the Gospel history. But above
    all there are given (something Le Clerc only does occasionally) at the head
    of each page the year and as far as possible the time of the year, the month,
    the day and in the Passion Narrative also the hours of what is reported. At
    the same time all conceivable methods of counting are considered (e.g.
    since the creation of the world, Roman consuls, the years in which Tiberius
    was born, took office, but also the year in which Jesus and the Baptist were
    born, and the years in which they began their ministry).

7   The printed text is, as far as I can see, Elzevir's text of 1624.

8   The only exception I have met is the transposition of the Vulgate verse

Matt. 5: 5 before 5: 4.

9   Preface, pp. iiif.

10   John 18: 12 comes between 18: 9 and 18: 10 to achieve the parallel position with Matt. 26: 50 and Mark 14: 46; John 18: 25–7 comes immediately after 18: 18 and so makes the account of Peter's threefold denial a self-contained unit also in John, as it is in the other Gospels. In John 19, v. 18*b* and vv. 23f. exchange places: in this way the sequence in Matthew (similarly Mark and Luke) of crucifixion, division of garments and attachment of the inscription is obtained also for John and in addition John 18: 18*b* is now parallel with Matt. 27: 38. John 20: 30f. are put after John 21 between vv. 24 and 25 and in this way the difficulty of the double ending is avoided.

11   That he was aware of the problems involved in this distinction can be seen by his shame-faced comment 'quod et olim fecerat' in the paraphrase to Matt. 21: 12 and parallels (p. 356).

12   E.g. canon 9: 'Similia fecit ac dixit saepius Christus, similibus occasionibus ita postulantibus'; cf. what is said above about the Lord's Prayer.

13   E.g. canon 7: 'Varietas paucularum circumstantiarum non ostendit in varias historias dispescendas esse narrationes non per omnia similes, si cetera consentiant', to be compared with canon 8: 'Similitudo paucularum circumstantium, quae ad summam rei parum faciunt, non ostendit unam a variis Evangelistis narrari historiam, si cetera dissideant.' It therefore only depends on what the harmonizer considers to be 'pauculae circumstantiae' and what he does not. In the case of the stories of the anointing for example this would not seem to be easy to make clear.

14   At most one could criticize the lack of a table from which one could quickly see where a particular text has been inserted.

15   Nevertheless he had predecessors as can be seen from Le Clerc's reproach (praef. p. iii) that other harmonies had been satisfied with juxtaposing similar words and deeds, and had shown no interest in the correct sequence of the events.

16   The 'self-imposed Rules' (*regulae a se conditae*) might be a play on Le Clerc's twenty-three canons.

17   From the preface to the second edition (1797), pp. vf.:

'auctores harmoniarum in hoc praecipue elaborarunt, ut tempus et ordinem, quo res gestae ab Evangelistis in literas relatae evenerint et invicem se exceperint, definirent; id quod a meo consilio alienissimum est. Ingenue enim profiteor, Lectoresque admonitos esse cupio, "harmoniam", quam proprie dicunt, in hocce libello neutiquam esse quaerendam. Quamvis enim non ignorem, quantum laboris viri perdocti harmoniae secundum regulas a se conditas in ordinem redigendae impenderint, ego tamen non solum exiguam utilitatem, imo nullam fere quam non mea etiam Synopsis praestet, e minuta esta diligentia percipi posse arbitror; sed valde etiam dubito, an ex Evangelistarum libellis harmonica componi possit narratio, veritati quoad chronologicam pericoparum dispositionem satis consentanea et firmis fundamentis superstructa. Quid enim? si nullus Evangelistarum ordinem temporis accurate ubique secutus est? et si sufficientia non adsint indicia, e quibus constare possit, quisnam et quibusnam in locis a chronologico ordine recesserit? Atque in hac me esse haeresi fateor.'

[This second edition of 1797 was the only one available to Prof. Greeven when he wrote this paper. However, the actual history of the publication of the Synopsis was as follows:

In 1774 Griesbach produced the first volume of his critical text of the New Testament in Greek under the title *Libri historici Novi Testamenti Graece. Pars prior, sistens synopsin Evangeliorum Matthaei, Marci et Lucae … Io. Iac. Griesbach, Halae, 1774.* The preface to this volume is dated 1 May 1774. Thus he chose to issue the first volume of his new critical text in the form of a 'synopsis' of the Gospels.

Then, in 1776, he reissued the identical text, and the preface still dated 1 May 1774, as a separate volume, the complete title of which was *Synopsis Evangeliorum Matthaei, Marci et Lucae, Textum Graecum ad fidem codicum, versionum et patrum emendavit et lectionis varietatem adiecit Io. Iac. Griesbach, Theologiae Prof. Puel. Halae, apud Io. Iac. Curt. MDCCLXXVI*, pp. xxxii + 295, plus five unnumbered pages containing his Conspectus Sectionum. In other words, the Synopsis now appeared as an independent work and no longer as the first part of his critical edition of the New Testament. In the bound copy in the British Museum, the text of John immediately follows but with a new pagination beginning at p. 1. Ed.]

18   Presented in his *Commentatio qua Marci evangelium totum e Matthaei et Lucae commentariis decerptum esse monstratur, 1789.*

19   See the *Commentationes theologicae* published by Velthusen, Ruperti and Kuinoel, vol. I (Leipzig, 1794).

20   Griesbach's significance for textual criticism is considered in a separate essay, chapter 7, so that it is unnecessary here to go into the copious text-critical information with which his synopsis is endowed. Nor need we consider here the work which underlies his text of the Gospels.

21   Planck, *Entwurf einer neuen synoptischen Zusammenstellung der drei ersten Evangelien nach Grunsätzen der höheren Kritik* (Göttingen, 1809).

22   Preface, pp. 3ff.

23   Therefrom were published *Fragmente eines Ungenannten* by G. E. Lessing (Braunschweig, 1774/8).

24   See also what follows this excerpt. Preface, pp. 3ff.

25   This is almost exactly the initial hypothesis of J. G. Eichhorn, as he presented it in 1794 (*Über die drei ersten Evangelien*), before he replaced it in his *Einleitung in das NT* in 1804 by a considerably more complicated one; cf. W. G. Kümmel, *Das Neue Testament. Geschichte der Erforschung seiner Probleme* (Freiburg, 1958; 2nd ed., München, 1970), p. 92.

26   The enumeration of the passages is not orientated according to the individual pericopes as in Eusebius but each passage embraces an uninterrupted part of the text of a Gospel without regard to its extent. Thus e.g. Luke 9: 51 – 18: 14 forms a single section, although several elements which have been placed elsewhere naturally do not appear.

27   Here Planck is wrong. Like others he has been deceived by the number of chapters. Although Matthew has four more chapters than Luke, the length of text of the latter exceeds that of Matthew by 6.3%; see Morgenthaler (note 99), p. 89.

28   W. M. L. de Wette and Fr. Lücke, *Synopsis Evangeliorum Matthaei, Marci et Lucae cum parallelis Joannis pericopis ex recensione Griesbachii cum*

selecta lectionum varietate concinnaverunt et breves argumentorum nota-tiones adjecerunt... (Berlin/London, 1818).

29 This would have amounted to the procedure applied e.g. in Huck's synopsis (from the third edition 1906).

30 Here can be seen how much historical interest still outweighed literary-critical interest: The difference of situation – here the Zebedees' question, there the Last Supper – would not allow a serious comparison of the logia. Only one 'cf.' was achieved, and this only in Luke, not in Matthew or Mark.

31 A table of comparison according to the original arrangement of the Gospels is in no way made superfluous by the new arrangement nor is it replaced by the full table of contents.

32 In his *Synopsis evangeliorum Matthaei Marci et Lucae cum Ioannis pericopis parallelis* (Halle, 1829), he writes (Praef., p. iv) about Griesbach's synopsis: 'Et quanquam difficultates non desint, quae illa ordinis institutione effici-antur, in plurimorum tamen theologorum manibus eadem illa versatur; neque Synopsis, per de Wettium et Lueckium, ut Griesbachianam ordinis rationem emendarent, concinnata... omnibus partibus satisfecit, ita ut Griesbachii liber a. 1822 typis recudendus esset.' The versatile, hard-work-ing young man is at the same time working on a new edition of Melanc-thon's *Loci theologici* (*loc. cit.*, p. 240).

33 However in part 3 the separate complete printing of each Gospel with the parallels is abandoned and Griesbach's sequence of sections is restored.

34 Naturally this is not accomplished altogether consistently; e.g. the two genealogies appear next to each other at Luke 3 with the same type, because in Griesbach the line on the left of the page was not added.

35 G. Ph. Chr. Kaiser, *Über die synoptische Zusammenstellung der vier kanonischen Evangelien* (Nürnberg, 1828) (only division into pericopes with a statement of contents, no text).

36 Praef., p. iii. David Schulz (1779–1854) was a representative of waning rationalism, professor of theology and philology in Halle (1809), of theo-logy in Breslau (from 1811, cf. RGG^3, vol. V, col. 1580f.).

37 H. N. Clausen (senior lecturer in Copenhagen), *Quatuor evangeliorum tabulae synopticae. Juxta rationem temporis, quoad fieri potuit, com-posuit, annotationibusque ex perpetua sectionum singularum collatione instruxit...* (Copenhagen, 1829), 185 pp.

38 Already before Clausen G. Chr. R. Matthäi, *Synopse der vier Evangelien nebst Kritik ihrer Wundererzählungen...* Göttingen, 1826), had produced an historical–exegetical synopsis, containing only a list of the 139 sections with brief indications of their contents; this was only a by-product of his principal concern, namely to provide an explanation of the miracle stories, which does not interest us here.

39 Here Clausen is repeating an argument of Le Clerc; cf. above p. 25.

40 It is not by chance that Clausen as well as Roediger appeals to H. E. G. Paulus, whose book *Das Leben Jesu, als Grundlage einer reinen Geschichte des Urchristentums* had appeared in 1828 (Heidelberg), prepared for by his *Philologisch-kritischer und historischer Kommentar über die drey ersten Evangelien...* (Lübeck, 1800–4).

41 *Zum Gebrauch bei akademischen Vorlesungen: Synoptische Tabellen über die drei ersten Evangelien* is published by Ed. Köllner (Giessen, 1849).

Inasmuch as he appeals to Planck's tables (n. 21) for his enterprise, he takes over without special proof, also, the latter's hypothesis of the Proto-Gospel, except that he calls it – in Planck's sense – 'Hebrew Matth.'

42 J. Gehringer, *Synoptische Zusammenstellung des griechischen Textes der vier Evangelien nach den Grundsätzen der authentischen Harmonie* (Tübingen, 1842), wants not only to produce a harmony of the Gospels but simultaneously to demonstrate that Matthew and Luke used Mark as source; cf. also Sommer (n. 46) and Anger (n. 55).

43 Gehringer (n. 42); J. H. Friedlieb, *Quatuor evangelia sacra Matthaei, Marci, Lucae, Ioannis in harmoniam redacta* (Breslau, 1847) (I could only obtain the second edition (Regensburg, 1869)); J. G. L. Chr. Krafft, *Chronologie und Harmonie der vier Evangelien, nach dem Tode des Vf. s* ed. von C. H. A. Burger (Erlangen, 1848). Also C. Tischendorf in his *Synopsis evangelica ex quatuor Evangeliis ordine chronologico concinnavit...* (Leipzig, 1851) is mainly interested in 'Historie' according to the preface. The text of his synopsis naturally corresponds to his critical edition and changes in the course of the different editions (7th ed., 1896) as his work on it proceeds. Apart from John, Tischendorf also offers the parallel texts Acts 1: 3–12 and 1 Cor. 11: 23–5. Incidentally he gives (pp. ix–xii) the most complete index of earlier harmonies and synopses since Fabricius (n. 5); it includes forty-seven names, from Tatian to W. Stroud.

44 Sommer (n. 46); Anger (n. 55).

45 Gehringer (n. 42); M. H. Schulze, *Evangelientafel als eine übersichtliche Darstellung der synoptischen Evangelien in ihrem Verwandtschaftsverhältnis zu einander, verbunden mit geeigneter Berücksichtigung des Evangeliums Joannes...* (Leipzig, 1861), wants to strengthen with his synopsis the thesis that Mark as the original of all Gospel writing was followed by Luke, imitating and supplementing, whereas Matthew was to be seen as the compiler of both. He pursues this aim not only in his introductory theses but, especially, in full footnotes.

46 Marginal mention only is made of the treatment by J. D. Schlichthorst, *Über das Verhältnis der drei synoptischen Evangelien zu einander im Allgemeinen und über die Composition und den inneren Charakter des Matthäus insbesondere* (Göttingen, 1835). Here Matthew is declared to be 'not synoptic' (like John) and an attempt is made to show the exact agreement between Mark and Luke – who both depend on the same source, which they use independently – by means of a comparative table. J. G. Sommer's *Synoptische Tafeln für die Kritik und Exegese der drei ersten Evangelien* (Bonn, 1842), has a special place among the synopses in table form. In his extensive introduction (21 pp.) he gives a critical survey of previous synopses in order to justify his own enterprise. Until that time one factor that was important for the solution of the Synoptic Problem had been insufficiently considered, namely the total arrangement of the material in the individual Gospels. This is obviously much easier to show by means of tables than through a fully printed text. Sommer's *Synoptische Tafeln*, which also allow smaller details to be recognized, have therefore the task of not only facilitating the finding of parallels, like similar aids in earlier synopses, but also represent a necessary additional instrument for the synopsis, without which the agreement and difference of the overall

arrangement of the material in the Gospels can only with difficulty be made apparent. Krafft (n. 43) also does not give the text, but only a running commentary on the 256 sections of his harmony, a commentary which limits itself so exclusively to chronology and harmonizing that, for example, in section 24 'Das zweite Wunder Jesu in Galiläa. Joh. 4, 46-54' he does not allude by a single word to the wonderful occurrence itself. That this healing might be connected with the story of the centurion of Capernaum remains completely outside the horizon of this work.

47 Gehringer (n. 42); Friedlieb, Krafft, Tischendorf (n. 43).

48 Schulze (n. 45); Anger (n. 55).

49 Sommer (n. 46).

50 Only Friedlieb (n. 43) strictly keeps to this rule; Gehringer (n. 42) follows it inasmuch as he makes an exception only at Matt. 5: 13; Mark 9: 5; 11: 25-6. Tischendorf (n. 43) too is still quite close to Griesbach. He has only a few repetitions and these are everywhere limited to smaller and very small units. In Matthew, twenty-nine verses appear twice, in Mark, ten, in Luke, eighty-five, in John, not one. This can easily be seen from the tables given at the end of the book. For Anger, cf. nn. 56, 58.

51 Gehringer (n. 42); Friedlieb (n. 43). Tischendorf (n. 43) alternates between parallel columns and additional material in notes, without there being any apparent reason for the different treatment. Schulze (n. 45) places the texts in columns next to one another but without equalization, and in a manner so cumbersome to use – the reader now having to turn one page now two – that it is often difficult to attribute the chapter references to the right Evangelist. Anger's arrangement is very much easier to survey (n. 55).

52 But not Tischendorf (n. 43), who only puts the smaller units mentioned in n. 50 in brackets, if they are not added as a note. In the more extensive parallels it is only possible to deduce from the table at the end whether or not a pericope is in its original position. Gehringer (n. 42) and Schulze (n. 45) omit every method of identification.

53 Gehringer (n. 42); Friedlieb, Tischendorf (n. 43); Schulze (n. 45); also Anger (n. 55).

54 In this respect Le Clerc's *Harmonia* is already notably progressive. Also Griesbach, followed by de Wette–Lücke and Roediger, who, however, do not surpass him, tries to put corresponding beginnings of sentences or catch-words where possible on the same level.

55 R. Anger, *Synopsis evangeliorum Matthaei, Marci, Lucae cum locis qui supersunt parallelis litterarum et traditionum evangelicarum Irenaeo anti- quiorum...* (Leipzig, 1852).

56 John's Gospel, however, as the most important and abundant witness for the synoptic tradition is classed with the 'alii Novi Testamenti loci'.

57 Prolegomena, p. 1.

58 Therefore Anger too does not meet de Wette–Lücke's requirement that the text of the individual Gospels must be capable of being read in its original order even in a synopsis.

59 H. Sevin, *Die drei ersten Evangelien synoptisch zusammengestellt* (Wiesbaden, 1866), would not require mention if the author had not based his rather modest work on the Codex Sinaiticus (with 300 to 400 corrections almost exclusively purely orthographic). The great events of the research

into the text reach out, though in this case not convincingly, into the field of the Greek synopsis of the Gospels: in 1862 there appeared Tischendorf's folio edition of the famous manuscript, in 1865 his octavo edition.

60 W. G. Rushbrooke, *Synopticon, An exposition of the common matter of the Synoptic Gospels* (London, 1880). For what follows, cf. foreword, pp. v–xii.

61 Naturally this must not be taken too literally. For even what is common only to Mark and Matthew, or Mark and Luke, even the little that is unique to Mark, Rushbrooke attributes to 'the triple tradition'. John is also printed in so far as he has material parallel to Mark. In the case of the story of the Anointing, Mark–Matthew–John even form 'a triple tradition', the Lucan version being put opposite for comparison.

62 The *Synopticon* was bound to arouse interest, not least owing to its generous, not to say luxurious, format. The folio volume consists of pages printed (with very few exceptions) on one side only, with a framed type-area. In the story of the Anointing (see n. 61), which, surprisingly, is not counted as part of the 'triple tradition of the Synoptic Gospels' (unlike, for example, the Feeding of the Four Thousand which is narrated only in Mark and Matthew), even gold print is used!

63 P. Feine *RE*[3], vol. XIX (1907), p. 280 (Art. 'Synopse'); B. M. Metzger *RGG*[3], vol. II (1958), col. 770 (Art. 'Evangelienharmonie'); W. G. Kümmel, *Einleitung in das Neue Testament*, 17th ed. (Heidelberg, 1973), p. 13.

64 The synopses of Wright (n. 73) and Heinecke (n. 77), which like Rushbrooke divide the matter into sections (the former without even mentioning him), otherwise pursue quite different goals with different means.

65 In appendix A′ in which Matthew is found next to Luke and common material is emphasized with 'capitals' a much better overall view may be obtained.

66 Pages of lists of Addenda and Corrigenda to the main part, which were added to the appendixes that appeared later, show the type-setting to have been tiresome beyond measure.

67 H. J. Holtzmann, *Hand-Commentar zum Neuen Testament*, vol. I, 'Die Synoptiker. Die Apostelgeschichte' (Freiburg, 1889); here the second edition of 1891 is cited.

68 A. Huck, *Synopse der drei ersten Evangelien* (Freiburg, 1892).

69 Huck was a most effective defender of the two-source theory; W. G. Kümmel, *loc. cit.* (n. 63), p. 22.

70 In H. A. W. Meyer's critical–exegetical commentary: on Matthew, 8th ed. (Göttingen, 1885), ed. B. Weiss; on Mark and Luke, 7th ed. (1883), ed. B. Weiss, and 8th ed. (1892), ed. B. and J. Weiss.

71 This appeared in 1901 in an entirely revised third edition, with which Huck's synopsis no longer fitted.

72 A few exceptions to this were removed in the fourth edition of 1910.

73 A. Wright, *A Synopsis of the Gospels in Greek...* (London, 1896); here the second revised and expanded edition of 1903 is used.

74 K. Veit, *Die synoptischen Parallelen. Ein alter Versuch ihrer Enträtselung* (Gütersloh, 1897). Veit in his preface, in which he justifies his enterprise with the 'lack of an appropriately arranged edition of the text', surprisingly

makes no mention of Huck's Synopsis which had appeared in 1892.

75   E.g. in the comparison of the Gospel of Thomas with the Sahidic text of the Canonical Gospels in W. Schrage, *Das Verhältnis des Thomas-Evangeliums zur synoptischen Tradition und zu den koptischen Evangelien-Übersetzungen*, ZNW Beiheft 29 (Berlin, 1964). Compare pp. 81f. (five parallel lines underneath each other – the general practice) with p. 116 (two columns next to each other – an exception).

76   Viewed theoretically one might be inclined to consider both methods of comparison basically of equal value. But this would be a mistake. It is significant that the eye – at least of the Westerner – is used to following a horizontal line of signs, not a vertical one. The to-and-fro of the comparative glance would therefore find it easier to function horizontally than vertically.

77   R. Heineke, *Synopse der drei ersten kanonischen Evangelien mit Parallelen aus dem Johannesevangelium* (Giessen, 1898). Heinecke does not seem to have known Veit's synopsis (n. 74) which appeared in 1897. At least he says nothing about it in his preface (April 1898).

78   W. Larfeld, *Griechisch-deutsche Synopse der vier neutestamentlichen Evangelien nach literarhistorischen Gesichtspunkten und mit textkritischem Apparat* (Tübingen, 1911).

79   The extra-canonical material is, however, not considered at all. From the canon only Acts 1: 1–20 and 1 Cor. 11: 23–5; 15: 3–8 are brought in.

80   The royal official (John 4) naturally has nothing to do with the centurion from Capernaum, not to speak of the different stories of Anointing.

81   Preface, p. v.

82   According to the revised Luther text, the numerous divergences of which from 'Nestle' are noted in the text.

83   E. DeWitt Burton and E. J. Goodspeed, *A Harmony of the Synoptic Gospels in Greek* (Chicago/London, 1920; 15th ed., 1967). The same authors had already produced a synopsis in English, and the Greek synopsis follows its pattern exactly.

84   The omission of such a juxtaposition at Luke 4: 5–8 // Matt. 4: 8–10 is an exception caused by the close proximity of the texts (they are found on the reverse sides of the same page). In both passages however the arrangement of the type is made as if they were put in juxtaposition: that is, arrangement according to corresponding lines.

85   For the sake of brevity I may be permitted to refer to my essay ('Erwägungen zur synoptischen Textkritik' in *NTS* 6 (1960), 281–96, especially pp. 288ff.

86   M.-J. Lagrange, *Synopsis evangelica. Textum graecum quattuor evangeliorum recensuit et juxta ordinem chronologicum Lucae praesertim et Johannis concinnavit...* (Barcelona/Paris, 1926).

87   These appeared from 1903 in *Études Bibliques*.

88   Exceptions: John 6 comes before John 5; 20: 30f. behind 21: 23.

89   G. Bornkamm in *ThLZ* 82 (1957), 270f. on: M.-J. Lagrange, *L'Évangile de Jésus-Christ. Avec la Synopse évangélique*, trad. par C. Lavergne (Paris, 1928; 2nd ed., 1954). The same translator had already taken care of a translation of the Greek synopsis into French together with M. Langlois: *Synopse des quatre Évangiles en français d'après la synopse grecque du...*

Lagrange (Paris/Gembloux, 1927).

90 P. Benoit and M.-E. Boismard, *Synopse des quatre Évangiles en français avec paralleles des apocryphes et des pères* (Paris, 1969).

91 It is probably an oversight that John 12: 3 and Mark 14: 3, but not Matt. 26: 6f. are printed next to Luke 7: 36–50.

92 J. Weiss, *Synoptische Tafeln zu den drei älteren Evangelien mit Unterscheidung der Quellen in vierfachem Farbdruck* (Göttingen, 1913), from the second edition revised by R. Schütz (3rd ed., 1929).

93 J. Weiss (ed.), *Die Schriften des Neuen Testaments neu übersetzt und für die Gegenwart erklärt* (Göttingen, 1906), vol. I, 'Die drei älteren Evangelien' (J. Weiss).

94 W. R. Farmer, *Synopticon. The verbal agreement between the Greek Texts of Matthew, Mark and Luke contextually exhibited* (Cambridge, 1969).

95 W. R. Farmer, *The Synoptic Problem. A Critical Analysis* (New York, 1964).

96 De Solages (n. 98) gives the same advice, p. 3*b*.

97 The confusion in the use of the colours, of which Morgenthaler (n. 104, *loc. cit.*, p. 25) complains, I do not therefore find so terrible. 'Traffic directions', which he misses there, could take much wind out of the sails of the student's own work – and joy in discovery – and might tempt him away to standard coloured works.

98 B. de Solages, *Synopse Grecque des Évangiles. Méthode nouvelle pour résoudre le problème synoptique* (Leiden, 1959). I had the simultaneous English edition (Leiden, 1959) before me.

99 R. Morgenthaler, *Statistik des neutestamentlichen Wortschatzes* (Zürich, 1957; 2nd ed., 1973).

100 Morgenthaler goes further into the uses of statistics in the past (see n. 104, *loc. cit.*, parts 1 and 4).

101 This happened more fully, e.g., in Morgenthaler's statistical synopsis (n. 104). Precisely in the French-speaking area much seems to have been set in motion by 'structuralism', also with respect to quantitative analyses. Thus the Benedictine J. Froger, *La critique des textes et son automatisation* (Paris, 1968), has suggested a method of textual criticism which makes use of set theory. His model is a Molière text artificially 'corrupted' for this purpose. An attempt to use it showed that the method failed when more than one or two contaminations were present. Contamination is, however, the daily bread of New Testament textual criticism.

102 See note 86.

103 Morgenthaler himself says in his description of de Solages' synopsis how far he can follow him and where he goes his own way (n. 100, *loc. cit.*, pp. 18–25).

104 R. Morgenthaler, *Statistische Synopse* (Zürich, 1971). It is perhaps not superfluous to note that 'statistical' and 'statistics' are used here, as also by de Solages, in the generally accepted sense: by counting to the end, number values are obtained which, by addition, sub-division and comparison with other values, and with the parts and the whole, reveal certain facts or characteristics in what is counted. But also all the heavy equipment of the mathematical discipline 'statistics' with its various 'mean values', with its concepts 'variance' or 'standard deviation', with the help of which the 'sample' is exactly described right up to the measure of a 'normal distribu-

tion', to which (so the expectation) the texts of the same author will be related in the same way, those of different authors in different ways — this too has already been applied to New Testament texts, though not yet to the Synoptics. G. Herdan in his work – used also by Morgenthaler and cited by him – *The Advanced Theory of Language as Choice and Chance* (Berlin/New York, 1966) in chapter 13 (pp. 219–49) gives an application to the Pauline letters (A) and to the New Testament as a whole (B). Together with K. Grayston, Herdan investigated not only 'The Authorship of the Pastorals in the Light of Statistical Linguistics' (*NTS* 6 (1959), 1–15), but also discussed de Solages' synopsis as 'an important contribution to stylostatistics' (*NTS* 7 (1960), 97f.).

105 Kurt Aland, *Synopsis Quattuor Evangeliorum, locis parallelis evangeliorum apocryphorum et patrum adhibitis*, 1st ed. (Stuttgart, 1963).

106 A new revision (the eleventh edition) by the author of this paper is due in 1978.

107 See above at n. 36.

108 The author for obvious reasons does not want to enter here into a consideration of the advantages and disadvantages of Aland's synopsis.

4 Bo Reicke: Griesbach's answer to the Synoptic Question

1 J. J. Griesbach, *Fontes unde evangelistae suas de resurrectione Domini narrationes hauserint: Paschatos solemnia*... (Jena, 1783); reprinted in J. J. Griesbach, *Opuscula academica*, ed. J. Ph. Gabler, vol. II (Jena, 1825), pp. 241–56 (quotations below are from this edition).

2 Idem, *Commentatio qua Marci evangelium totum e Matthaei et Lucae commentariis decerptum esse monstratur* (Jena, 1789–90).

3 Idem, *Commentatio* (n. 2)... *locupletata*: J. C. Velthusen *et al.* (eds.), *Commentationes Theologicae*, vol. I (Leipzig, 1794), pp. 360–434; reprinted in Griesbach, *Opuscula* (n. 1), pp. 358–425 (quotations below are from this edition).

4 H. Owen, *Observations on the Four Gospels* (London, 1764), p. 32: Matthew–Luke–Mark; A. F. Büsching, *Die vier Evangelisten mit ihren eigenen Worten zusammengesetzt und mit Erklärungen versehen* (Hamburg, 1766), pp. 99, 108, 118ff.: Luke–Matthew–Mark.

5 Griesbach (n. 3), p. 365.

6 H. Grotius, *Annotationes in libros evangeliorum* (Amsterdam, 1641), p. 8: Hebr. Matthew–Greek Mark; p. 594: Matthew–Mark–Luke.

7 G. C. Storr, *Über den Zweck der evangelischen Geschichte und der Briefe Johannis* (Tübingen, 1786; 2nd ed. 1810), pp. 274, 294.

8 Griesbach, *Fontes* (n. 1), p. 243; *Commentatio* (n. 3), p. 397.

9 R. Simon, *Histoire critique du texte du Nouveau Testament* (Rotterdam, 1689), pp. 71–87.

10 G. E. Lessing, 'Neue Hypothesen über die Evangelisten als bloss menschliche Geschichtsschreiber betrachtet' (1778), *Theologischer Nachlass* (Berlin, 1784), 45–72, p. 68.

11 J. G. Eichhorn, 'Über die drei ersten Evangelien', *Allgemeine Bibliothek der biblischen Litteratur*, vol. V (Leipzig, 1794), pp. 759–996.

12 J. B. Koppe, *Marcus non epitomator Matthaei*, Programme Univ. Göttingen (Helmstadii, 1792); reprint in D. J. Pott and G. A. Ruperti (eds.), *Sylloge*

commentationum theologicarum, vol. I (Helmstadii, 1800), pp. 35–69, esp. p. 66; Griesbach (n. 3), pp. 360f.

13 J. G. Herder, *Vom Erlöser der Menschen, nach unseren drei ersten Evangelien* (Riga, 1796), pp. 202, 205; idem, *Von Gottes Sohn, der Welt Heiland, nach Johannes Evangelium. Nebst einer Regel der Zusammenstimmung unserer Evangelien aus ihrer Entstehung und Ordnung* (Riga, 1797), pp. 306, 341, 376.

14 Valuable bibliographical information on the development of the Synoptic Problem in Germany and Great Britain before and after A.D. 1800 is found in J. C. L. Gieseler, *Historisch-kritischer Versuch über die Entstehung und früheste Geschichte der schriftlichen Evangelien* (Leipzig, 1818), pp. 30–52.

15 Griesbach (n. 1), pp. 243, 248.

16 *Ibid.,* pp. 244, 247.

17 Pp. 248, 251, 253.

18 Pp. 255–6.

19 Griesbach (n. 3), p. 359.

20 *Ibid.,* p. 365.

21 Pp. 365–9.

22 Griesbach (n. 3), pp. 371–7.

23 *Ibid.,* p. 378, n. 2.

24 Pp. 378–84.

25 Pp. 384f.

26 P. 386.

27 P. 394.

28 P. 394.

29 P. 397.

30 P. 398.

31 Pp. 395ff.

32 P. 400.

33 Pp. 402–12.

34 Pp. 412–22.

35 H. E. G. Paulus, review of *Commentationes theologicae* (n. 3): *Neues theol. Journal,* 5 (1795), 211–30; = idem, 'Nachweisung der Entstehung des Markus-Evangeliums aus den beiden des Matthäus und Lukas', *Theologisch-exegetisches Conservatorium* (Heidelberg, 1822), pp. 73–85; see also idem, *Philologisch-kritischer und historischer Kommentar,* vol. I, 1 (Lübeck, 1800; 2nd ed., 1804), pp. 263f.; idem, *Exegetisches Handbuch über die drei ersten Evangelien,* vol. I, 1 (Heidelberg, 1831), pp. 25–37. In the commentaries mentioned, however, Paulus was not willing to regard Matthew as the source of Luke.

36 H. Saunier, *Über die Quellen des Evangeliums des Marcus. Ein Beitrag zu den Untersuchungen über die Entstehung unserer kanonischen Evangelien* (Berlin, 1825), pp. 35–7.

37 *Ibid.,* pp. 44–8.

38 P. 54.

39 P. 66.

40 P. 74.

41 Pp. 172f.

42 Pp. 177–80.

43 P. 187.

44 K. G. W. Theile, *De trium priorum evangeliorum necessitudine,* vol. I (diss., Leipzig, 1825), p. 8.

45 W. M. L. de Wette, *Lehrbuch der historisch kritischen Einleitung in die kanonischen Bücher des Neuen Testaments* (Berlin, 1826), pp. 128-71; 5th ed., with larger pages (1848), pp. 131-79; 6th ed., ed. H. Messner and G. Lünemann (1860), pp. 144-95.

46 De Wette (n. 45), 6th ed., pp. 144-9.

47 In the sixth edition, pp. 150-2, with references to fifteen representatives of Griesbach's theory from 1805 through 1853.

48 *Ibid.,* pp. 152f.

49 Pp. 154-9.

50 Pp. 159-84.

51 Pp. 184f. In the second paragraph quoted above, the numbers in square brackets [1-4] were added by the author of this paper.

52 P. 185.

53 P. 186.

54 Pp. 187-90.

55 Pp. 191-5.

56 F. Neirynck, 'The Griesbach Hypothesis' (an unpublished paper circulated in mimeographed form by the author at the Colloquium), n. 78. This note reads:

'As it can be seen from this Bibliography, the Griesbachian Hypothesis continued to be defended, after Strauss and Baur, also by Roman Catholics: Kuhn (Tübingen), Schwarz (Tübingen), Maier (Freiburg), Langen (Bonn), Grimm (Würzburg), Nippel (Tübingen). They tended to correct the hypothesis by the assumption of Mark's contact with an original Petrine tradition (see also Köster and others) – and they were hardly members of "the wicked company it [the Griesbach Solution] kept in the old days"; cf. D. L. Dungan, "Mark – The Abridgement of Matthew and Luke", *Perspective* 11 (1970), 89.'

57 E. Zeller, 'Über den dogmatischen Charakter des dritten Evangeliums', *Theologische Jahrbücher* 2 (1843), 59-90.

58 A. Ritschl, *Das Evangelium Marcions und das kanonische Evangelium des Lucas* (Tübingen, 1846), pp. 55-150.

59 F. C. Baur, *Kritische Untersuchungen über die kanonischen Evangelien, ihr Verhältnis zu einander, ihren Charakter und Ursprung* (Tübingen, 1847), pp. 608-13.

60 *Ibid.,* p. 441.

61 P. 535.

62 Pp. 535, 567.

63 Pp. 605-9.

64 K. A. Credner, *Einleitung in das Neue Testament* (Halle, 1836), pp. 201-5.

65 C. H. Weisse, *Die evangelische Geschichte kritisch und philosophisch bearbeitet,* vol. I (Leipzig, 1838), pp. 3, 56, 83.

66 C. G. Wilke, *Der Urevangelist oder exegetisch kritische Untersuchung über das Verwandtschaftsverhältnis der drei ersten Evangelien* (Dresden and Leipzig, 1838), p. v.

5 J. J. Griesbach: Commentatio qua Marci Evangelium totum e Matthaei et Lucae
commentariis decerptum esse monstratur

Introduction by Bo Reicke

1 J. J. Griesbach, *Libri historici*, vol. I (Halle, 1774), p. vii.
2 *Ibid.*
3 E. and C. Bertheau, 'Eichhorn, Johann Gottfried', *RE*, vol. V (1898), pp. 234–7.
4 J. G. Eichhorn, 'Über die drey ersten Evangelien', *Allgemeine Bibliothek der biblischen Litteratur*, vol. V (Leipzig, 1794), pp. 759–996.
5 R. Simon, *Histoire critique du texte du Nouveau Testament* (Rotterdam, 1689), pp. 71–87.
6 G. E. Lessing, 'Neue Hypothese über die Evangelisten als blos menschliche Geschichtsschreiber betrachtet' (1778): *Theologischer Nachlass* (Berlin, 1784), pp. 45–72.
7 J. A. Wagenmann, 'Johann Benjamin Koppe', *AdBiog*, vol. XVI (1882), pp. 692–3.
8 J. B. Koppe, *Marcus non epitomator Matthaei*, Programme Univ. Göttingen (Helmstadii, 1792); reprint in D. J. Pott and G. A. Ruperti (eds.), *Sylloge commentationum theologicarum*, vol. I (Helmstadii, 1800), 35–69, pp. 65–7.
9 Th. Schott, 'Gottlob Christian Storr', *AdBiog*, vol. XXXVI (1893), pp. 456–8; M. A. von Landerer and O. Kirn, 'Tübinger Schule, ältere', *RE*, vol. XX (1908), pp. 148–59.
10 G. C. Storr, *Über den Zweck der evangelischen Geschichte und der Briefe Johannis* (Tübingen, 1786; 2nd ed., 1810), pp. 274, 294.

Griesbach's Commentatio

1 Extat haec recognita commentatio in Commentatt. theol. a Velthusen Kuinoel et Ruperti editis, Vol. I, Lips. 1794. p. 360. sqq. G.
2 In Programm. paschali anni 1783 (vid. supr. p. 241).
3 De consensu Evangeliorum Libr. I. cap. 2.
4 *Supplement to the credibility of the gospel history.* Vol. I, cap. 10.
5 In Programm. Gotting. MDCCLXXXII. quod inscriptum est: *Marcus non epitomator Matthaei.*
6 *Ueber den Zweck der evangel. Geschichte Iohannes* § 85. seqq. collata ejusdem Viri doctissimi dissertatione priore *in librorum N. T. historicorum aliquot loca.* Tubing. 1790. pag. 58 seqq. ubi hypothesi a nobis propositae opponuntur nonnulla, quae posthaec suo loco in examinandis obiectionibus adversus sententiam nostram prolatis non negligemus.
7 *Allgemeine Bibliothek der biblischen Literatur*, Vol. 5. Part. 5. Sed ad finem nondum perducta est haec de Evangeliis commentatio. (Paulo post autem finita est haec commentatio part. 6. eiusd. Vol. V G.)
8 l.c. pag. 823.
9 Ibid pag. 920.
10 Temporis spatium, quo primaevi scripti ebraici et nostrorum Evangeliorum natales inter se distant, angustius nobis videtur, quam ut tot archetypi recensiones novas ac locupletiores, tot recensionum permixtiones, tot denique earum versiones capere queat. Librorum conscribendorum et

divulgandorum modus, coetuumque christianorum per longe dissitas provincias dispersorum nec communi quodam vinculo inter se connexorum conditio ac status, isto aevo, si quid iudicamus, tam velocem libelli alicuius non solum propagationem sed etiam in tam multiplices formas conversionem, vix admittebant. Si Evangelia nostra non ante seculum secundum medium conscripta essent, facilius hypothesi Eichhornianae assentiremur.

11 Ex Cel. *Eichhornii* sententia, ni fallimur, non archetypus sed versiones ejus praesto fuerunt nostrorum Evangeliorum auctoribus. Matthaeus saltim ebraicum archetypum non adhibuit. Nam in graeco Matthaei textu, si Viri doctissimi iudicio standum est, plura deprehenduntur παροραματα, e vocum ebraicarum archetypi similium permutatione eruta. Quis vero Matthaeum ipsum tales errores commisisse sibi persuadeat? Atqui si Matthaeus graeca archetypi versione usus est, idem sano de Luca et Marco statuendum erit.

12 De his argumentis, *quatenus* ad impugnandam *nostram* de Marci Evangelio hypothesin adhiberi possent, infra nonnulla dicenda erunt, eamque ob causam eorum mentionem hoc loco fecimus. Cardo autem rei vertitur in eo, ut dispiciatur, (1) utrum indubia adsint fontis *ebraici* indicia, (2) num e diverso eandem rem enuntiandi modo, item ex omissionibus et ἐναντιοφανειαις nonnullis cogi possit, alterum auctorem altero usum non esse. Nam utrumque hoc si recte negatur, non est cur hypothesin a nobis defensam novae huic postponamus.

13 *In den Beyträgen zur Beförderung des vernünftigen Denkens in der Religion.* Partic. XVI. pag. 57.

14 Sicubi longiores sermones retinuit, veluti cap. 4. et 13. tamen in his quoque brevitati studuit. Certe, si locos Matthaei parallelos compares, Marcum utroque loco laudato haud pauca resecuisse deprehendes.

15 Neque tamen omnia, quae propius ad Iudaeos et Palaestinenses spectant, penitus a suo libello excludere potuit. Cum enim Christus nunquam alios habuisset auditores quam Iudaeos, ipseque sapientissime institutionem suam semper attemperasset audientium conditioni, fieri non poterat, quin sermonibus ipsius tantum non omnibus inesset aliquid, quod ad Iudaeos maxime pertineret. Praeterea, cum omnes Christianorum coetus isto tempore collecti una cum Exgentilibus etiam Exiudaeos complecterentur, inter Marci quoque lectores procul dubio fuere iudaicis sacris addicti. Horum causa transfundere e Matthaei Evangelio in suum Marcus quaedam potuit, quae ad Iudaeos potissimum horumque cogitandi vivendive modum respicerent. Interim (*a*) haud pauca huius generis prorsus intacta reliquit, (*b*) in iis, quae retinenda censuit, brevior esse solet Matthaeo, (*c*) nonnullos sermones, ad Iudaeos spectantes, duntaxat propter eximias quasdam et perutiles sententias, in ipsis obvias transscripsisse videtur; (*d*) multa, quae Palaestinensibus Iudaeis dicta fuerant, ab aliis etiam non sine utilitatis fructu legi poterant. Haec qui attendere velit, de nonnullis Marci locis, quos *Storrius V. V.* in dissertatione modo laudata pag. 65. nostrae thesi opposuit, nullo negotio judicium feret. Nempe Marci 2, 16–18. [*sic*] servatum fuit propter commata 17. 20. 27. 28. Quae cap. 3, 22–30. leguntur, omittere Marcus noluit, quia extra Palaestinam quoque Christianae religionis hostes Iesum et Apostolos magicis artibus daemonumque ope miracula patrasse caussabantur. Narratio de Nazaretanis cap. 6, 1–6. utilis

esse poterat omnibus, qui mirarentur, quid sit, quod tam pauci e populari-
bus Iesu tanti doctoris monitis aures praebuissent dociles. Mandata, quae
Dominus, cap. 6, 8–11. apostolis, cum eos primum futuri officii quasi
rudimentum ponere iuberet, dederat, haud indigna sane erant, quae omnium locorum Christianis innotescerent; quamquam Marcus, Lucae imitatus
exemplum paucis versibus complexus est, quae Matthaeus verbosa oratione
persecutus erat. Marci 8, 1–23. servatum fuit ob vs. 15–23. Cap. 8, 11. 12.
non solum reprehenduntur omnes quorumcunque locorum homines σημεια
ἐπιζητουντες, verum referri etiam hic locus potest inter eos, e quibus patet,
Iesum nunquam eo consilio miracula edidisse, ut vanae spectatorum curiosi-
tati satisfaceret; qua de re infra Sect. II. observ. 3. plura dicentur. Tandem
cap. 12, 38–40. praeeunte Luca paucissimis tantum Marcus attingit sermonem Domini, quo Pharisaei et Scribae reprehendebantur; quem locum
Matthaeus copiosissime tractaverat.

16   Omittuntur haec capita integra, quia Marcus res a Christo, tanquam doctore
     publico, gestas enarrare tantum voluit.

17   Marcus, ad Matth. 4, 21. progressus, seponit Matthaeum et transit ad
     Lucam, quoniam orationem Christi in monte habitam, quae apud Mat-
     thaeum hic sequitur, praeterire decreverat. Nimis enim verbosa videbatur
     ei, exiguum libellum scripturo, et multa praeterea complectitur, quae
     proxime ad eos tantum homines pertinebant, qui Christum coram in
     monte loquentem audirent.

18   Quae leguntur Marc. 1, 14. parallela sunt loco Luc. 4, 14. Iis vero quae
     sequuntur Luc. 4, 15–30. nempe sermone in synagoga Nazaretana habito,
     accommodatione loci Esaiae, et exemplis ex historia Eliae et Elisaei petitis,
     his igitur omnibus Marcus suos lectores facile carere posse censebat. Prae-
     terea Marc. 6, 1–6. de Nazaretanis narrantur nonnulla e Matthaeo, quae
     cum Luc. 4, 15 sqq. comparari possunt. Hinc patet, quomodo Marcus, a
     Matthaeo ad Lucam transiliens, ad Lucae 4, 31. devenerit.

19   Omittitur, quia apud Marcum cap. 1, 16–20. jam praecesserat narratio e
     Matthaeo ducta, huic, quae apud Lucam h. l. legitur, haud absimilis.

20   Vide notam x. (pag. 203 not. 22).

21   Marcus hic abrumpit filum, propter orationem montanam h. l. apud
     Lucam sequentem, et transit ad Matthaeum.

22   Causa cur Marcus, a Luca rediens ad Matthaeum, ab eo commate capitis
     12, quod tabula indicat, novam quasi telam exorsus sit, in aprico posita
     est. Scilicet Luca duce (Luc. 6, 11). Marcus pervenerat usque ad capitis
     sui 3 comma 6, ita tamen, ut quoad narrationis ordinem Lucam quidem
     secutus esset, at Matthaeum tamen simul, ubi hic eadem cum Luca
     traderet, semper contulisset. Iam locus Marci modo laudatus cap. 3, 6.
     7. parallelus est Matthaei 12, 14. 15. Quae sequuntur Marc 3, 7–12. uberius
     et fere παραφραστικως exprimunt commata Matthaei cap. 12, 15–21. sed
     ita, ut Marcus (1) consulto omitteret locum prophetae comm. 17–21
     laudatum, (2) simul conferret Luc. 6, 17–19. et (3) de suo adderet comm
     9. circumstantias quasdam. Nimirum, cum comma suum 6. (parallelum
     Matth. 12, 14. et Luc. 6, 11.) scripsisset Marcus, statim in perlegendo
     Lucae commentario, quem inde a Luc. 5, 31. ad cap. 6, 11. ducem secutus
     fuerat, perrexisse videtur usque ad Luc. 6, 20. ubi oratio incipit montana,
     quam cum omittere decrevisset seposito Luca ad illum se convertit Mat-

thaei locum, qui suo commati 6. parallelus est, scil. Matth. 12, 15. Hanc, ut diximus, paraphrastice expressit, insertis nonnullis, quae e Lucae loco, quem modo perlustraverat, (Luc. 6, 17-19) menti ipsius adhuc obversabantur. Iam cum scripsisset comma suum 12, quod exacto respondet Matthaei commati 16, progrediendum fuisset (praetermisso prophetico loco) ad Matthaei comm. 22. 23. Sed hic Marcus animadvertit, catalogum Apostolorum, quem modo apud Lucam legerat, nondum in suo extare libello. Matthaeus quidem alio iam loco (Matth. 10, 2-4.) eum anticipaverat; sed illum locum (imo omnia a Matth. 4, 23. ad cap. 12, 14.) Marcus transsilierat. Ne igitur sui lectores tali catalogo plane carerent, praeeunte Luca (Luc. 6, 12-16.) antequam hunc seponeret, Apostolorum delectum et nomina heic (Marc. 13 - 19.) enarravit. His insertis, redit ad eum Matthaei locum, in quo, ut vidimus, substiterat, scilicet Matth. 12, 22. Hic, admonitus a Matthaeo (Matth. 12, 23. ἐξίσταντο παντες, και ἐλεγον μητι οὗτος ἐστιν κ. τ. λ.) singulares quasdam περιστασεις a Matthaeo vel neglectas vel saltim perobscure indigitatas, quas ipse penitius cognitas haberet, inserendas esse putavit Marc. 3, 20. 21. Quo peracto facem iam praeferente Matthaeo, (cap. 12, 24 seqq.) strenue pergit Marcus cap. 3, 22. usque ad cap. 4, 20.

23 Omittitur, quia sententias his similes Marcus legerat in oratione montana, Matth. 7, 16-20. quam a suo libro abesse volebat.

24 Omittitur haec oratio Christi, utpote ad Palaestinenses, quibus Christum coram loquentem audire contigit, potissimum spectans. Praeterea similis his, quae h. l. apud Matthaeum leguntur (comm. 38. 39.) recurrunt mox apud eundem cap. 16, 1-4. unde Marcus ea in suum librum (cap. 8, 11. 12.) transtulit.

25 Antecedentia et consequentia e Matthaeo decerpta sunt; haec vero quinque commata Lucas suppeditavit. Nempe praecedentia, Marc. 4, 1-20. quae desumta erant e Matth. 13, 1-23. respondens Lucae 8, 1-15. Lucam igitur cum Matthaeo contulerat Marcus. Iam vero apud Lucam commate proxime sequente, nimirum cap. 8, 16. inveniebat parabolam elegantem eandemque brevissimam, quam excipiebant comm. 17. 18. gnomae nonnullae itidem perbreves sed memorabiles. Tria haec commata, ad quae Matthaeus eum quasi deduxerat, a suo libello abesse noluit Marcus.

26 Parabola, quae habetur Matth. 13, 24-30. et mentionem iniicit *agricolarum dormientium*, in memoriam revocabat Marco aliam de *agricola dormiente* parabolam brevitate sua non minus quam elegantia commendabilem, et cum argumento parabolarum et gnomarum proximo antecedentium et sequentium magis adhuc, quam illa apud Matthaeum parabola, consentientem. Hanc igitur in locum substituit alterius, quae praeterea explicationem uberiorem (Matth. 13, 36-43) quam Marcus, brevitati studens, in libellum suum transfundere nolebat, adiunctam haberet.

27 Sat multas parabolas e Matthaeo iam descripserat Marcus. Cum vero Matthaeus porro parabolis adderet parabolas, Marcus velut fatigatus hunc ducem aliquantisper valere iussit, et ad Lucam se recepit.

28 In decerpendo Luca Marcus pervenerat usque ad Luc. 8, 18. Narratiunculam comm. 19-21. his omisit, quia supra iam (Marc. 3, 31-35) eo loco et ordine, quo apud Matthaeum eam invenerat, in suos commentarios retulerat. Itaque devenit ad comma proxime sequens Luc. 8, 22. Hic

igitur pergit.

29 Quae Marci capite 5. continentur, leguntur quidem etiam apud Matthaeum, sed partim alio loco et ordine, partim paucioribus verbis. Manifestum erit unicuique tres Evangelistas comparanti, Marcum haec omnia non Matthaeo accepta referre, sed Lucae.

30 Marcum nimia parabolarum Matthaei cap. 13. copia quasi obrutum, Lucae se adiunxisse comitem, nota c. (p. praec. not. 27) vidimus. Verumtamen cum Matthaeum potissimum sibi elegisset, ad cuius ductum memorabilia Christi scripto consignaret, iam ad Matthaeum suum redit, et quidem ad eum ipsum locum, quo parabolae istae finiuntur, nempe ad Matth. 13, 53. 54. Interim Lucam non tamen plane negligit, sed diligenter eum cum Matthaeo confert. Hinc pericopae sequentes mox ex hoc mox ex illo sunt decerptae.

31 Haec solus habet Marcus. De his vero, quae apud Marcum tantum occurrunt, posthaec disseretur.

32 In hac pericopa, Matthaei potissimum vestigia premit, collato tamen Luca.

33 Omittitur prolixior haec Christi oratio apud Marcum.

34 Omittuntur haec Lucae capita. Continentur enim iis, qua partem maximam, orationes Christi verbosiores, quibus paucae tantum de rebus a Christo gestis narratiunculae adspersae sunt.

35 Marcus hic Matthaeum adhibet ducem, et praeterit ea, quae Lucae sunt peculiaria, velut Luc. 19, 1–28. Sed Lucas etiam praesto ipsi fuit. Vide e. gr. Marc. 10, 15–29.

36 Omittitur satis verbosa Christi oratio.

37 Marci 12, 37. 38. parallelum erat Lucae 20, 44. 45. Hinc Marcus iam pergit Luc. 20, 45.

38 Prolixiores sermones, quos Matthaeus exhibet, praetermittit Marcus, et in eorum locum substituit perbrevem oratiunculam, eiusdem fere cum sermonibus apud Matthaeum extantibus argumenti.

39 Quae inde ab hoc commate leguntur apud Marcum, dubia sunt. Si vero genuina esse censes, facile videbis a tabula nostra, ea esse partim ex Matthaeo partim e Luca desumta et in epitomen quasi redacta, (quod posterius tamen a more Marci abhorrere videtur,) adspersis etiam nonnullis, quae in neutro illorum occurrunt.

40 Quae de custodibus tradit Matthaeus, omittit Marcus, uti etiam Matth. 27, 62–66. narrationem de sepulcro custodibus munito silentio praeteriverat. Recte enim iudicabat lectores ab Hierosolymis remotos, ad quorum aures non pervenerant rumores a Matthaeo cap. 28, 15. memorati, non magis has narratiunculas esse desideraturos, quam illam, de Iudae proditoris morte et de agri Haceldama dicti emtione. Matth. 27, 3–10.

41 Si genuina essent postrema Marci commata, nec authentica clausula Evangelii, quae versum 8. excipiebat, intercidisse videretur, mirari omnino fas esset, quid sit quod Marcus, qui commate 6. [sic] et cap. 14, 28. mentionem fecerat promissi, discipulos in Galilaea visuros esse Dominum, prorsus sileat de itinere in Galilaeam, quanquam apud Matthaeum relatum legerit, vidisse omnino discipulos, uti promissum fuerat, Christum in Galilaea.

42 Notatu inprimis dignum est, Marcum ne tum quidem ab ordine, quem praeivit Matthaeus, recedere, ubi hic plane arbitrarius est. E. gr. cap. 14, 12. [sic] commemorat Matthaeus, suspicatum esse Herodem, Iesum, multis

miraculis clarum, esse Ioannem baptistam a mortuis resuscitatum; et hac arrepta occasione caedem Ioannis velut in transcursu enarrat. Eandem rem eodem modo et loco et ordine, qui sane quam maxime fortuitus est et arbitrarius, Marcus quoque refert cap. 6, 14.

43   Forte additamento hoc monere voluit lectores, quo sensu accipi debeat sententia proxime sequens. Praeterea comma hoc abest a codicibus nonnullis.

44   V. supra p. 203 not. 22.

45   Vid. not. 26 pag. 204 et not. 38 p. 205.

46   Vid. not. 22 pag. 203.

47   *Allg. Biblioth. der bibl. Literatur*, vol. 5. Sect. 5. pag. 770.

48   STORRII V. V. diss. laudata, pag. 66. 67.

49   Haud multo aliter hac de re iudicat STORRIUS V. V. in libro egregio *über den Zweck der evangel. Geschichte und der Briefe Iohannis* pag. 249 sqq. et 265, ubi luculenter ostendit, pleraque omnia, quae de Marco a Petri ore pendente apud veteres scriptores leguntur, valde dubia esse et suspecta. Attamen idem Vir doctissimus p. 266. coll. p. 366. e Iustini Martyris loco quodam colligi posse censet, non omni fundamento destitutam esse istam traditionem. Hinc in dissertatione supra allegata, pag. 61. 'Marcum', inquit, 'scripsisse, ὡς Πετρος ὑφηγησατο αὐτῳ, historica argumentatione efficitur in libro *über den Zweck* §. 56.' (hoc est eo ipso, quem modo excitavimus, libri loco) et paulo post pag. 66. 'opinionis nostrae', inquit, 'tanto minus nos poenitet, quod a GRIESBACHIO historica quibus nitimur argumenta non labefieri sed intacta relinqui videmus.' Ne igitur historicorum argumentorum examen plane declinasse videamur, paucula saltim de eorum pretio monebimus.

50   Saltim si ita intelligatur: e sermonibus Paulli innotuisse Lucae ea, quae de rebus gestis et orationibus Iesu in Evangelio suo narravit.

51   Scilicet Evangelium Marci complectitur την δια λογου παραδοθεισαν τοις ρωμαιοις διδασκαλιαν Πετρου!

52   Eandem fabulam, omissa tamen revelationis mentione, e Clemente seu potius ex Eusebio mutuatus est Hieronymus (catal. viror. illust. 8.) 'Marcus', ait, 'discipulus, et interpres Petri, iuxta quod Petrum referentem audierat, rogatus Romae a fratribus, breve scripsit Evangelium; quod cum Petrus *audisset*, probavit et ecclesiis legendum sua auctoritate edidit.'

53   Consentientem nobiscum habemus b. *Michaelis* in Introduct. in N.T. Edit. 4. tom. 2. pag. 1052.

54   *Storrii* dissert. laudata. pag. 64.

55   *Koppii* Progr. Marcus non epitomator Matthaei. pag. 9.

56   Ven. *Storrius über den Zweck der evangel. Gesch.* passim et in dissert. laudata pag. 63. et 66.

57   *Ueber den Zweck etc.* pag. 274. et in Dissert. laud. pag. 63.

58   Conf. praesertim col. *Eichhornium.* l. c. praecipue pag. 772. 781. seq. et praeter hunc, quod ad errores in transferendo ebraico archetypo commissos *Michaelem*, Rev. *Boltenium*, aliosque.

59   Vide *Michaelem, Koppium*, Ven. *Storrium*, nec non Cel. *Eichhornium* 11.cc.

60   Si nullo modo Marcus excusari potest, quid tum postea? Num eam ob rem negabimus, Matthaeum fuisse ab eo lectum? Minime vero; nam adhibitum hunc et Lucam ab eo esse, validis argumentis probatur. Quid igitur? Ingenue

fatebimur, virum optimum, sed in scribendis libris plane inexercitatum, minus dextre in negotio inusitato esse versatum, atque neglexisse et omisisse nonnulla, quae cum caeteris a Matthaeo aut Luca petitis retinenda fuissent. Equidem vero profiteor, nullum me observasse locum, qui excusationem omnino nullam admitteret.

61   Dissert. laud. pag. 65.

62   Quam ob rem Marcus, progressus usque ad Matth. 4, 21. iam pergat Luc. 4, 31. ostendimus Sect. II. not. 17 p. 203.

63   De omissa pericopa Luc. 5, 1–11. vide Sect. II. not. 16 p. 203.

64   Propter orationem montanam, quam Marcus suis lectoribus minus necessariam esse iudicabat, a Luca redit ad Matthaeum.

65   Haec Marcus narrat solus. Conf. tamen Sect. II. p. 204 not. 22 in fine.

66   Cur Marcus a Luc. 6, 16. transeat ad Matth. 12, 24. diximus Sect. II. p. 203 not. 22.

67   Causam, ob quam Marcus filum Matth. 13, 35. abruptum annectat Luc. 8, 22. indicatam vide Sect. II. p. 204 not. 27 et 28.

68   *Lardnerus, Townsonus, aliique, quibus iam praelusit Eusebius* Demonstr. Evang. L. 3. pag. 120.

6 Bernard Orchard: A demonstration that Mark was written after Matthew and Luke (A translation of J. J. Griesbach's *Commentatio*)

1   This revised version is to be found in the theological commentaries edited by Velthusen, Kuinoel, and Ruperti, vol. I (Leipzig, 1794), pp. 360ff. [It was republished in 1825 in P. Gabler's edition of the works of J. J. Griesbach, from which this translation has been made: *Jo. Jacobi Griesbachii Opuscula Academica* vol. II, pp. 358–425.]
In the Easter Programme for the Year 1783 [see P. Gabler's edition of the *Works* of J. J. Griesbach (1825), vol. II, p. 241.]

3   *De Consensu Evangeliorum*, book 1, chapter 2.

4   *Supplement to the Credibility of the Gospel History*, vol. I, chapter 10.

5   In the Dissertation, Göttingen 1782, entitled *Mark not the Abbreviator of Matthew* (*Marcus non epitomator Matthaei*).

6   *Über den Zweck der evangel. Geschichte Johannes,* §§ 85ff.; also compare the prior dissertation of the same scholar, *In Librorum N. T. historicorum aliquot loca* [*Re some Passages of the Historical Books of the N. T.*] (Tübingen, 1790), pp. 58ff., where certain matters contrary to our hypothesis are put forward, matters which we shall not neglect when later in their proper place we examine objections brought forward against our view.

7   *Allgemeine Bibliothek der biblischen Literatur*, vol. V, part 5. But this commentary on the Gospels has not yet been completed. (This Commentary was finished shortly after part 6 of the same vol. V. G.)

8   See p. 823 [of Eichhorn's work quoted in note 7].

9   See p. 920 [of Eichhorn's work quoted in note 7].

10   The space of time separating these primeval Hebrew writings and the origins of our Gospels seems to me too short for the formation of so many new and fuller recensions of the archetype, for so many mixtures of recensions and for so many versions of them. The mode of writing and spreading books, and the position and situation of Christian communities dispersed through widely separated provinces and having no common bond of communication

between one another, in that age, in our opinion hardly permitted not merely such a swift propagation of a book, but even less its rendering into such diverse forms. If our Gospels were not written before the middle of the second century, we might assent more readily to the Eichhorn hypothesis.

11   Unless we are deceived, it is Eichhorn's view that the versions of the archetype, not the archetype itself, were available for the authors of our Gospels. Matthew at least did not use the Hebrew archetype. For in the Greek text of Matthew, if the judgement of the most learned scholar is to be accepted, many oversights are discerned, that have been derived from the alteration of similar Hebrew words in the archetype. But who would persuade himself that Matthew himself has committed such errors? Surely if Matthew used the Greek version of the archetype, the same ought surely to be affirmed of Luke and Mark.

12   Some things will be said below about these arguments, in so far as they could be used to attack our hypothesis about the Gospel of Mark, and we have mentioned them in this place for that reason. The hub of the matter turns on this, that one must discover (1) whether there are signs clear beyond doubt of a *Hebrew* source, (2) whether from a different way of reporting the same thing, as well as from omissions and seeming contradictions, it can be proved that one author did not use the other. For if both these assertions can be rightly denied, there is no reason why we should postpone the hypothesis defended by us for the sake of this one.

13   *In den Beyträgen zur Beförderung des vernünftigen Denkens in der Religion*, Partic. XVI, p. 57.

14   Wherever Mark retained the longer sermons, as in chapters 4 and 13, nevertheless in these too he aimed at brevity. Certainly if you compare the parallel passages of Matthew, you will discover that Mark has cut back a number of things in each passage adduced.

15   However he could not entirely exclude from his book everything pertaining to Jews and Palestinians. For since Christ never had any other hearers but the Jews, and he himself always most wisely adapted his teaching to the condition of his hearers, it could not but occur that among his discourses there would be some things specially pertaining to the Jews. Moreover since all the assemblies of Christians that gathered together in those days contained converts from Judaism as well as from the Gentiles, there were among Mark's readers undoubtedly those who studied the Jewish Scriptures. For the sake of these Mark was able to transfer from the Gospel of Matthew to his own Gospel certain matters especially concerned with the Jews and with their manner of living and thinking. In this regard (a) he left out entirely a number of things of this sort, (b) among those he decided to retain he is usually more brief than Matthew, (c) he seems to have transcribed some discourses relating to the Jews precisely on account of the wonderful and valuable sentiments found in them, (d) many things which had been said to Palestinian Jews could also be read by others with great profit.

He who will take note of these things will easily deal with some passages of Mark which Storr (in the Dissertation just cited, p. 65 [see note 6 above]) opposed to our thesis. For Mark 2: 16-28 has been retained on account of verses 17, 20, 27, 28. Again, Mark did not want to omit the contents of 3: 22–30, because outside Palestine also the enemies of the Christian religion had accused Jesus and the apostles of performing miracles with the aid of the devils and magic arts. The story of the inhabitants of Nazareth, 6: 1–6, again, could be profitable to all who might wonder why it was that so few had lent willing ears to the warnings of such a great teacher as Jesus. Again, it was truly fitting that the commands which the Lord, 6: 8–11, had given to the apostles when he was ordering them to take the first steps as it were of their future function, should be made known to the Christians of all places; although Mark imitating the example of Luke summed up in a few verses what Matthew set forth in a lengthy discourse. Mark 8: 1–23 has been kept on account of verses 15–23. In Mark 8: 11, 12 not only are all 'seekers of signs' rebuked everywhere, but this passage can also be reckoned among those which make it clear that Jesus never wrought miracles for the sake of satisfying the vain curiosity of bystanders; more will be said about this matter in Section II. Finally, in Mark 12: 38–40 Mark, following Luke's example, relates in very few words only the Lord's discourse in which the Pharisees and Scribes were rebuked; whereas Matthew has treated it very fully.

Notes to table

16 These chapters are entirely omitted, because Mark meant to narrate only those deeds performed by Christ in his capacity as a public teacher.

17 Mark, having followed Matthew up to 4: 21, forsakes Matthew and passes over to Luke since he had decided to pass over Christ's Sermon on the Mount, which follows at this point in Matthew; for, as he meant to write a short book, it seemed to him too verbose, and, besides, it comprises many things which specially pertained only to those persons who heard Christ speaking on the mountain.

18 Mark 1: 14 is parallel to Luke 4: 14. Mark considered that his readers could easily do without all those materials which are found in Luke 4: 15–30, namely the sermon preached in the synagogue of Nazareth, including the adaptation of the passage from Isaiah, and the examples taken from the history of Elijah and Elisha. Moreover in Mark 6: 1–6 (about the people of Nazareth) are related some matters taken from Matthew which can be matched with Luke 4: 15ff. Hence it is clear why Mark, passing from Matthew to Luke, has arrived at Luke 4: 31.

19 Luke 5: 1–11 is omitted by Mark, because at Mark 1: 16–20 he had already included the story taken from Matthew, which Luke here relates in a not dissimilar manner.

20 See note 22 below.

21 Mark here breaks off the thread, on account of the Sermon on the Mount which here follows in Luke, and passes back to Matthew.

22 The reason has come to light why Mark, returning from Luke to Matthew, begins a new path as it were from this verse [24] of chapter 12, a fact which is indicated by the table. That is to say, following Luke (Luke 6: 11), Mark came as far as Mark 3: 6; in such a way, however, that he has followed Luke as regards the order of narration but, at the same time, always kept his eye on Matthew, wherever he was relating the same things

as Luke. Now the passage of Mark quoted here, 3: 6, 7, is parallel to Matt. 12: 14–15. What follows in Mark 3: 7–12 expresses more fully and expansively Matt. 12: 15–21, but in such a way that Mark (1) deliberately omitted the prophecy cited in 12: 17–21, (2) simultaneously matched Luke 6: 17– 19, and (3) added certain details of his own, 3: 9. Furthermore, when Mark had written his verse 3: 6 (parallel to Matt. 12: 14 and Luke 6: 11), he seems to have gone straight on in his reading of Luke's Gospel (which he had followed from Luke 5: 31 to Luke 6: 11) as far as Luke 6: 20, where the Sermon on the Mount begins; and since he had decided to omit it, he leaves Luke and goes back to that verse of Matthew which is parallel to his verse 3: 6, that is, to Matt. 12: 15. This verse, as we have said, he has expanded, inserting some details still present to his mind from the passage of Luke 6: 17–19, which he had already been over. And when he had written his Mark 6: 12, which exactly corresponds to Matt. 12: 16, he would have gone on, omitting the prophetic passage, to Matt. 12: 22–3. But here Mark realizes that he has not yet found a place in his book for the list of the apostles, which he had read in Luke. Matthew in fact had already anticipated it in another place (Matt. 10: 2–4), but Mark had passed over that place (in fact everything from Matt. 4: 23 to Matt. 12: 14). Lest therefore his readers should be without this list (Luke had already inserted it at Luke 6: 12–16, before he [Mark] had left off following him), he here narrates the choosing of the apostles and their names (Mark 3: 13–19). After this insertion, he returns to that place of Matthew, where, as we have seen, he had halted, namely Matt. 12: 22. Here, advised by Matthew (Matt. 12: 23, 'And all the crowds were astonished and said, "Is not this man etc." '), Mark thought he ought to insert his 3: 20f., viz. certain special details either neglected or at least obscurely described by Matthew, but which he knew thoroughly. Having done this, under the guidance of Matt. 12: 24f., Mark goes vigorously forward with him from 3: 22 to 4: 20.

23   [Matt. 12: 33–7] is omitted because Mark had read similar sentiments in the Sermon on the Mount at 7: 16–20, a sermon which he did not intend to incorporate in his book.

24   These words of Christ [Sign of Jonah, Matt. 12: 38–45] are omitted by Mark because they especially pertained to the people of Palestine, who happened to hear Christ speaking publicly. Moreover words similar to these (Matt. 12: 38, 39), recur before long in Matt. 16: 1–4, and from this passage Mark has transferred them to his own work at Mark 8: 11, 12.

25   The preceding and succeeding materials were taken from Matthew; but Luke has provided these five verses [Mark 4: 21–5]. As regards the preceding material, Mark 4: 1–20, which is taken from Matt. 13: 1–23, clearly corresponds with Luke 8: 1–15; Mark had therefore compared Luke with Matthew. But now in the very next Lucan verse, namely Luke 8: 16, Mark found a very brief and elegant parable, which was followed by some equally brief and memorable sayings, verses 17, 18. Mark did not want to omit from his book these three verses of Luke to which Matthew had as it were guided him.

26   Matthew's parable, 13: 24–30, which makes mention of 'sleeping labourers' recalled to Mark's mind another parable of 'a sleeping labourer,' as commendable for its elegance as for its brevity, and one that agrees still better

with the content of the parables and sayings that immediately precede and follow it than that parable of Matthew (13: 24–30). Therefore he substitutes this one in the place of the other which in any case has a fuller explanation attached (Matt. 13: 36–43) which Mark, pursuing brevity, did not desire to transfer to his book.

27 Mark had already copied quite enough parables from Matthew. When therefore Matthew proceeded to add parables to parables, Mark, apparently having had enough, said good-bye to this guide for a short while and returned to Luke.

28 In utilizing Luke, Mark had come to Luke 8: 18. Here he omitted the short story Luke 8: 19–21, because he had already brought it into his book at Mark 3: 31–5 in the place and order he had found it in Matthew. [Mark] therefore arrived at the next verse of Luke, namely 8: 22. He therefore proceeds.

29 What is contained in Mark 5 [Gerasene demoniac: Jairus' daughter] is also found in Matthew, but both in another place and order, and in fewer words [8: 28–34; 9: 18–26]. It will be clear to everyone comparing the three Evangelists that Mark is here dependent on Luke and not on Matthew.

30 We have seen above, note 27, that Mark has been (as it were) embarrassed by Matthew's excess of parables in chapter 13, and so attached himself to Luke. All the same since he had selected Matthew especially to guide him in his written record of the *memorabilia* of Christ, he now returns to Matthew, and indeed to that very place where the parables finish, namely Matt. 13: 53, 54. Meanwhile however, he clearly does not ignore Luke, but carefully compares him with Matthew. Hence the following pericopes are taken now from the one and now from the other.

31 Mark alone has this story. The peculiar Marcan material will be discussed later.

32 In this section, he follows chiefly in the footsteps of Matthew, but all the while comparing with Luke.

33 This longer discourse of Christ [Matt. 18: 10–35] is omitted by Mark.

34 These chapters of Luke [9: 51 – 18: 14] are omitted. For the most part, they contain the longer speeches of Christ, among which are scattered only a few short stories of his deeds.

35 Mark here follows Matthew, and passes over those things which are peculiar to Luke, such as Luke 19: 1–28. But Luke all the same was at hand for him. See, for example, Mark 10: 15–29.

36 This rather long discourse of Christ [23: 1–39] is omitted.

37 Mark 12: 37, 38 was parallel to Luke 20: 44, 45. Mark now continues at Luke 20: 45.

38 Mark passes over Matthew's longer discourse, and puts in its place a very brief little discourse [Mark 13: 33–6] having almost the same content as the discourse in Matthew [24: 36 – 25: 46].

39 This and the remaining verses of Mark [16: 9–20] are dubious. If you regard them as genuine, you will easily see from our table that they are taken partly from Matthew and partly from Luke, and are, as it were, reduced to a summary (which seems, looking back, to be inconsistent with Mark's usage) and interspersed with a few things which do not occur in either.

40 Mark omits Matthew's verses about the guards, just as he had passed over in silence the story of the tomb being provided with guards, Matt. 27: 62-6. For he correctly judged that readers far from Jerusalem, whose ears the rumours mentioned in Matt. 28: 15 had not reached, would no more be interested in these brief little stories than in the one about the death of Judas the betrayer and the purchase of the field called Hakeldama described in Matt. 27: 3-10.

41 If the last verses of Mark were genuine and the authentic conclusion of the Gospel which followed verse 8 had not, as it would seem, perished, it would indeed be right to wonder why it is that Mark, who in Mark 16: 6-7 and 14: 28 had expressly mentioned the promise that the disciples would see the Lord in Galilee, should be quite silent about the journey into Galilee, although he had read in Matthew that the disciples indeed saw Christ in Galilee as he had promised.

[Here end the notes to the table]

42 It is worth noting that Mark does not even depart from the order which Matthew has already adopted when this is clearly arbitrary. For example, in Matt. 14: 1-2 Matthew says that Herod suspected that Jesus, famous for his many miracles, was John the Baptist raised up from the dead; and seizes this occasion to relate in passing, as it seems, the execution of John. Mark also relates in 6: 14 the same thing in the same manner, place and order, though it is clearly an exceedingly arbitrary and fortuitous one.

43 Perhaps he [Mark] wanted to warn the readers by this addition ['The Sabbath was made for man...'], in what sense the following sentence ought to be understood. Moreover this verse [2: 27] is missing in some codices.

44 See note 22 above.

45 See note 26 and note 38.

46 See note 22 above.

47 *Allg. Biblioth. der bibl. Literatur*, vol. V, sect. 5, p. 770.

48 Storr, dissertation, pp. 66, 67 [see note 6 above].

49 Not much different is the judgement of Storr in his distinguished work *über den Zweck der Evangel. Geschichte und der Briefe Johannis*, pp. 249ff., 265, where he shows lucidly that in general everything that we read in the ancient writers about Mark depending on the utterance of Peter is exceedingly dubious and suspect. However, the same scholar, pp. 266, 366, reckons that it can be gathered from a certain passage of Justin Martyr that this tradition is not entirely without foundation. Hence in the dissertation quoted above, p. 61, he says the assertion that 'Mark wrote as Peter dictated to him is verified by historical argumentation in my book *über den Zweck*, § 56' (that is, from the very passage we have just cited), and a little further on, p. 66, says 'I have all the more reason to be pleased with my view, because we see that the historical arguments on which we lean are not destroyed but are left intact by Griesbach.' Lest therefore we may seem to have openly avoided an examination of the historical arguments, we shall at least pronounce something about their value.

50 At least if it is understood in the sense that Luke learnt from the discourses of Paul what he related in his Gospel about the actions and words of Jesus.

51   That is to say the Gospel of Mark embraces 'the instruction of Peter given by word of mouth to the Romans'!

52   Jerome (*Catal. vir. illustr.* 8) has borrowed the same fable, though omitting any mention of the revelation, from Clement, or rather from Eusebius. He writes: 'Mark, the disciple and interpreter of Peter, wrote a short Gospel at the request of the brethren at Rome, based on what he had heard Peter say; and Peter, after *hearing it*, approved and published it by his own authority to be read in the churches.'

53   J. D. Michaelis agrees with us in his *Introduction to the New Testament*, 4th ed., vol. II, p. 1052.

54   Storr, dissertation quoted previously, p. 64 [see note 6 above].

55   Koppe, Dissertation, *Marcus non epitomator Matthaei (Mark not the Abbreviator of Matthew)*, p. 9.

56   Storr, *Über den Zweck der Evangel. Gesch, passim,* and in the dissertation quoted, pp. 63 and 66 [see note 6, above].

57   *Über den Zweck* etc., p. 274, and in the dissertation quoted, p. 63 [see note 6 above].

58   See particularly Eichhorn, *loc. cit.* esp. pp. 772, 781ff. and besides him, Michaelis, Rev. Bolten, and others, as regards errors committed in translating the Hebrew archetype.

59   See Michaelis, Koppe, Storr and Eichhorn in the appropriate places.

60   If Mark cannot be excused in any way, what of it? Surely this would not allow us to deny that he had read Matthew? Indeed not; for his use of Matthew and Luke is proved by valid arguments. What then? We shall admit quite simply that this excellent person [Mark] was clearly inexperienced in writing books, not properly trained for an unfamiliar task, and that he left out and omitted a number of items which should have been retained together with others sought out by Matthew or Luke. All the same, I do not recall any instance where there is not some reason or other for the omission.

61   *Dissertation,* p. 65 [see note 6 above].

62   Why Mark, having gone as far as Matt. 4: 21, then goes with Luke 4: 31, was explained in Section II, note 17.

63   Re the omission of Luke 5: 1–11, see Section II, note 16.

64   Because Mark deemed the Sermon on the Mount unnecessary for his readers, he returns from Luke to Matthew.

65   Mark alone narrates this incident; but see Section II, note 22 at the end.

66   We have explained why Mark goes from Luke 6: 16 to Matt. 12: 24, Section II, note 22.

67   See Section II, note 27 and note 28 for the reason why Mark ties the thread broken at Matt. 13: 35 to Luke 8: 22.

68   Lardner, Townson, and others, for whom Eusebius, *Demonstr. Evang.* Bk. 3, p. 120 had already prepared the way.

7   G. D. Kilpatrick: Griesbach and the development of text criticism

1   F. H. A. Scrivener, *Introduction to the Criticism of the New Testament,* 4th ed. (London, 1894), vol. II, p. 224.

2   See *Opuscula Academica,* vol. II (Jena, 1825), pp. 62–6, and compare Gabler, *ibid,* pp. xx–xxvi.

3   G. D. Kilpatrick, *Scripture Bulletin* 5 (1974), 5.
4   B. H. Streeter, *The Four Gospels* (London, 1936), p. 26.
5   Kirsopp Lake, *HTR* 21.4 (October 1928).
6   Streeter, *The Four Gospels,* p. 39.
7   Kirsopp Lake, *HTR* 21.4 (October 1928), 324.
8   Scrivener, *Introduction,* vol. II, pp. 224f.
9   B. F. Westcott and F. J. A. Hort, *The New Testament in the Original Greek* (Cambridge and London, 1881), vol. II, pp. 1–140.
10 H. Lietzmann, *Handbuch zum Neuen Testament* (Tübingen, 1912).
11 F. C. Burkitt, 'Text and Versions', *Encyclopaedia Biblica* (London-New York, 1899–1903), vol. IV, col. 4991f.
12 F. C. Burkitt, *The Gospel History and its Transmission,* 3rd ed. (Edinburgh, 1907), pp. 40–58.
13 Streeter, *The Four Gospels* (1937), pp. 309–29.
14 C. H. Turner, 'Marcan Usage', *JTS* 25–9 (1924–8).
15 Turner, *JTS* 25 (1923/4), 377.
16 Turner, *JTS* 26 (1924/5), 20.
17 *Ibid,* p. 20.
18 Turner, 'A Textual Commentary on Mark i', *JTS* 28 (1926/7), 146–7.
19 Turner, *JTS* 29 (1927/8), 14.
20 J. W. Burgon, *The Traditional Text of the Holy Gospels* (London, 1895; 2nd ed., 1896), vol. XIV.
21 Scrivener, *Introduction,* vol. II, p. 226.

8 Gordon D. Fee: Modern text criticism and the Synoptic Problem

1   See the review of my monograph on P[66] by J. N. Birdsall, *JTS* 22 (1971), 198–200.
2   *An Introduction to the Textual Criticism of the New Testament* (E. T., London, 1937), pp. 91–2.
3   The UBS *Greek New Testament,* 3rd ed. (Stuttgart, 1975), ed. K. Aland et al. Cf. B. M. Metzger (ed.), *A Textual Commentary on the Greek New Testament* (London and New York, 1971), pp. xiii–xxxi.
4   E.g., B. M. Metzger, *The Text of the New Testament,* 2nd ed. (New York, 1968); J. H. Greenlee, *Introduction to New Testament Textual Criticism* (Grand Rapids, 1964).
5   See e.g. F. C. Grant, 'The Greek Text of the New Testament', *An Introduction to the Revised Standard Version of the New Testament,* ed. L. A. Weigle (International Council of Religious Education, American Standard Bible Committee, Chicago, 1946), pp. 37–43; cf. R. V. G. Tasker (ed.), *The Greek New Testament, being the text translated in the New English Bible* (New York, 1961; Oxford and Cambridge, 1964), pp. vii–x.
6   See E. C. Colwell, 'Genealogical Method: Its Achievements and Its Limitations', *JBL* 61 (1947), 132.
7   K. W. Clark, 'The Effect of Recent Textual Criticism upon New Testament Studies', *The Background of the New Testament and Its Eschatology,* ed. W. D. Davies and D. Daube (Cambridge, 1954), pp. 37–8.
8   In 1954 Clark, 'Recent Textual Criticism', p. 37, called this 'the most influential factor in recent criticism'. For an excellent survey of the history of this idea see C. M. Martini, *Il problema della recensionalità del codice B*

alla luce del papiro Bodmer XIV (Rome, 1966), pp. 1–41. Cf. G. D. Fee, 'P⁷⁵, P⁶⁶, and Origen: The Myth of Early Textual Recension in Alexandria', *New Dimensions in New Testament Study*, ed. R. N. Longenecker and M. C. Tenney (Grand Rapids, 1974), pp. 19–45.

9   This was first argued by J. W. Burgon, *The Revision Revised* (London, 1883), see esp. pp. 252–7. See also Colwell, 'Genealogical Method'; Fee, 'P⁷⁵, P⁶⁶, and Origen'; and J. N. Birdsall, 'The New Testament Text', *The Cambridge History of the Bible*, vol. I, 'From the Beginnings to Jerome' (Cambridge, 1970), 308–16.

10   Cf. Birdsall, 'The New Testament Text', p. 310.

11   *The New Testament in the Original Greek*, vol. II, 'Introduction, Appendix', 2nd ed. (London, 1896), pp. 115–19.

12   *Ibid*, pp. 32, 227–50.

13   *Ibid*, p. 41.

14   *Ibid*, p. 32.

15   See especially, Martini, *Il problema*; Fee, 'P⁷⁵, P⁶⁶, and Origen'; and C. L. Porter, 'Papyrus Bodmer XV (P⁷⁵) and the Text of Codex Vaticanus', *JBL* 81 (1962), 363–76.

16   *New Testament in the Original Greek*, pp. 250–1.

17   *The Text of the Greek Bible*, 2nd ed. (London, 1949), p. 208.

18   This is a loosely used word in textual criticism. In 'P⁷⁵, P⁶⁶, and Origen', pp. 22–3, I noted that it is sometimes used to mean 'a "revision," implying both the creation of variants as well as the selection of similar readings where variation already exists, or it may mean an "edition," implying not emendation of the text but selection from good and bad manuscripts and/ or good and bad readings'. By neither definition is B a recension.

19   See especially the various studies by G. D. Kilpatrick and J. K. Elliott. By Professor Kilpatrick: 'Western Text and Original Text in the Gospels and Acts', *JTS* 44 (1943), 24–36; 'Atticism and the Text of the New Testament', *Neutestamentliche Aufsätze: Festschrift für Prof. Josef Schmid*, ed. J. Blinzler, et al. (Regensburg, 1963), pp. 125–37; 'An Eclectic Study of the Text of Acts', *Biblical and Patristic Studies in Memory of Robert Pierce Casey*, ed. J. N. Birdsall and R. W. Thomson (Freiburg, 1963), pp. 64–77; 'The Greek New Testament of Today and the *Textus Receptus*', *The New Testament in Historical and Contemporary Perspective*, ed. H. Anderson and W. Barclay (Oxford, 1965), pp. 189–208; 'Style and Text in the Greek New Testament', *Studies in the History and Text of the New Testament in honor of Kenneth Willis Clark*, Studies and Documents 29; ed. B. L. Daniels and M. J. Suggs (Salt Lake City, 1967), pp. 153–60; ' "Kurios" in the Gospels', *L'Évangile hier et aujourd'hui. Mélanges offerts au Professeur Franz-J. Leenhardt* (Geneva, 1968), pp. 65–70; 'Some Problems in New Testament Text and Language', *Neotestamentica et Semitica, Studies in Honour of Matthew Black*, ed. E. E. Ellis and M. Wilcox (Edinburgh, 1969), pp. 198–208; 'Language and Text in the Gospels and Acts', *VC* 24 (1970), 161–71.

By Dr Elliott: *The Greek Text of the Epistles to Timothy and Titus*, Studies and Documents 36 (Salt Lake City, 1968); 'ΔΙΑΩΜΙ in 2 Timothy', *JTS* 19 (1968), 621–3; 'The Use of ἕτερος in the New Testament', *ZNW* 60 (1969), 140–1; 'Nouns with Diminutive Endings in the New Testament',

NovT 12 (1970), 391-8; 'Κηφᾶς: Σίμων Πέτρος: ὁ Πέτρος: An Examination of New Testament Usage', *NovT* 14 (1972), 241-56; 'Phrynichus' Influence on the Textual Tradition of the New Testament', *ZNW* 63 (1972), 133-8.

Dr Elliott has recently called the results of this method a 'radically eclectic text' ('The United Bible Societies Greek New Testament: An Evaluation', *NovT* 15 (1973), 300). This is a useful article in that he has brought together the resultant text of a great many of the studies listed in this note.

For critiques of this method, see G. D. Fee, 'Rigorous or Reasoned Eclecticism - Which?' *Studies in New Testament Language and Text, Essays in Honour of George D. Kilpatrick on the Occasion of his sixty-fifth Birthday* (Leiden, 1976), pp. 174-97; and C. M. Martini, 'Eclecticism and Atticism in the Textual Criticism of the Greek New Testament', *On Language, Culture and Religion: In Honor of Eugene A. Nida*, ed. M. Black and W. A. Smalley (The Hague/Paris, 1974), pp. 149-56.

20   *The Text of the Epistles* (London, 1953), pp. 212-13.

21   *Papyrus Bodmer II (P⁶⁶): Its Textual Relationships and Scribal Characteristics*, Studies and Documents 34 (Salt Lake City, 1968).

22   'P⁷⁵, P⁶⁶, and Origen', pp. 40-4.

23   This is true, but needs to be sharply qualified. For the most part this support is of readings which were *already* known to have existed in the second century through the versions. Very few purely Byzantine readings have in fact received such support.

24   *The Last Twelve Verses of Mark*, SNTS Monograph Series 25 (Cambridge, 1974), p. 48.

25   C. R. Williams, 'The appendices to the Gospel according to Mark: a study in textual transmission', *Connecticut Academy of Arts and Sciences, Transactions* 18 (New Haven, 1915), p. 403; cited by Farmer, *ibid.*

26   See esp. his 'Marcan Usage: Notes, Critical and Exegetical, on the Second Gospel', *JTS* 25 (1924), 377-86; 26 (1924/5), 12-20, 145-56, 225-40, 337-46; 27 (1925/6), 58-62; 28 (1926/7), 9-30, 349-62; 29 (1927/8), 275-89, 346-61. See also 'A Textual Commentary on Mark i', *JTS* 28 (1926/7), 145-58.

27   See above, n. 19.

28   See e.g. E. Ruckstuhl, *Die literarische Einheit des Johannesevangeliums*, Studia Friburgensia 3 (Freiburg, 1951), pp. 190-205; W. Nicol, *The Sēmeia in the Fourth Gospel*, Suppl. NovT 32 (Leiden, 1972), pp. 14-25.

29   See esp. F. Neirynck, *The Minor Agreements of Matthew and Luke against Mark with a Cumulative List*, Bib. Ephem. Theol. Lovan. 37 (Leuven, 1974), pp. 199-288.

30   Again, Hort has noted this problem (*New Testament in the Original Greek*, p. 21): 'There is much literature, ancient no less than modern, in which it is needful to remember that authors are not always grammatical, or clear, or consistent, or felicitous.'

31   *Ibid.*

32   See several studies by Boismard: 'A propos de Jean v, 39', *RB* 55 (1950), 388-408; 'Lectio brevior, potior', 58 (1951), 161-8; 'Dans le sein du Père (*Jo.* 1, 18)', 59 (1952), 23-39; 'Problèmes de critique textuelle concernant

le quatrième évangile', 60 (1953), 347–71; 'Le papyrus Bodmer II', 64 (1957), 363–98. Cf. Kilpatrick's contribution to this Colloquium.
33 See esp. 'Atticism'.
34 Cf. my critique in 'Rigorous or Reasoned Eclecticism', pp. 189–91.
35 *New Testament in the Original Greek*, pp. 107–15.
36 See esp. 'Le papyrus Bodmer II' (n. 32 above).
37 See 'The Text of John in Origen and Cyril of Alexandria: A Contribution to Methodology in the Recovery and Analysis of Patristic Citations', *Biblica* 52 (1971), 357–94; 'The Text of John in *The Jerusalem Bible*: A Critique of the Use of Patristic Citations in New Testament Textual Criticism', *JBL* 90 (1971), 163–73.
38 This has been further confirmed by F. T. Gignac, 'The Texts of Acts in Chrysostom's Homilies', *Traditio* 26 (1970), 308–15; and also by the Tura papyrus materials of Didymus which show how often the New Testament text of *de Trinitate* in Migne reflects a Byzantine corruption of Didymus' basically Alexandrian text.
39 See esp. 'The Text of John in *The Jerusalem Bible*', pp. 170–2.
40 Examples abound. Some are noted in the two articles cited in n. 37. A typical example is the use of Origen to support the omission of καὶ ἡ ζωή in John 11: 25. This dubious support first appeared in a critical apparatus after the discovery of P⁴⁵. It would never have occurred either to Tischendorf or von Soden, on the basis of the evidence, that Origen supports this omission. For, Tasker notwithstanding (*JTS* 37 (1936), 149), there is *no* evidence that Origen knew a Greek text with those words missing. It is true that five times throughout the John commentary Origen cites ἐγώ εἰμι ἡ ἀνάστασις without καὶ ἡ ζωή; but by the same token he thrice cites ἐγώ εἰμι ἡ ὁδός without καὶ ἡ ἀλήθεια καὶ ἡ ζωή. In the single occurrence of the citation in the commentary *on chapter 11*, he says: '... καὶ τῷ εἰρημένῳ ὑπὸ τοῦ κυρίου πρὸς τὴν Μάρθαν λέγοντος· ἐγώ εἰμι ἡ ἀνάστασις καὶ ἡ ζωή' (*GCS* 4, 400.10).
41 One cannot assume, of course, that any of the Gospel writers used the 'original' text of his predecessor. But such a factor is hidden and will be forever unknown to us.
42 *The Four Gospels, A Study of Origins*, rev. ed. (London, 1930), pp. 325–9.
43 'Western Text', pp. 29–30.
44 *The Synoptic Problem* (New York and London, 1964), pp. 325–8.
45 There is always the possibility, of course, that the Gospel writers had access to a Greek text of the LXX which read ὑποκάτω.
46 'Western Text', p. 27.
47 'The New Testament Text', p. 330.
48 Preserved in J. A. Cramer, *Catenae in evangelia Matthaei et Marci* (Oxford, 1840), p. 273.
49 His text reads· καὶ μετὰ ὀλίγα· ἀπὸ τότε ἤρξατο ὁ Ἰησοῦς κηρύσσειν καὶ λέγειν, μετανοεῖτε, ἤγγικε γὰρ ... In the following paragraph he says, citing Matthew: καὶ ἀπὸ τότε ἤρξατο κηρύσσειν, καὶ λέγειν, οὐχὶ, τὸ μετανοεῖτε, καὶ τὰ ἐξῆς, ἄλλα μόνον τό, ἤγγικεν ἡ βασιλεία τῶν οὐρανῶν.
50 'The United Bible Societies Greek New Testament', p. 295.
51 'Atticism', p. 126.
52 See my 'Rigorous or Reasoned Eclecticism', pp. 189–91. I have now dis-

covered a third example from Chrysostom. In *hom. 52 in Jo. 2* (M. 59, 289)
he cites John 8: 13 ἀπεκρίθησαν καὶ εἶπον αὐτῷ where all others read
εἶπον οὖν αὐτῷ. It is also noteworthy that Chrysostom not only has the
septuagintal idiom, but in each case has the Johannine form of it! Thus he
is also conforming to an author's style.

53   J. B. Orchard has recently argued that this latter is less significant because
the material is often so ambiguous ('J. A. T. Robinson and the Synoptic
Problem', *NTS* 22 (1975/6), 346–52). I would here argue that this matter
cannot be easily dismissed. I am using these data here as Orchard himself
argues we must, namely 'for the confirmation of the investigation' (p. 352).

54   *The Tendencies of the Synoptic Tradition*, SNTS Monograph Series 9
(Cambridge, 1969).

55   'The Priority of Mark and the "Q" Source in Luke', *Jesus and Man's Hope*
(Pittsburgh, 1970), p. 132.

56   C. H. Talbert and E. V. McKnight, 'Can the Griesbach Hypothesis Be
Falsified?' *JBL* 91 (1972), 338–68.

57   G. W. Buchanan, 'Has the Griesbach Hypothesis Been Falsified?' *JBL* 93
(1974), 550–72.

58   Farmer, *Synoptic Problem*, p. 223.

59   Streeter, *Four Gospels*, pp. 162–4.

60   *The Originality of St. Matthew* (Cambridge, 1951), p. 68.

61   See J. B. Orchard, 'J. A. T. Robinson and the Synoptic Problem'.

9 Thomas R. W. Longstaff: At the Colloquium's conclusion

1   The three areas chosen were: (1) Greek synopses of the Gospels, (2) the
Synoptic Problem, and (3) text criticism of the New Testament, all areas
where Griesbach himself had made important contributions to New
Testament scholarship.

2   K. Veit, *Die synoptischen Parallelen: Ein alter Versuch ihrer Enträtselung*
(Gütersloh, 1897), and Reuben J. Swanson, *The Horizontal Line Synopsis
of the Gospels* (Western North Carolina Press, Inc., Dillsboro, N.C., 1975).

APPENDIX

Additional entries to the Bibliography

[*For the sake of completeness the editors add to the bibliography in chapter 10:-*]

46a   LONGSTAFF, Thomas R. W. 'The Minor Agreements: An Examination of the Basic Argument', *Catholic Biblical Quarterly* 37. 2 (April 1975), 184–92.

46b   'Empty Tomb and Absent Lord: Mark's Interpretation of Tradition', in *Society of Biblical Literature: 1976 Seminar Papers*. Cambridge, Massachusetts, 1976.

46c   'A Critical Note in Response to J. C. O'Neill', *New Testament Studies* 23. 1 (October 1976), 116–17.

46d   *Evidence of Conflation in Mark? A Study in the Synoptic Problem*, Society of Biblical Literature Dissertation Series, 28. Missoula, Montana, 1977.

47   COPE, O. Lamar. *Matthew: A Scribe Trained for the Kingdom of Heaven*, Catholic Biblical Quarterly Monograph Series, 5. Washington, D.C., 1976.

48a   ORCHARD, Bernard. *Matthew, Luke and Mark*. Koinonia Press, 1976. (19 Langdale Drive, Bury, Greater Manchester, England)

48b   'J. A. T. Robinson and the Synoptic Problem', *New Testament Studies* 22. 3 (1976), 346–52.

49   REICKE, Bo. 'Griesbach und die synoptische Frage', *Theologische Zeitschrift* 32. 6 (1976), 341–59

50   DELLING, Gerhard, 'Johann Jakob Griesbach: seine Zeit, sein Leben, sein Werk', *Theologische Zeitschrift* 33 (1977), 81–99.

51   FARMER, William R. 'Modern Developments of Griesbach's Hypothesis', *New Testament Studies* 23 (April 1977), 275–95.

52   RIESNER, Rainer. 'Wie sicher ist die Zwei-Quellen-Theorie?', *Theologische Beitrage* 8 (1977), 49–73.

53   STOLD, Hans-Herbert. *Geschichte und Kritik der Markushypothese*. Göttingen, 1977.

INDEX

Eichhorn, J. G. xii, 52f., 56, 61, 71, 75, 83, 104f., 114, 176, 186 (nn. 58, 59), 188 (nn. 81, 84), 191 (n. 25), 198 (n. 11), 201 (nn. 3, 4), 206 (nn. 58, 59), 213 (nn. 58, 59)
Eichstädt, H. C. 183 (n. 22)
Eliot, G. 178
Elliott, J. K. 166, 215 (n. 19), 217 (n. 50)
Ellis, E. E. 215 (n. 19)
Elzevir 189 (n. 7)
Epiphanius 52
Erasmus, D. 69
Ernesti, J. A. 183 (n. 16), 186 (n. 59)
Eusebius 23, 52, 84, 86, 101, 115ff., 134, 142, 164f., 191 (n. 26), 207 (n. 68), 213 (n. 68)
Evanson, E. 176

Fabricius, J. A. 24, 189 (n. 5), 193 (n. 43)
Farmer, W. R. xiiff., 1ff., 45f., 158, 163, 168, 171f., 175, 181, 197 (nn. 94, 95), 216 (nn. 24, 25), 217 (n. 44), 218 (n. 58), 219
Fee, G. D. xiii, 172, 214 (n. 1), 215 (nn. 8, 9, 15, 18), 216 (nn. 19, 21, 22), 217 (nn. 34, 37, 39, 40, 52)
Feine, P. 189 (n. 3), 195 (n. 63)
Fichte, J. G. 188 (n. 81)
Fitzmyer, J. A. 168, 218 (n. 55)
Francke, A. H. 5, 182 (n. 9)
Francke, A. M. 182 (n. 9)
Fresenius, J. P. 6
Friedlieb, J. H. 193 (n. 43), 194 (nn. 47, 50, 51, 53)
Friedrich II 7
Fritzsche, K. F. A. 178
Froger, J. 197 (n. 101)
Fuller, R. H. xiii, 173

Gabler, J. P. 9, 12f., 16ff., 20, 73, 137, 176, 182 (nn. 2, 5), 184 (nn. 34, 36), 185 (nn. 47, 52), 187 (n. 61), 198 (n. 1), 207 (nn. 1, 2), 213 (n. 2)
Gaedertz, K. T. 188 (n. 79)
Gebhardt, O. von 39f., 42f., 186 (n. 59)
Gehringer, J. 193 (nn. 42, 43, 45), 194 (nn. 47, 50, 51, 52, 53)
Gfrörer, A. F. 179
Gieseler, J. C. L. 199 (n. 14)
Gignac, F. T. 217 (n. 38)
Goethe, J. W. von 5f., 13f., 68, 182 (nn. 3, 8, 12), 185 (n. 54), 187 (nn. 66, 68, 69, 70, 73, 75)

Goodspeed, E. J. 43, 196 (nn. 83, 84)
Grant, F. C. 214 (n. 5)
Grässer, E. 2
Grayston, K. 198 (n. 104)
Greenlee, J. H. 214 (n. 4)
Greeven, H. xiiif., 2, 170f., 196 (n. 85), 198 (nn. 106, 108)
Gregory the Great 9
Griesbach, D. R. 6, 182 (n. 9)
Griesbach, F. S. 8, 14, 183 (n. 13), 185 (n. 55), 186 (n. 57), 187 (n. 72), 188 (n. 79)
Griesbach, K. K. 5f.
Grimm, J. 181, 200 (n. 56)
Grotius, H. 51, 198 (n. 6)

Hartung, F. 186 (n. 56), 187 (nn. 66, 67), 188 (n. 84)
Hasert, C. A. 179
Hasse, F. C. A. 20
Hegel, G. W. F. 66
Heineke, R. 42, 195 (n. 64), 196 (n. 77)
Heracleon 164
Herdan, G. 198 (n. 104)
Herder, G. 71
Herder, F. G. 186 (nn. 58, 59), 188 (n. 81)
Herder, J. G. 52, 62, 199 (n. 13)
Heuermann, A. 187 (n. 69)
Heyd, W. von 188 (n. 82)
Hezel, W. F. 18
Hoche, R. 183 (n. 20)
Holtzmann, H. J. 38f., 179f., 195 (nn. 67, 71)
Hornig, G. 184 (n. 43), 185 (n. 44)
Hort, F. J. A. 43f., 137ff., 145ff., 154ff., 214 (n. 9), 215 (nn. 11, 12, 13, 14, 16), 216 (nn. 30, 31), 217 (n. 35)
Housman, A. E. 152
Huck, A. 38ff., 42f., 45, 47, 192 n. 29), 195 (nn. 68, 69, 71, 72), 196 (n. 74)

Immanuel, F. 20
Irenaeus 9, 62, 84ff., 115ff.

Jerome 52, 86, 117, 206 (n. 52), 213 (n. 52), 215 (n. 9)
John the Elder 84, 101, 115, 134
Jonas, F. (185, n. 54), 186 (n. 57), 187 (nn. 63, 71, 76), 188 (nn. 78, 79, 80)
Jung, R. 182 (n. 4)
Justin Martyr 35, 76, 85, 106, 116, 164, 206 (n. 49), 212 (n. 49)

Kahnis, K. F. A. 180